IT'S EVEN WORSE THAN YOU THINK

WHAT THE TRUMP ADMINISTRATION IS DOING TO AMERICA

DAVID CAY JOHNSTON

Simon & Schuster

NEW YORK   LONDON   TORONTO   SYDNEY   NEW DELHI

Simon & Schuster
1230 Avenue of the Americas
New York, NY 10020

First Simon & Schuster hardcover edition January 2018

SIMON & SCHUSTER and colophon are registered trademarks
of Simon & Schuster, Inc.

For information about special discounts for bulk purchases,
please contact Simon & Schuster Special Sales at 1-866-506-1949
or business@simonandschuster.com.

The Simon & Schuster Speakers Bureau can bring authors to your
live event. For more information or to book an event, contact
the Simon & Schuster Speakers Bureau at 1-866-248-3049
or visit our website at www.simonspeakers.com.

Manufactured in the United States of America

1   3   5   7   9   10   8   6   4   2

Library of Congress Cataloging-in-Publication Data is available.

ISBN 978-1-5011-7416-2
ISBN 978-1-5011-7417-9 (ebook)

For the late, great Wayne Barrett,
who blazed the trail on Trump reporting

CONTENTS

PART I

A PRESIDENT
LIKE NO OTHER

The Trump Factor

A single factor defines Donald Trump's presidency, making it unlike the forty-four administrations before. Be they great, middling, or corrupt, the presidents past all shared a trait missing in the Trump presidency.

In 1789, when America began its experiment in the then radical idea of self-government, George Washington set a tone that he hoped would endure among all those who in the future would be temporarily imbued with the powers of the presidency, avoiding any hint of the debauchery and high-handedness of European monarchs whose claim of a God-given right to reign was challenged by the new nation. When Washington desired a piece of land the nascent federal government owned, he did what everyone else who wanted that real estate did. Washington submitted a bid, the winning one, as it turned out.

Thomas Jefferson, who in the Declaration of Independence gave us the lofty ideal that all men are created equal even as he owned slaves to the end of his life, pointed the nation west toward its manifest destiny with the Louisiana Purchase and applied the principles of scientific thought as he strived for the best policies to benefit the nation and its people.

Abraham Lincoln freed the slaves, whom the Confederacy leaders declared that the Christian God commanded them to own, before the shock of his assassination bequeathed us three amendments expanding our Constitutional rights to all.

Theodore Roosevelt, in a time of concentrated wealth the world had never seen amid desperate want, railed against the rich not for having money, but for abusing their fortunate status. He used government to rein in the worst impulses of the "malefactors of wealth."

Franklin D. Roosevelt overcame the handicap of a patrician upbringing to recognize the need to recover from the nation's worst economic crisis with lasting economic reforms before preparing the people to prosecute a war against the murderous Nazi racists and their allies.

Dwight Eisenhower saw a nation pregnant with economic opportunity and gave it stretch marks in the 55,000 miles of Interstate highways while sending in the 101st Airborne Division to protect the first African American children going to Little Rock's Central High School.

John F. Kennedy implored us to "ask not what your country can do for you, ask what you can do for your country" and set us on a trajectory toward the moon.

Lyndon Johnson overcame the racist environment of his youth to marshal votes for the Civil Rights Act, the Voting Rights Act, as well as Medicare so that the disabled and elderly would not suffer needlessly and die early, even as he lost his way in Vietnam.

Richard Nixon signed the Clean Air and Clean Water Acts, created the Environmental Protection Agency, and came out for national health care even as his many crimes enveloped him, until at long last he showed his patriotic respect for our Constitution by resigning.

Ronald Reagan, certain that the New Deal was holding back a richer future, persuaded the nation for better or worse to move in a new direction that, while Reagan could not have anticipated this, set us on the path to the Trump presidency.

Even the worst of the presidents shared one common trait vital to democracy that is missing from the Trump administration.

Chester Arthur came from New York political corruption, but when the assassination of James Garfield elevated Arthur to president, he told his cronies never to darken the White House door. Unwilling to sully the office he unexpectedly occupied, Arthur began professionalizing the federal workforce, reducing patronage by persuading Congress to enact the Pendleton Civil Service Reform Act.

Warren G. Harding is remembered for the Teapot Dome scandal that benefited his crooked friends in business, but he also promoted nascent enterprises that would increase national wealth and opportunity, including aviation, cars and paved roads for them to drive on, and radio broadcasting.

John Adams came closest to Trump (and Nixon) with the four Alien and Sedition Acts that restricted immigration and gave him a path to prosecute political enemies—as Trump says he wants to do. One of those four laws remained on the books long enough to give legal cover to the internment of Japanese Americans in 1942. Still, the Adams administration was free of scandal, managed government finances prudently, and launched the modern Navy.

What distinguishes these American presidents from Trump? Some did great deeds and inspired great ambitions among the people, while others got lost in the small stuff. Some were reformers, others determined guardians of the status quo. Some spoke eloquently, lending grace to civic debate, while others were coarse, even verbal clods. Some, like Barack Obama, were personally scrupulous, their administrations free of scandal, while others, like Bill Clinton, couldn't control their impulses.

What they had in common was that their administrations were about America and its people. Some presidents made America great, while others tried and missed the mark. Some took great political risks to move the country forward, as when Lyndon Johnson could not abide the oppression of fellow citizens a century after the Civil War just because of the color of their skin. Johnson knew his actions would cost Democrats the South for generations, but did what he thought was in the nation's best interests even if it would harm his party.

We can look back at these presidents and applaud or be appalled by their conduct. But we must always take care to judge them by the standards of their day, not by conditions today. Viewed properly in the context of their times, the last forty-four presidents all pursued policies that they believed would make for a better America tomorrow.

The Trump presidency is about Trump. Period. Full stop.

He says so himself all the time, but because he mixes it in with lines about how he loves everyone and what a terrific job he will do, millions of Americans believe he is at one with them even though he is not even at one with himself. But listen skeptically and carefully and it becomes clear that Trump boasts that his term in office is all about him, about how great he is, about how large the crowds are, about his negotiating skills, about his authority to start a nuclear war, as he pledged on the campaign trail that he would. Trump is desperate for others to fill the void inside himself. He has a sad need for attention and, preferably, public adoration.

There is so much work to do as president that lack of sleep and quick aging have become hallmarks of the presidency. Trump is not one to stay up past midnight reading policy memos and calling on the vast array of government experts to ask their help in understanding difficult issues of economics, geopolitics, science, trade, or anything else. Instead the White House staff has confirmed that he spends hours each day in front of a television, the remote control flicking from one channel to another so Trump can see the latest news about himself. When he doesn't like what he sees, he sends out nastygram tweets, often in the wee hours before dawn.

Tony Schwartz, the writer of Trump's bestselling book *The Art of the Deal,* understands these motivations. Schwartz told the documentary filmmaker Libby Handros that the simple fact is that "Donald Trump would be a very unhappy man if no one paid attention to him."

Trump has also lived a life of thumbing his nose at conventions and law enforcement, learning lessons as a boy from his father, Fred, whose business partner was an associate of the Gambino and Genovese crime families. He has long been in deep with mobsters, domestic and foreign, along with corrupt union bosses and assorted swindlers. Trump even spent years deeply entangled with a major international drug trafficker who, like many of the others, enjoyed their mutually lucrative arrangements.

This life experience helps explain why he and his staff often talk as if the position of president is dictatorial, a profoundly anti-American notion. Instead of a president of specific duties and constitutionally limited authority, Trump and his aides talk as if he is an absolute ruler, or should be, to whom all must bend the knee. Indeed, one of his longest and closest aides said exactly that. Omarosa Manigault, who met Trump as a contestant on his show *The Apprentice* and became a repeat guest over the years, was the Trump campaign's director of African American outreach.

"Every critic, every detractor, will have to bow down to President Trump," Manigault told the documentary television program *Frontline.* "It's everyone who's ever doubted Donald, whoever disagreed, whoever challenged him. It is the ultimate revenge to become the most powerful man in the universe," she said. Instead of rebuking Omarosa, Trump made her director of the White House Office of Public Liaison, a post that means she deals with special interest groups.

He also brought to the White House his philosophy of life, a philosophy totally at odds with political compromise, of appreciating that others in office have different interests and needs in their home districts. Over many years and in many forums Trump has laid out his life philosophy in some detail. And his behavior is consistent with his stated views on life.

Trump himself has reduced his life philosophy to a single word—revenge.

"I love getting even," Trump advised in one of his books, adding "go for the jugular, attack them in spades!" Repeatedly he has said in talks and in his books that destroying the lives of people he considers disloyal gives him pleasure. That Trump does not recognize ethical limits on conduct, the propriety George Washington modeled, derives from his fundamental character, narcissism. But unlike the mythic figure who came to a tragic end drowning in the pool that mirrored his visage, Trump's narcissism has so far helped him get to where he has for decades said he belonged—in the White House.

Over many years in paid public appearances and in books bearing his name on the cover, Trump rejected the idea of turning the other cheek, saying that those who do are "fools" and "idiots." This philosophy was ignored by the many pastors who endorsed Trump and accepted his statement that he is a Christian. That is worth pondering because revenge is explicitly rejected by Jesus and runs counter to the whole theme of the New Testament. The Golden Rule has no place in the life of Donald Trump. Revenge is the philosophy of dictators and mob bosses everywhere and always, used to keep others in line with threats of economic ruin, violence, or worse. That Trump by his silence gave tacit approval to what Omarosa said about Americans bowing down and that he then put her on the government payroll reinforces the facts showing that the Trump presidency is unlike anything that came before, a presidency built on open public contempt for Constitutional principles. As president, he brought into the White House a host of people with fringe ideas, some of them Islamophobes, some white nationalists, some xenophobes, and many of them sharing Trump's ignorance of science. As we shall explore ahead, many of them had no qualifications whatsoever for the posts he appointed them to; he just called them "terrific." For those posts that required Senate confirmation, he got the advice and consent of a majority of senators despite testimony revealing some of them as modern know-nothings and one of them being determined to destroy the agency he now runs.

From ambassadorships to agency heads, Trump has left the vast majority of the nearly four thousand positions under his control vacant. But the long-term concern involves the many appointees, known as the politicals, who seldom make the news. Many of these jobs were filled at the behest of people around Trump, as happens in all administrations. But this time is different.

The Trump administration deposited political termites throughout the structure of our government. Their task, in the words of Trump's first White House strategic adviser, Steve Bannon, is the "deconstruction of the administrative state." By that, Bannon has explained, he means to undo the tax, trade, regulatory, and other means by which the federal government carries out its duties. The endgame is not just a smaller government, which Republicans always say they want, but a weak government, a government that looks first after the best-off in the land, not those most in need of a helping hand in the form of a sound education, clean water, and the other basics of a healthy society in the twenty-first century. These termites operate out of sight, in some cases in extraordinary secrecy, to bully or scare scientists into leaving, remove from public access important public records, and for all anyone knows destroy many of them. Such records are often necessary to enforce environmental, worker safety, and other laws.

The administration, however, has wrought one significant change to expand equality in America. Thanks to Trump the mentally ill now have virtually the same gun rights as the sane.

This book is my attempt to examine the Trump administration's policies in a cohesive narrative, the opposite of Trump's incoherent statements, which in polite company are called word salad. Much of what follows has been reported glancingly in the news, some of it not reported at all.

This is an administration that actively looks for the least qualified and the most aggressive termites to eat away at the structure of government.

To overhaul the federal Department of Education, Trump choose an heiress with no background in education theory or administration, but an intense desire to promote schooling that is corporate run and free to be religious. To run Housing and Urban Development, he picked a retired surgeon with no administrative experience, no housing expertise, and who has said that the Egyptian pyramids were not tombs for dead pharaohs but granaries. At Treasury, Trump chose for secretary a Wall Street banker who made much of his fortune aggressively foreclosing on homeowners. To run the Environmental Protection Agency, he chose a lawyer who had vowed to destroy it.

After firing an FBI director who would not pledge personal loyalty to him and close part of the Russia investigation, Trump appointed as FBI director a lawyer who earned more than $17 million the previous year defending corrupt banks involved in money laundering and other white-collar crimes the FBI is known to investigate.

For surgeon general, a job where a principal duty is to persuade Americans to not take up smoking, Trump named a physician who owned tobacco company stocks.

So many facts from the Trump administration are unknown or little known. That is because while Trump rails against honest reporting that he calls "fake news," he benefits from organizations that traffic in made-up stories, twisted facts, or simple silence on matters they cannot explain away.

A glimpse of this showed up in August when pollster Peter D. Hart put a dozen people of varying political views in a room in Pittsburgh. All said they were embarrassed by Trump, but those who voted for him stood by him, at least for the moment. Most interesting was what Hart discovered when he asked the focus group about Robert Mueller, the special prosecutor heading the Russia investigation that Trump has been so eager to stop. Four people, all Trump voters, had no idea who he was. Few things benefit Trump more than ignorance.

The Hart focus group reminded us of what every con artist knows: people see what they want to see, hear what they want to hear, believe what they want to believe, and let their hopes and wishes vanquish their skepticism. Unless and until some fact they cannot reconcile slaps them hard in the face, the con's marks will keep seeing the world through the credulous and distorted lens they fashioned for themselves.

His entire life Trump has been a con artist. In *The Art of the Deal* he

brags about deceptions that enriched him. He has boasted about not paying banks that loaned him billions of dollars. He conned thousands of
people desperate to learn what Trump said were the secrets of his success
into paying up to $35,000 to attend Trump University. In a promotional
video, Trump said his university would provide a better education than
the finest business schools with a faculty he personally picked. Lawsuits
forced Trump's testimony and documents that showed that there were no
secrets he shared with the "students." The faculty never met Trump. These
professors turned out to be fast-food managers and others with no experience in real estate, the focus of the "university." Because of the lawsuits,
Trump paid back $25 million to the people he conned so the scam would
not follow him into the White House.

To con a wider audience, Trump relies on faux news organizations.
People who get their news from these sources believe, reasonably, that he
is under siege for doing the right thing.

Many millions of Americans, including about half of Republicans according to many polls, believe that Trump is their champion and is being
railroaded by Democrats who collude with the journalists whom Trump
calls the "enemies of the people." The more extreme among them say that
the Democrats want to destroy America by imposing Sharia law. That
crazy beliefs have currency in the Trump era provides great fodder for
television comedians. The jokes, however accurate in fact and skewering
in tone, amuse those who have not bought into Trump, but only strengthen
the resolve of those who project onto Trump their hopes and dreams. To
those unaware of the factual basis for the humor, it comes across as mean,
dishonest, and despicable.

In this context consider the plight of congressional Republicans, some
of whom say in private Trump is unsuited for the presidency, as ignorant
as he is unstable. To go against Trump when half of their constituents believe he is a demigod or at least their last best hope for a better future is
to risk political suicide. And they know that if they do publicly disagree
with Trump they can expect a primary challenge that may well end their
careers. Trump knows that to remain in power he must cow the Republicans so they dare not say the word *impeachment*.

Many of those who believe in Trump come from the 90 percent whose
economic fortunes dwindled over the last half century, turning up only

starting in 2013, while the richest of the rich have built fortunes that even John D. Rockefeller, Andrew Carnegie, and J. P. Morgan Jr. could not have imagined. The vast majority suffer real economic pain, which I documented in a series of books that revealed government policies few knew about that stealthily take money from them and transfer it to the already very rich. Their very real grievances include the fact that policies embraced by both political parties ignored their plight or made it worse. In 2012 the average income that the bottom 90 percent reported on tax returns was slightly less, after inflation, than what the same demographic reported in 1967.

A major source of Trump's influence comes from people who distrust respected news organizations and instead rely on those that have been shown to have little regard for fact, especially when it comes to Trump. To discourage the faithful from consulting the work of journalists that Trump cannot dispute, he simply damns them all with the term "fake news" so his supporters will not even bother.

The biggest influence is Rupert Murdoch's Fox News, its faux day-time newscasts and evening entertainment shows propaganda for Trump. What is reported is often one-sided, inaccurate, or just made up. Until not long before he was fired for sexual harassment, Fox president Roger Ailes talked daily with Trump.

There is also the fast-growing website Breitbart, which promotes racially charged stories and whose chairman served as Trump's strategic director in the White House. Trump has told tales that can be found at racist websites like the neo-Nazi Daily Stormer. Trump has at times spread made-up news from Sputnik, a Russian propaganda operation, without citing his source. But troubling as it is that any American leader would spread disinformation from a hostile foreign power, that is not the most disturbing example of how Trump consumes fake news. Trump has cited as reliable, and has appeared as a guest on, an Internet show called InfoWars. There host Alex Jones rants at length about such vital issues of the day as his discovery that "interdimensional beings" secretly control the American elites. Jones says not to worry, that because of his courageous reporting the hidden truth about these creatures is, finally, starting to come out. We will examine the role all this plays in the Trump era.

What has happened to American democracy has perplexed and

stunned people in many countries who looked upon America, flaws and all, as a beacon of hope and a society interested in justice. Even former president George W. Bush has complained about the crudeness of public discourse today. Trump's victory also gave cause for a party in the Kremlin—and when word of this secret Kremlin victory party got out, the government-controlled television news ran video of one of two senior Russian officials being seized in meetings, bags thrown over their heads, their whereabouts unknown ever since.

In June 2016 Hillary Clinton, in an address on foreign policy, said, "Moscow and Beijing are deeply envious of our alliances around the world, because they have nothing to match them. They'd love for us to elect a President who would jeopardize that source of strength. If Donald gets his way, they'll be celebrating in the Kremlin. We cannot let that happen." The Chinese have seized upon Trump's erratic behavior and his cancellation of the Trans-Pacific Partnership to promote their own trade deal, orienting fifteen Pacific Rim economies and India away from Washington and toward Beijing.

There is much more, so let's get to it.

Kleptocracy Rising

As President Donald Trump's inaugural motorcade left the Capitol for the White House, it passed more military and police guards than civilians. Here and there knots of people gathered behind the barricades, many booing as the presidential limousine, known as The Beast, passed them by.

On one side of the street protesters waved homemade placards decrying racism, sexism, and corruption; demanding Trump release his tax returns; and making lurid fun of an imagined bromance between the new American president and Russian leader Vladimir Putin. One man held a little effigy of Trump, devil's horns growing out of its yellow hair. Across the street, the ranks of Trump supporters were thinner and subdued, especially compared to the boisterous enthusiasm eight years earlier when nary a protester turned out for Barack Obama's first inauguration.

About five blocks short of the White House, Trump ordered The Beast stopped. A few people chanted "USA! USA!"

A Secret Service agent opened the door. Trump stepped out, wearing a dark blue overcoat, his signature red tie hanging unfashionably below his belt. From the other side his wife, Melania, emerged in her stunning, form-fitting ice blue dress by Ralph Lauren with matching suede pumps and long cuffed gloves, revealing her highly sophisticated sense of fashion and bottomless budget for clothes. The rest of the family stepped out, too.

This was not some random point along the route, but one carefully chosen to send a message. The Trumps' stroll occurred outside the Old Post Office and Clock Tower, which Trump had just converted into the Trump International Hotel Washington.

On the night before the inauguration, Team Trump dined at the hotel.

Sean Spicer, who was about to become White House press secretary, endorsed the hotel. "It's an absolutely stunning hotel. I encourage you to go there if you haven't been by," he exclaimed.

This was an official signal that no boundaries would be drawn between presidential duties and personal profits. The family's two-minute turn on the Pennsylvania Avenue asphalt outside the president's newest hotel sent a clear signal to those seeking to curry favor with him and his family that they should first pay tribute. The message radiated quickly, enveloping this acquisitive administration at home and abroad.

The Al-Sabah family seemingly had already gotten the message. The Al-Sabahs own enough oil-rich real estate in the Middle East that their family does business as a country called Kuwait. Each year the Kuwaiti government hosts a lavish party to mark its national day, an event held in Washington as well to express its thanks to America for Operation Desert Storm. This first Gulf War easily ousted Saddam Hussein's invading army, recovering much of what they stole, including the gold bathroom sink faucets that American soldiers reinstalled in the emir's bathroom before he returned to his palace.

For years, the Kuwaitis hosted their annual soirée at the Four Seasons hotel, one of Washington's swankiest. But after the 2016 elections the Kuwaitis decided they would get much more value for the money by moving the affair to Trump's hotel.

President Trump stopped by the hotel for dinner a few times, reinforcing the message of seamlessness between his official duties and his private business. In official appearances, the president often talked about how terrific his properties are, using the White House and the presidential seal as props to promote his profiteering.

Trump's strategy has made the hotel a phenomenal success.

Trump had leased the property from the federal government for sixty years. Reports the Trump Organization filed before the opening projected losses of $2.1 million in the first four months of 2017. Instead it generated a profit of almost $2 million, documents obtained by *The Washington Post* showed.

Trump's hotel charges the highest room rates in Washington even though nothing distinguishes it from other high-end lodging establishments, other than the name over the entrance.

Average room rates at Trump hotels fell during much of 2016, but right after the election rates soared 20 percent. Similar hotels increased rates by about one percent compared to the prior year. After Trump took office luxury hotel prices in America were flat, except for Trump hotels, where rates soared by as much as 40 percent, *The Economist* magazine concluded after analyzing published rates.

Documents filed with the government's property management arm, the General Services Administration, revealed that at Trump's Washington hotel the average revenue per guest night was $653. That was triple the average of all District of Columbia hotels and well above what other high-end hotels charged.

At night, the Trump bar and restaurant hummed. Steaks cost $60. Trump's cash registers rang up more than $68,000 per day selling food and beverages, a total in the first 120 days of $8.2 million. The tabs were run up by lobbyists, executives, foreign diplomats, and other favor seekers with deep expense accounts who found it the best place to meet Trump cabinet members and other appointees with their own deep pockets.

The hotel business Trump promoted by stopping The Beast showed how kleptocracies begin in plain sight. But while the keen-eyed swamp dwellers in Washington understood, many people watching the live television broadcast missed the message because the video pool camera in a truck ahead of The Beast stayed focused on the family, not the surrounding buildings. The reason for the stop got little serious discussion.

Interestingly, the massive granite-walled building that became a Trump hotel connected the president to a crooked nineteenth-century industrial titan turned politician whose avaricious behavior bore striking similarities to Trump's. The site for the Old Post Office had been chosen by Senator Leland Stanford of California, who became one of the capital's swamp dwellers after making a fortune cheating American taxpayers. Stanford and his cronies tripled their fee per mile for much of the Central Pacific Railroad track by sending Washington maps showing that the flatlands outside Sacramento were High Sierra mountains. Trump himself had previously faked accounting records, filed at least two fraudulent income tax returns, and made false claims to escape property tax bills.

When completed in 1899, the Romanesque Revival structure was the first in America's capital built using steel frame technology. Trump Tower and the Trump Plaza apartments in Manhattan were among the first high-rises there made of concrete, all of it Mafia-supplied cement.

Stanford used immigrant labor from China for dangerous work with dynamite and other tasks, and many of them died, according to congressional testimony, their wages unpaid. Trump used illegal immigrants with sledgehammers (but no hard hats or other safety gear) to demolish a twelve-story Manhattan department store so he could build Trump Tower. A federal judge, after a trial, held that Trump engaged in a conspiracy to cheat those men out of their full $4 an hour pay.

Stanford personally completed the transcontinental railroad by driving the Golden Spike into the last rail section in 1869. Trump puts his name on his buildings in faux gold capital letters.

Stanford started what became one of the world's great universities, named for his dead son. Trump started a faux university named for himself that taught nothing of value and collapsed in scandal.

In many ways the new administration, like Trump himself, would prove to be crass. But when it came to enriching himself and his family through his official position, Trump applied subtle techniques, like frequently visiting Mar-a-Lago and his golf courses, where the Secret Service paid full price for everything, including the golf carts to follow the president around his links. Though as a candidate he vowed never to leave the White House and never play golf or visit his golf courses because there was so much work to do, he spent seven of the first nine weekends as president at his properties, setting a pattern that has continued.

During the transition, Trump doubled the fee to become a Mar-a-Lago member to $200,000, showing the power of the presidency for someone determined to maximize such a profitable opportunity. Candidate Trump castigated Bill and Hillary Clinton for making money because of their positions, calling what they did criminal. They raked in money from speeches, but at least they waited until they were out of office to cash in.

During the transition, Trump pledged that he would not expand his businesses, would not be opening new hotels and the like. "No new deals will be done during my term(s) in office," he tweeted.

Trump had long been known to never let a penny slip past his fingers.

He once deposited a check for 13 cents, a fake refund sent him by the satirical magazine *Spy* to test the avariciousness of the rich and famous. Of the fifty-eight well-heeled Americans to whom *Spy* sent increasingly smaller checks, only Trump and his pal Adnan Khashoggi, the Middle East arms merchant, cashed theirs.

Events would soon show that all that had changed was the size of the stakes. Ivanka Trump's clothing line would get an official endorsement from White House adviser Kellyanne Conway, who later had to apologize. Frequent visits to Trump properties would remind those seeking favors of where to spend their money. And the deal making did not stop; it was just nominally done by Trump's oldest sons.

No opportunity to profit from the Trump candidacy was too crass. When son Eric showed up at a Trump-branded golf course in Scotland, the staff were issued "Make Turnberry Great Again" hats, playing off the president's campaign slogan.

White House promotion of the Trump Washington hotel got to be too much for Diane Gross and her husband, Khalid Pitts. They owned one of the hottest bistros in Washington. It was hopping until Trump became president.

Cork Wine Bar gets rave reviews, offers more than fifty wines by the glass, and often has diplomats, lobbyists, and officials waiting for tables. But business slowed once Trump took office, the couple said in a lawsuit filed in District of Columbia Superior Court.

"A significant portion of Cork's business involves serving meals and alcoholic beverages, and hosting events, often for large groups of individuals and organizations, including many from outside the United States, who have business of one kind or another with—including seeking to influence the policies of—United States Government and its elected officials," they said in court papers.

Trump's hotel would simply have been another competitor had Hillary Clinton won the Electoral College as well as the popular vote. But because Trump became president, Gross and Pitts complained, "many organizations and individuals, including citizens of nations other than the United States, substantially increased the use of" the Trump hotel to the detriment of Cork Wine Bar.

"The perception of many of the customers and prospective customers of the hotel, substantially aided by the marketing efforts of officers and employees of the hotel," as well as the president, his family, and his associates, was "that it would be to their advantage in their dealings with President Donald J. Trump and other agencies of the United States Government" to patronize his hotel and not Cork Wine Bar.

"Rather than take any significant steps to avoid exploiting public office for private gain," their lawsuit continued, Trump, his family, and White House staff and advisers "continued to promote the hotel to maximize its exposure and income-producing potential."

Their complaint cited examples of Trump bringing up the hotel in official White House meetings where television cameras were present, reinforcing the impression among favor seekers that doing business there would be smart.

One lobbyist, evidently a frequent but unnamed Cork Wine Bar customer, was quoted in the lawsuit. "Reading between the lines isn't that tough here," he told Gross and Pitts. "The senior [White House] staff hang out in the lobby bar at the hotel. They are seeing who spends time and money there and who books large parties there and large blocks of rooms for delegations.

"Point is," the lobbyist was quoted as saying, "someone is paying attention to the person who orders the $1,000 bottle of wine."

The couple also complained that Trump was in violation of the sixty-year lease of the Old Post Office, which was owned by the federal government. Section 37.19 of the lease "specifically forbids" any federal employee from receiving any gain or benefit from the lease.

"No member or delegate to Congress, or elected official of the government of the United States," the lease states, "shall be admitted to any share or part of this lease, or to any benefit that may arise therefrom."

There was an exception for shareholders in publicly traded corporations. Trump owns his businesses, making that clause irrelevant.

Trump signed many Old Post Office documents without reading them, he acknowledged in a separate lawsuit. And while he put his more than five hundred business entities into a supposedly blind trust, that trust consists largely of Trump-named businesses managed by his two oldest sons. Previous presidents owned stocks and bonds, which were put into blind trusts, sometimes with orders to sell and buy mutual funds instead. But Trump's properties were not shielded the same way.

The blind trust was also modified shortly after Trump took office. The changes allow him to withdraw as much cash as he wants at any time. Trump told *Forbes* that his sons fill him on how much money his businesses are making. Given those facts, what Trump created was an eyes-wide-open blind trust.

The language in the contract making Trump ineligible because he was president seemed cut and dried. That is exactly what a contracting officer for the federal Government Services Administration, the GSA, which leased the Old Post Office to Trump, wrote in a letter that the agency made public. Still, Kevin M. Terry found Trump in "full compliance" with the lease terms because Trump had put his interest into that revocable trust.

Gross and Pitts saw a conflict of interest problem for the GSA. Its top official served at the pleasure of the president. And they had no doubt that a GSA interpretation forcing the president to sell his lease interest to his hotel would not please him.

The couple suggested three remedies. One would be shutting down the hotel, including its bar and restaurant, until Trump left office, the cleanest, if most costly, solution. Another solution would be for Trump and his family to "promptly and fully" sell their interests. Or they said, Trump could resolve the issue by "resigning as president of the United States."

Even a sale of the leasehold posed ethical problems. Who would determine if it was a sweetheart deal or a proper arm's length negotiation? And how would anyone know unless every detail of any transfer was made public?

Trump's lawyers moved to dismiss the lawsuit, making contradictory arguments that he was in a position of privilege, immune to such a civil action as president, and yet at the same time that he was not enjoying any special benefit as president.

His lawyers argued that the Constitution's supremacy clause barred the lawsuit. A local court "may not declare conduct unlawful because it is performed by the President, for that is a transparent attempt to directly regulate the Presidency," they wrote, invoking a long-established doctrine about the limited immunity the president, like other officials, enjoys for official actions.

"The premise of this lawsuit is that D.C. common law prohibits the President of the United States from owning an interest in a hotel, precisely because he is President of the United States," Trump's lawyers wrote. However, the core of the Cork Wine Bar complaint was that the president was using his office for unfair competition and was in violation of the lease.

Simultaneously, Trump's lawyers argued that Cork Wine Bar had no case because Trump's hotel was just another business competitor, one located more than a mile from their establishment, which had nothing to do with his being president.

Taken together Trump's lawyers crafted a legal argument for eating your cake and having it too. They were saying Trump's office made him immune, but he had no advantages compared to any other citizen.

Scott Rome, the lawyer representing Cork Wine Bar, said his clients believe the lease's clause barring any elected official "is strong evidence that the government itself, in drafting the Lease, understood that such ownership by an elected official would be problematic and would result in unfair competition.

"Trump should choose to be President or choose to continue to own or operate businesses," Rome said. "If he chooses to keep his businesses while President, he should not be permitted to claim presidential immunity when he gets sued for their operation."

Rome also recalled a controversy when another business owner became president. "Jimmy Carter gave up his peanut farm."

To quell doubts about the integrity of his decisions as president, Carter in 1977 put his peanut business into a blind trust. He even gave the trustee authority to sell the business. Nonetheless a special prosecutor, Paul J. Curran, spent six months investigating Carter's business, discovering that Carter's brother Billy had been helping himself to more money than he was supposed to get and also found some routine small business accounting issues. "No indictment can or should be brought against anyone," Curran's 180-page report concluded.

If Carter had to sell, or *divest*, in legalese, his small business in Georgia, why should Trump get special privileges? Trump's vastly larger businesses, operating on five continents, and the Washington hotel lease raise much bigger questions, Rome said. Many others noted that these businesses created huge opportunities for corruption.

Cork Wine Bar's case, still pending at this writing, was not the only lawsuit challenging the connections between official business and the president profiting off his personal businesses. Others raised issues about anticorruption clauses in the Constitution. One of them involved a mere $150 payment and the opinion of a former Justice Department lawyer who later was a Supreme Court justice, as the next chapter explains.

Emoluments

Ensuring the integrity of the United States government was one of the major concerns of the Framers, who put three anticorruption clauses in the Constitution.

When the first American Republic began in 1781 under the Articles of Confederation, the founders of the modern world's first democratic society fretted about how to ensure against official corruption. They wrote and spoke about their worry that hidden or open payments to officials could interfere with the moral judgment of even the best of men. That was why they took such care with the corrupting effect of money. They wanted to limit payments, apart from government salaries, that could influence how the public's business would be conducted. The Articles contained two emoluments clauses as anticorruption measures.

When the Constitution was drafted in 1787, establishing the second American Republic in which we still live, this concern was even greater. The Constitution contains three emoluments clauses, relating to concerns foreign and domestic. The domestic clause applies to only one person—the sitting president.

In drafting the foreign emoluments clause, the Framers knew full well the history of corrupting payments between foreign monarchs and others in Europe. Concerns about this type of influence were so great that in the early 1800s the states nearly ratified a Constitutional amendment that would have stripped the citizenship of any American who accepted payments from foreign governments and their agents without the explicit consent of Congress.

Fast forward to 1986. During the Reagan era, the issue of foreign emoluments so troubled the National Aeronautics and Space Administration that it sought a formal ruling by the Justice Department. The issue? Could a NASA scientist accept a $150 payment from an Australian university for reviewing, on his own time, a doctoral thesis on aerosol sprays. The task of evaluating whether this tiny sum violated the Constitution fell to a Justice Department lawyer named Samuel Alito, who two decades later would become a Supreme Court justice. Alito may have to rule on emoluments clause issues raised by Trump's presidency.

Alito pointed out that the Australian university was not a foreign government, though it was funded by one, and the scientist would be reviewing the dissertation on his own time in a field in which he was a renowned authority. Alito also observed that the NASA scientist was sought because of his expertise, not his government position.

Because of these limiting circumstances, Alito wrote, "we do not believe that it presents the opportunity for 'corruption and foreign influence' that concerned the Framers and that we must presume it exists whenever a gift or emolument comes directly from a foreign government or one of its instrumentalities."

Questions of corruption and foreign influence are on the front burner today because of the extensive business holdings of Donald Trump and his actions encouraging foreign powers, lobbyists, and other favor seekers to spend money at his Washington hotel and other properties.

The domestic emoluments clause that applies only to the president states that beyond his government salary the president may not receive "any other Emolument from the United States, or any of them." Those last six words bar payments from the federal government or any of the fifty states to the president.

Without doubt Trump has been profiting from spending at his properties by foreign governments, like the party the Kuwaiti government held at his hotel in the Old Post Office described in the previous chapter. Also Trump has been profiting from federal, state, and local governments spending money at his properties as part of presidential security details. When Trump stays at Mar-a-Lago, his country clubs, or Trump Tower, these governments rent rooms, buy meals, and use golf carts for which they pay full retail prices.

Trump controls the amount of money he collects this way. He could not leave the White House except to travel to the presidential retreat at Camp David. He could forgo golf while in office, as he repeatedly promised at campaign rallies. That would reduce his domestic emoluments in dollar terms. Instead, during his first 202 days in office, Trump spent sixty-five days at Mar-a-Lago, his New Jersey golf course, or Trump Tower. That's almost one day in three.

Lawsuits accusing Trump of violating the Constitution's emoluments clauses have been filed by attorneys general from sixteen states and by 196 senators and representatives, Democrats all; a bipartisan ethics watchdog organization called Citizens for Responsibility and Ethics in Washington, or CREW; and a growing list of business owners who compete with Trump hotels and restaurants.

Their lawsuits and public statements describe calculated, willfully blind violations of the anticorruption emoluments clauses. Trump's lawyers, both his private counsel and Justice Department lawyers representing him as president, all contend there is nothing going on, and even if there was, the Constitution provides no pathway for these aggrieved parties to press their case in any court. Trump's lawyers say the plaintiffs lack standing, meaning they have no right under the law to bring a case enforcing the Constitution. Trump's position is that the plaintiffs cannot show they have suffered any personal or direct harm.

The very different ways these sides see the same set of facts are a crucial issue of democratic self-governance. The emoluments issues may seem abstract—a word the president's lawyers invoke—but they go to the very nature of the United States of America and whether we are a nation of laws or of people, whether elected office is for public service or it permits profiteering.

Trump is the first president to pose numerous questions about whether he is receiving income from foreign governments, which the Framers felt was inherently corrupting. He is also the first to present the issue of profiting from spending by federal, state, and local governments with payments that the Framers denied to the president. How these cases are resolved will likely have an enormous influence on whether the American Republic endures not just in the current era but in the future when other rich men—and women—known more for their presumed wealth than any record of public service may get enough votes to occupy the White House.

*   *   *

In modern America *emolument* is a hoary word few people have ever used in conversation. Trump's private and Justice Department lawyers narrowly define emolument. In court papers, the Justice Department argues that the foreign emoluments clause does "not prohibit any company in which the president has any financial interest from doing business with any foreign, federal, or state instrumentality." In other words, anything short of a flat-out bribe is legal, just so long as the transaction is run through one of the more than five hundred companies owned by the president. That is the official line at the United States Justice Department.

During the Constitutional Convention in Philadelphia, that's not how the word was understood. Back then *emolument* was in common use. Dictionaries from the era when the Constitution was written show that *emolument* had a broad meaning, including profit, gain, benefit, and advantage.

Sir William Blackstone's *Commentaries* was well known to the Framers and remains in print today. John Mikhail, a Georgetown University law professor who has extensively researched the emoluments clause, found that "the majority of Blackstone's usages of 'emolument' involve benefits other than government salaries or perquisites," including profits from business and rents from land.

Blackstone's broad view is also favored by the chief ethics officers in the George W. Bush and Barack Obama administrations, Richard W. Painter and Norm Eisen. As leaders of Citizens for Responsibility and Ethics in Washington, they describe Trump's conduct as a "flagrant abuse" of the Constitution for personal profit. CREW argued that not only was Trump prohibited from any connection to his Washington hotel under the lease, his whole business empire offends the Constitution's emoluments clauses. One clause concerns money from foreign powers and their agents, which would include corporations, while the other concerns his pay. The president receives a fixed salary during his term and "shall not receive within that Period any other Emolument from the United States, or any of them."

Trump's businesses have made lots of money from the federal government and the states when they pay for staff and security during his stays on his properties. CREW's lawsuit says the extensive business holdings create "countless conflicts of interest, as well as unprecedented influence by foreign governments," which it said violate the Constitution. Its lawsuit addresses both the foreign and domestic emoluments clauses.

"As the Framers were aware, private financial interests can subtly sway even the most virtuous leaders, and entanglements between American officials and foreign powers could pose a creeping, insidious threat to the Republic," CREW's lawsuit argues. "The Foreign Emoluments Clause was forged of the Framers' hard-won wisdom. It is no relic of a bygone era, but rather an expression of insight into the nature of the human condition and the essential preconditions of self-governance. And applied to Defendant's diverse dealings, the text and purpose of the Foreign Emoluments Clause speak as one: this cannot be allowed."

Painter, the Bush ethics chief, who now teaches law at the University of Minnesota, is almost apoplectic at Trump's conduct and the failure of his fellow Republicans to speak up.

"I'm not anti-corporation, but I recognize that corporations in this economy are global. They are not going to be loyal to America or anyone else, they are going to be loyal to their bottom line," Painter said. "Enormous concentrations of wealth and corporate wealth will follow the money, there is no concern about patriotism. That doesn't mean corporations are bad, but if we have corporations choosing our elected officials we will be in deep trouble."

Painter is also vexed by how corporations and foreign powers can influence the larger Trump family and, though them, official actions. "We have this Chilean billionaire who wants to open a mine in Minnesota," Painter said, referring to Andrónico Luksic, whose family is likely the richest in Chile. "So, what does he do? He buys up a house that Jared Kushner and his wife, Ivanka Trump, want and rents it to them," Painter said, referring to Trump's son-in-law and first daughter, both White House employees. The Obama administration blocked the Luksic family from opening what would be a huge mine to extract copper and nickel. Trump could overturn that by fiat. Luksic said no connection exists between the mine and the house rental.

To Painter this is an example of the kind of foreign influence that requires vigilance by the citizenry or the United States government will be up for sale.

Trump's advocates at the Morgan Lewis law firm propose a narrow interpretation of the Constitution under which any president could benefit from favor seekers becoming customers just so long as these are arm's length arrangements. This view fails to consider several important points. One is that the volume of business alone can be crucial, especially in times of financial stress. Another is the assumption that the arm's length standard can be enforced in a world where different customers pay different prices and forensic auditors are relatively few and expensive. A third is that the public and the government have no inherent right to audit Trump's books as a private business to see if deals really are arm's length. Also, the Morgan Lewis argument ignores the history of the emoluments clauses, which were designed to be preventatives, not tools for exposing corruption after it occurs.

That Trump uses his properties to enrich the family was obvious the evening he launched a missile strike in Syria while dining on the taxpayers' dime at Mar-a-Lago with President Xi Jinping of China. That very day the Beijing government granted Ivanka Trump three trademarks for her jewelry, handbags, and spa brands. In the first six months of the Trump presidency, China granted, provisionally or in full, at least twenty-four trademarks to her company Ivanka Trump Marks LLC. More than forty other intellectual property grants were pending in summer 2017, government records showed. In all the Trump family owned more than a hundred Chinese trademarks and Trump was seeking even more, including in Macau, a special administrative region of China that has surpassed Las Vegas as the planet's top gambling city.

Matthew Dresden, an intellectual property lawyer in Seattle, found the speedy Chinese approvals unusual. "The speed with which these appeals were decided is mind-blowing," he told the Associated Press. "I have never seen any decisions made that quickly." A Chinese intellectual property lawyer in Shanghai, You Yunting, said, "Considering the political element, the authorities are definitely not going to admit special treatment, but the possibility cannot be excluded."

Trump's tone on China changed markedly between April 2016, when he was a candidate, and the next April, when he hosted Xi at Mar-a-Lago. Candidate Trump castigated China for an "economic assault" on America and promised voters he would face down Chinese leaders, making them stop what he said was their currency-manipulating, steel-dumping, North

Korea–coddling ways. A year later, President Trump, the owner of more than a hundred Chinese trademarks, spoke glowingly in a television interview about how he and Xi shared "the most beautiful piece of chocolate cake that you've ever seen" at Mar-a-Lago. And he pledged cooperation between the two nations, even calling Xi for a history lesson about the thousands of years of differences between China and Korea.

A month before the Xi dinner, an observation by Ivanka in Vancouver, British Columbia, at the opening of a Trump-branded hotel owned by Malaysian investors, gave some unintended insight into her father's about-face. "You can't have a great partnership if you are not on the same page," she said.

In negotiating trade deals, Trump was inherently conflicted by this shower of trademarks in his duty to the United States and what he has often said is his duty to his business interests.

Trump has even drawn the Justice Department into acting as a de facto agent for his properties. Hotelier Eric Goode filed a lawsuit asserting unfair competition because since Trump took office, Goode's Bowery Hotel in New York City was losing business to Trump's hotel across from Central Park. The claim was a stretch because the two hotels are three miles apart. The Justice Department responded with an observation more marketing than legal. Trump's hotel gets five diamonds from the American Automobile Association, the government lawyers wrote, while Goode's rates only four.

Trump's defenses in these matters include that he has put his properties into a trust run by his grown sons and that he will give away profits earned from foreign governments. The disgorgement policy is laid out in a glossy eight-page brochure filled with promotional photos. The text is skimpy, forty sentences at best, that narrowly define when an attempt would even be made to identify foreign government business. For example, if a foreign government used direct billing, its payments would be considered for disgorging profits. However, if paid with a credit card, they would not.

Representative Elijah Cummings, a Maryland Democrat who took the lead in pressing the emoluments issue on Capitol Hill, said, "Complying with the United States Constitution is not an optional exercise, but a requirement for serving as our nation's President." Under the emoluments clause gifts can be accepted when Congress grants permission. Cummings offered a simple way out for Trump—ask Congress to grant its consent to accept money at his hotels and golf courses from foreign governments and their agents.

The Maryland attorney general's office said that in addition to the corrupting influence of owning the hotels and golf courses, Trump has pitted the interests of states with Trump properties against those without. "No state should be in competition with another state," when it comes to the president's business, said Raquel Coombs, a spokeswoman for Attorney General Brian Frosh.

An American-educated law professor who teaches in Ireland and is sympathetic to Trump's position offered an interesting historical point about the Old Post Office lease deal, one that illustrates the difference between Trump's conduct and the scrupulousness of George Washington. Seth Barrett Tillman of Maynooth University Department of Law noted that George Washington wanted to buy a piece of land the nascent federal government owned when he was president. Washington submitted a bid at public auction, just like everyone else seeking the parcel.

Washington won the auction, but he did so fair and square—and while taking care to not use his position as president for personal advantage. In contrast, Trump uses his privileged position to acquire additional revenue while continuing his lifelong practice of trying to avoid paying what he owes to governments and to other businesses for goods and services.

Refusals to Pay

Once they take office, most presidents try to behave with propriety. Even Chester Arthur, as noted earlier, told his corrupt cronies in 1881 to get lost. Harry Truman left office with less money than the little he had going in. As we have seen, Jimmy Carter was so scrupulous that he sold his peanut business lest anyone think he was taking advantage of his position as president. For two years Bill Clinton and his wife paid more than twice as much federal tax as the law required out of an excess of caution about reputation.

Not so Donald Trump. As president, he did not change his long history of refusing to pay contractors, fighting tax bills, and using two sets of wildly different estimates of the value of his properties. But as president he had to assign those values and certify to their accuracy, an ethical and legal obligation he tried to evade.

Like all high-level federal employees, Trump files an annual disclosure form with the Office of Government Ethics listing his income, assets, and debts. Its purpose is to "assist employees and their agencies in avoiding conflicts between official duties and private financial interests or affiliations." The front page of the form, in a bold box, twice warns about the consequences of lying, denying, or concealing. The form says:

> Falsification of information or failure to file or report information required to be reported may subject you to disciplinary action by your employing agency or other authority. Knowing and willful falsification of information required to be reported may also subject you to criminal prosecution.

The signature box reads:

I certify that the statements I have made on this form and all attached statements are true, complete, and correct to the best of my
knowledge.

Trump wanted to submit his financial disclosure without his signature.
Sheri Dillon, his lead lawyer at the Morgan Lewis law firm, wrote to the Office of Government Ethics saying that since Trump was filing voluntarily
a year before the next report was due, she saw no reason why a signature
was required. Marilyn Glynn, a retired veteran of the Office of Government Ethics, was astonished that Trump and his lawyer would even think
they could file an unsigned ethics form. "It would be as unusual as not
signing your taxes," Glynn said.

The form showed that Trump was worth nowhere near what he
claimed in the campaign when within days he said $8 billion, $7 billion,
$10 billion, more than $10 billion, and once $11 billion. The form showed
$1.4 billion.

When the report, properly signed, was filed, it showed that profits at
Mar-a-Lago had shot up by 23 percent from $30 million to $37 million.
That occurred after President-elect Trump doubled the fee for joining the
club to $200,000 and after the Secret Service, cabinet members, and other
federal employees paid for rooms, meals, golf carts, and drinks, and the
taxpayers picked up the tab for guests like the president of China and his
retinue.

The disclosure form set very high values on many Trump properties.
For example, he valued the golf course he plays while staying at Mar-a-
Lago at more than $50 million. The Palm Beach County property assessor
valued that Jupiter, Florida, property at $18.4 million in 2016. Concerned
about how much tax he would have to pay, Trump said that figure was too
high and appealed. He said its value was no more than $5 million. Trump
had first sued over the value of the property in 2014, saying the $25 mil-
lion valuation by the county assessor vastly overstated the golf course's
worth. Trump's property tax appeal papers say he paid $5 million for the
golf course when he acquired it in financial trouble in 2012.

So, which is it—more than $50 million or less than $5 million? What's
a mere 90 percent difference?

Trump sued the county again in 2017, when he was president, claiming the property was worth far less than what he put down on his Office of Government Ethics disclosure form. This time he didn't put a value on the property, reporter Jeff Ostrowski of *The Palm Beach Post* noted when he broke the story.

If the Jupiter course is worth $50 million, his property tax bill would be a tad more than $1 million. The assessor's valuation set the property tax at $383,171. Trump said he should pay no more than $104,000.

Trump valued his Westchester golf course, a short drive north of Manhattan, at more than $50 million on his presidential ethics form. But Trump also protested his property taxes, saying the local tax officials in Briarcliff Manor had grossly overvalued the property. Trump said it was worth only $1.35 million. That's roughly the value of two homes in the surrounding neighborhood. The golf course covers 140 acres, includes a 100-foot waterfall and a clubhouse that Trump claims has 1.7 acres of floor space.

There is no way to justify the claim that the golf course is worth less than $1.4 million. Yet that claim stood until David McKay Wilson reported it in the *Journal News,* the Westchester County Gannett newspaper, and Brian Ross of ABC and I gave it national attention. Trump then revised his tax protest, saying he was willing to agree to a value of $9 million, still at least an 82 percent discount from his ethics filings.

In California, Trump has said that he invested $264 million in his Palos Verdes Peninsula golf course, a sum out of proportion to the $14 million a year Trump says it collects in revenue. The Los Angeles County assessor set the value of the Palos Verdes property at $21.8 million. Trump argued that $10 million was appropriate. The assessor finally cut the value to $10.7 million, but only after the number of rounds of golf played on the course fell so severely that Trump had to cut prices. So, it seems, contrary to his claims, not every business Trump owns is a money machine.

We know the Palos Verdes value claims at both ends are absurdities, more evidence of how Trump just makes stuff up.

On the high end, anyone who actually put $264 million into a golf course property worth just $10 million would win from Trump his favorite sobriquet—loser. On the other end, a handful of residential lots he carved out of the property were sold in 2017 with an average price of about $1.5 million. If a lot for a single house is worth $1.5 million or more, then clearly more than 250 acres of golf links, the driving range, the parking areas and the nearly 40,000-square-foot clubhouse with its ocean view dining room are worth more than $10 million.

Then there is the story of the Doral, his Miami area golf course. The Doral brought in $115.9 million of revenue in 2016 plus $7.4 million in food and beverage sales for a total of almost $123.3 million. In addition to the "Blue Monster" golf course, the property includes 693 hotel rooms, unlike most of his golfing properties.

Trump bought the Doral with $104.8 million he borrowed from Deutsche Bank, the German money house infamous for laundering money for Russian oligarchs. The loan was for $106 million, slightly more than the purchase price, so Trump had only borrowed money in the deal, but none of his own.

He made extensive renovations that he said cost $250 million. More likely the costs were closer to the $19 million he borrowed during the renovation process. His purchase and improvement loans are on exceptional terms that most businesspeople would never get. The adjustable interest rate is about 3.5 percent, low for commercial property loans, with balloon payments due in 2023.

When Trump took office, the Doral was under a foreclosure order. Trump, as he often does, refused to pay contractors in full. Months after he became president he still owed millions to contractors on the Old Post Office conversion into the Trump Washington hotel. Most contractors just walk away when Trump refuses to pay. That's because Trump will spend far more to litigate than the amount in dispute to discourage contractors and small business owners he cheats from suing for what they are due.

One Doral contractor decided he was not going to be cheated. Trump had agreed to pay $135,000 to the Paint Spot, a Benjamin Moore dealer. After all the paint was delivered Trump owed $32,535.87.

After Trump repeatedly refused to pay, the Paint Spot owner filed a lien against the Doral, a common action by contractors to protect their interests. Trump lawyer Bruce Rogow argued that the Paint Spot lien was invalid. Rogow said the lien named the wrong Trump general contractor.

Court papers show that Juan Carlos Enriquez, the Paint Spot owner, was so diligent in making sure his rights were protected that he personally had gone to the Doral offices. He asked for the name of the business to put on his papers just in case there was a problem later with payment.

The lien he later filed did indeed name the wrong business entity—because Enriquez was given inaccurate information.

A Florida state judge ruled that Trump's firm knew that it owed the money. When Trump continued refusing to pay, the judge ordered a hearing to inquire as to why. Trump's designated witness told the judge the Paint Spot was not getting the money owed because Trump feels he "already paid enough." The judge ruled for Paint Spot.

Contract law does not work Trump's way. Imagine if it did. A boss might tell workers that their paychecks were short because they had been paid enough. Looked at from the buyer's point of view, you could have remorse about that new car you bought and tell the dealer you decided that your deposit was enough and you were not making any more payments. But this tactic of refusing to pay in full, and sometimes refusing to pay at all, has been a constant throughout Trump's life, involving him in hundreds of lawsuits accusing him of nonpayment. If everyone he stiffed sued, the number of cases would be much greater.

Trump appealed the order to pay the Paint Spot. An appeals court ruled against the president in April 2017. At long last President Trump's company, Trump Endeavor LLC, paid Enriquez with interest. Trump also paid Daniel Vega, the lawyer representing the Paint Spot, the amount the judge set as a reasonable cost of enforcing the contract—$280,000.

Vega said his client got paid only because he "had the fortitude to endure the massive pressure of potentially having to pay" Trump's legal fees if he lost the lawsuit.

Trump had previously lost another Florida lawsuit, this one over the Jupiter club. That lawsuit, which he continued to litigate as president, raises serious questions about his integrity.

When Trump bought the Jupiter course from the Ritz-Carlton hotel chain in 2012, many members resigned, as their membership allowed them to do. They asked for refunds of their membership deposits. Those were between $40,000 and $200,000 depending on the level of their membership. The membership contracts entitled members to get their money back. However, that could take years. Refunds are paid only on every fifth new membership sold. The membership contracts allowed people who resigned to continue playing golf and using the clubhouse, so long as they paid their dues, until they got their refunds.

Trump ordered them out immediately.

"As the owner of the club, I do not want them to utilize the club nor do I want their dues. In other words, if you choose to remain on the resignation list, you're out," he wrote in a letter after learning that many members applied for their refunds.

The issue before Kenneth A. Marra, a federal district court judge, was whether Trump now had an immediate duty to pay refunds because he barred the members from the property and refused their dues.

Judge Marra ruled in February 2017, just after Trump took office, that the contracts were crystal clear. He ordered Trump to pay the refunds with interest. "By categorically denying Class Members all rights to Club access [Trump] revoked or cancelled their memberships, thus recalling their memberships." That meant refunds should have been paid within thirty days.

Six months later Trump appealed. Trump argued that people seeking refunds should have continued paying their dues even though he had barred them from the property. That is, as a lawyer for the members who sued said, a "contorted" position. It is also classic Donald Trump. Had people paid for no play it would have cost them much or all of the refunds they had coming to them. And by appealing, Trump knew he would get to hold on to their money longer. He may even manage to delay the case long enough that the members settle for less than they are owed just so they get something back.

In New York's Westchester County there were other fights with Trump over his golf course. His Westchester National Golf Club kept the water level in golf course ponds at six feet above the approved level and did not properly maintain drains. The ponds overflowed during a 2011 rainstorm, sending a river of muddy water from the golf course cascading into the quaint downtown. The town sent Trump a $238,000 bill for cleaning up the mess. He refused to pay.

Gloria Fried, the receiver of taxes for Trump's golf course in Westchester, said it is disheartening for other taxpayers to cover the costs of Trump's efforts to get out of his obligations. "It is very difficult when you see someone who has all these assets at his disposal who would rather pay lawyers to avoid his civic duty of paying taxes," she said.

Residents of Briarcliff Manor, where the golf course is located, decided to try a new tactic. Their goal was to persuade Trump to quit seeking a dis-

count of 82 percent or more on his property taxes. Residents of the afflu-
ent suburb held a protest march on the president's seventy-first birthday
hoping it would shame him into changing his behavior.

There was not much of chance of that, as indicated by what happened
when Trump took the oath of office. That was when he interrupted his inaugural ride in the presidential limousine in front of his Washington hotel
to send a signal that he intended to use his office to enrich himself at the
expense of not just taxpayers, but also competitors in business.

Appointees

Filling the four thousand positions a new president is authorized to fill is a daunting task even for the best prepared candidates. Donald Trump said he did not expect to win and thus it was no surprise that he did not have an operation under way to identify the best talent along with places for those loyalists who had helped him become president.

But even a year after the election, the Trump administration has left many jobs vacant. Trump has the slowest rate of appointments of any modern president. And as time passes he is not catching up with those who came before him, but falling further behind.

By the time Congress took its regular August recess, Trump had not even nominated people for 368 of 591 key positions requiring Senate confirmation. Paul C. Light, a New York University professor who studies the federal workforce, said that "Trump is running at a subglacial speed." He had just 124 nominees confirmed, less than half the number for Presidents Bill Clinton (252), George W. Bush (294), and Barack Obama (310). The Partnership for Public Service, which tracks presidential appointments, noted that there was not a single case in which the White House had announced an appointment but not yet formally filed the nomination, so the appointments pipeline was empty, too.

Particularly troubling was Trump's dawdling on ambassadorships after he created a problem by firing every current ambassador the moment he took his oath. While he had the power to do so, traditionally incoming presidents leave sitting ambassadors, especially career diplomats, in place until the Senate confirms their replacements. That ensures a steady flow of information and assures foreign leaders about continuity between administrations.

After more than seven months in office Trump had nominated only 36 of 188 ambassadors.

This meant that in foreign capitals when multibillion-dollar investment decisions were being discussed, political intrigues were unfolding, and informal changes in policy were under way, the United States often had no one with authority at the dinner tables, cocktail parties, or official government proceedings where they could pick up intelligence. Just knowing who sat where, or who was absent, at functions often provides valuable insights into foreign affairs. Not having ambassador-rank representatives on the scene posed serious economic and national security risks to the United States and was not consistent with Trump's claims that he would always put America first.

The failure to promptly fill these positions, and many others, raised more than the issue of Trump's lackadaisical approach to governing and ignoring basic duties while he spent hours watching television to learn what was being said about him.

His neglect also brought into question whether he was violating his oath to "faithfully execute" the duties of his office as Article II, Section 2 of the American Constitution clearly states.

The Constitution does not employ the discretionary verb *may* or the merely authorizing word *can,* but a verb that imposes a duty to act. And it uses that mandating verb twice: "he shall nominate, and by and with the Advice and Consent of the Senate, shall appoint Ambassadors, other public Ministers and Consuls, Judges of the supreme Court, and all other Officers of the United States, whose Appointments are not herein otherwise provided for, and which shall be established by Law."

Another big reason for the slowness in filling important posts is Trump's mercurial nature and how it creates unnecessary problems. Instead of thoughtful, even calculated, official actions, Trump's volatile emotions often drive his decisions. So does whatever he heard from the last person he spoke to. So one of the first things General John Kelly did as White House chief of staff was to control who sees the president and what papers they put in front of him.

At first Chris Christie, the New Jersey governor, led the team developing names for the four thousand positions a president controls, ranging from cabinet members to ceremonial posts. Then Trump dumped Christie, who was tarnished by scandals including one over political retribution that sent two of his closest aides to prison.

Trump assigned the task to Indiana governor Mike Pence, the vice president–elect, who started the process anew with less than ten weeks to go before they took office. There is evidence that Pence was not especially engaged in this crucial task or, if he was, that he was less than truthful about his role. Pence has said he was not aware of doubts about the loyalty and integrity of General Michael Flynn, Trump's choice for national security adviser, even though the transition team received written memos about him and Obama warned Trump about Flynn.

Trump took no responsibility for the delays. He blamed the Democrats, tweeting "Dems are taking forever to approve my people, including Ambassadors. They are nothing but OBSTRUCTIONISTS! Want approvals."

There were three factual problems with that tweet. One was that the Senate can only confirm people who are nominated and Trump was not putting forth names promptly or even at a steady pace. Second, Republicans controlled the Senate and were approving some nominees even before their ethics and other paperwork was completed. Third, every person Trump nominated was approved by the Senate.

Most presidents name about two career diplomats for each political appointee. The politicals are usually super-rich campaign donors who get plum posts like European capitals or island paradises. For countries with contentious economic, military, or other issues with America, presidents tend to assign career diplomats with skills suited to a specific country.

Of the positions Trump filled in his first seven months, politicals dominated, getting twenty-one of the thirty-six coveted positions. He chose one of his bankruptcy lawyers, David Friedman, to be ambassador to Israel. The Tennessee campaign finance director, businessman William Francis Hagerty IV, got Japan. Scott Brown, the former *Cosmo* magazine centerfold who was defeated in the 2013 Massachusetts Senate race by Elizabeth Warren and went on to become a major Trump campaign cheerleader, went south to New Zealand. And a billionaire real estate developer, Doug Manchester, got the Bahamas, a lovely group of islands beloved by South American drug lords.

Friedman, Hagerty, Brown, and Manchester had no diplomatic experience.

Another ambassadorship was a savvy political choice. Trump named Nikki Haley, the governor of South Carolina, to the United Nations. That allowed Henry McMaster to move up from lieutenant governor. McMaster had given a speech nominating Trump at the GOP convention in Cleveland and was the first Palmetto State leader to endorse him.

At the State Department, Rex Tillerson, the CEO of ExxonMobil before he became secretary of state, was pushing people out the door fast. He started trimming the payroll almost immediately. Trump clearly approved. When Vladimir Putin told America to send more than 150 diplomats packing, which also ended the jobs of about 600 Russian locals, Trump said he was delighted.

"I want to thank him because we're trying to cut down on payroll, and as far as I'm concerned, I'm very thankful that he let go of a large number of people, because now we have a smaller payroll," Trump said. "There's no real reason for them to go back. So I greatly appreciate the fact that we've been able to cut our payroll of the United States. We'll save a lot of money."

The White House later said Trump was joking. Maybe so, but his remarks were consistent with Tillerson's purge at State as well as Trump's approval of almost everything that Putin does.

Slashing diplomats, especially senior people with deep knowledge built up at taxpayer expense about the foibles and strengths of players in countries big and small, comes at a price. Getting into the Foreign Service requires serious skills and brainpower. Less than 5 percent of those who apply ultimately get hired, Office of Personnel Management records show.

Mieke Eoyang, a lawyer and former House intelligence committee staffer who has worked in these areas for two decades, warned that "institutional memory is fading. We are losing many of the senior people who make the building work."

She said many young people were also trying to decide if they should leave. "The fast risers see that they will not be getting promoted," Eoyang said.

Administrations come and go, but the diplomatic interests of the United States endure. Diplomatic missions can leave important marks that last for decades and they can also roil relations with countries, creating lasting enmity.

Jeff Hauser, executive director of the Revolving Door Project, which tracks people who come from industry to government and then return, said the Trump administration was adept at getting around Senate confirmation hearings.

"They are appointing a lot of what are called special government employees," Hauser said. "They can put someone on the payroll for not more than 130 days. That way they don't have to go through a Senate confirmation process, which the person might not survive. It's a way of getting around oversight by the Congress and journalists because who pays attention to a short-term employee?"

Hauser pointed to the example of Keith Noreika. He was made Acting Comptroller of the Currency. When his temporary assignment ran out, the Trump administration left him in place.

Before his special government employee position as the nation's top banking regulator, Noreika was a lawyer defending JPMorgan Chase, Wells Fargo, and eighty other banking clients. The temporary appointment, Hauser said, enables Noreika to scoop up valuable information for when he returns to the private sector. Political appointees have always done that, or always have been able to do that. What makes Noreika different is that he and many others got no scrutiny from the Senate.

Compounding this, Hauser and others said, are much weaker ethics rules under Trump. Walter Shaub quit as director of the Office of Government Ethics after a series of clashes with the administration, which wanted to keep financial matters of its appointees hush-hush, waivers granted so people who owned stocks in companies they would be regulating could keep their shares, and other policies that Shaub considered offensive to honest and open government. They were also, he said, unlike those of any presidents in the previous four decades at least.

Shaub called Trump's eyes-wide-open blind trust, in which his sons would run his businesses and tell their dad about profits, "wholly inadequate" because "that's not how a blind trust works. There's not supposed to be any information at all."

After resigning in disgust in July, Shaub told the British newspaper *The Guardian*, "The fact that we're having to ask questions about whether he's intentionally using the presidency for profit is bad enough because the appearance itself undermines confidence in government."

Trump's conduct "risks people starting to refer to us as a kleptocracy. That's a term people throw around fairly freely when they're talking about Russia, fairly or unfairly, and we run the risk of getting branded the same way. America really should stand for more than that."

PART II

JOBS

Hiding in the Budget

In his inaugural address, Donald Trump pledged that his every decision would put American workers first. But his very first budget directly contradicts that promise. It's a document few people even in Washington read, an official policy declaration that rarely makes the news.

The story of this hidden betrayal illustrates the importance of journalists paying attention to government. It is not enough just to cover politics and controversies. Often the most important news goes unannounced, lying right out in the open in the government documents most journalists are loath to uncover and read.

Only by examining the official record can voters know if politicians use their power to fulfill their promises or break them. For example, we can see with absolute clarity that the Trump budget request for the U.S. Trade and Development Agency directly contradicts his campaign promises to American workers as well as investors in the businesses that employ them.

Each year a justification for each federal agency must be laid out in the budget requests the administration sends to Congress. The Trump administration's first report on the Trade and Development Agency says its "mandate is to support job creation at home and promote economic development abroad." The trade agency does this "by leveraging U.S. industry expertise to build mutually beneficial, trade- and investment-based partnerships with emerging markets" overseas.

Some 18,000 American workers owe their jobs to exports fostered by the agency, according to the Trump administration.

Efforts by the agency's fifty-eight employees generated a $3 billion increase in American exports to poor countries in 2016, according to the Trump administration. That brought total exports the agency fostered to

$53.4 billion, a healthy 5.7 percent increase over the previous year, again according to the Trump administration.

Agency operations cost taxpayers $75 million. That means American exporters sold $752 worth of goods and services overseas for each dollar invested by taxpayers. However, the Trump budget report credited the agency with only $85 of exports per taxpayer dollar spent, with no explanation for the lower figure.

Given the high rate of return on the taxpayer dollar, even by the smaller ratio cited in the budget report, one might expect the Trump administration to request more money for this agency so it could help grow American exports even more and help create more jobs. Instead, the Trump administration asked Congress to shut it down. It asked Congress to appropriate only $12.1 million, money needed to pay severance and terminate leases.

Why?

"The Administration believes that the Agency's mission is more appropriately served by the private sector," its budget report said.

"While the administration wants U.S. businesses to invest in emerging markets to grow their businesses and create American jobs, these businesses have incentive to invest and should rely on private sector financing. In general, the United States should not provide taxpayer subsidies," it explained, adding that the agency was doing nothing more than putting "the Government in the business of picking winners and losers, potentially distorting the free market."

Government interventions that distort markets occur continually, as explained in *Free Lunch* and *The Fine Print,* my books exposing how the political donor class uses the federal, state, and local governments to gain unfair advantages against competitors, restrict competition, and jack up prices. Those books champion competitive markets, which are essential for generating the benefits of capitalism, and expose the troubling trend in America toward corporate socialism with gains going to owners and executives while losses are sloughed off onto taxpayers.

There is no such thing as a "free market," much as that term of art in economics is loosely bandied about all the time by politicians and journalists. And no free market exists in world trade—not anywhere, not ever.

"Free market" is an abstract ideal, not a reality, a useful tool in the algebra of economics. This ideal helps in analyzing how government rules and practices shape human behavior and investment decisions. All markets operate subject to rules and those rules guide market decisions.

What matters in commerce is a level playing field. Market capitalism suffers when rules tilt the field of competition in favor of this company or that industry. Among the many ways that businesses seek to angle the playing field in their favor are campaign donations, jobs for the friends and family of office holders, and handing out favors like travel on corporate jets to those who make or influence the rules.

In world trade the idea of a "free market" is absurd. Small countries with fragile markets create all manner of formal and, often more importantly, informal rules that distort markets. Those rules may be beneficial or extremely harmful, but in international trade they must be obeyed or navigated around because each nation is sovereign. American exporters to these countries often must contend with kleptocratic government leaders demanding payoffs, which if met would put them in criminal violation of the Foreign Corrupt Practices Act. Then there are the petty and practical problems of customshouse inspectors who want their palms greased before goods can go from ship to shore and many other real-world interferences in markets. And, of course, in export deals there's the need for basic intelligence—whom to work with and whom to avoid in the developing country? Does a country have the foreign reserves to pay for American goods, for example?

Because each country has its own culture, its own rules, and its own internal logic, it is far more efficient for the American government to employ experts in trade, international law, and diplomacy to help American companies navigate their way to successful sales in emerging market countries. Otherwise a business lacking the scale to develop in-house the disparate skills required to make deals would have to forgo opportunities to make those sales. Likewise, American firms may not engage with countries whose size as a market makes the costs of working in unfamiliar commercial terrain prohibitive. The trade agency smooths those paths while advancing the national interest of building a robust economy that exports high-value American-made products and services. Eliminate this agency and American workers (and investors) lose. So do taxpayers, because if exports fall, so do the taxes collected from export companies and their workers.

The Trump administration officials know this, assuming they know a whit about the harsh realities of global commerce. And yet, in large part Trump paved his road to the White House with promises of new trade practices that he said would favor the United States, which he claimed had been taken advantage of by so many other countries, to create more American jobs.

Aside from the larger questions about trade, shutting down a federal agency that helps sustain 18,000 American jobs directly contradicts the Trumpian promise to always act in support of American workers.

In response to the North Korean nuclear weapons program, Trump tweeted in September 2017 that "The United States is considering, in addition to other options, stopping all trade with any country doing business with North Korea." To fulfill such a threat, the U.S. would have to suspend trade with China, India, Russia, and a host of other countries including Brazil, Chile, France, Mexico, Pakistan, and Saudi Arabia.

China buys 8 percent of America's exports, totaling nearly $170 billion in 2016. China is the third largest buyer of American exports.

Perhaps Trump's tweets can be set aside as passing thoughts, if not utter nonsense. But the Trump budget proposal to close the Trade and Development Agency is formulated policy, and it clearly undercuts his "America First" claims. So why did the Trump administration adopt this policy? A hint of the reasons the Trump administration would sabotage American workers appears in the trade agency's reports on its successes in promoting American exports to poor countries. The trade agency does more than encourage exports of high-value American goods like telecommunications and transportation systems. It also promotes certain kinds of energy projects.

The trade agency "supports efforts to expand energy generation by helping its partner countries develop renewable energy resources, invest in cleaner forms of traditional energy and modernize electric grids." During the 2015 budget year the trade agency "committed over half of its energy investments to renewable power. These project preparation activities have the potential to unlock over $4.3 billion in financing and produce over 2,400 megawatts of new renewable energy."

That focus could mean lots of jobs for American green energy companies—wind, solar, and biomass. It would help encourage more investment to make renewable energy cheaper. It also would help reduce emissions of carbon dioxide and toxic by-products from burning coal, petroleum coke (petcoke), and even natural gas.

That does not sit well with Trump and the political termites his administration has put to work inside our government, eating away at its structure. Trump has attacked renewable energy again and again. A major stated goal of his term in office will be much greater extraction and use of fossil fuels. And more than any other form of carbon, Trump loves coal. He boasts that he has wrought a revival of American coal mining, a tenuous claim, but in his mind a certainty. And Trump is undaunted by the mounting evidence of climate change and global warming. He insists that climate change is imaginary and certainly not caused by burning fossil fuels. And those beliefs, it seems, outweigh the value of jobs for Americans that enable green energy in poor countries.

Immediately after taking the oath of office, Trump declared that "from this moment on, it's going to be America First. Every decision on trade, on taxes, on immigration, on foreign affairs, will be made to benefit American workers and American families. We must protect our borders from the ravages of other countries making our products, stealing our companies, and destroying our jobs. Protection will lead to great prosperity and strength."

It appears that Trump's inaugural address promise that every decision would favor American workers came with a hidden caveat not included in the speech everyone heard or in the official White House text but buried in an obscure budget document that no one was expected to notice. Only because of a Freedom of Information request did this justification document become public.

Other actions Trump took that contradicted his inaugural address and his campaign promises were done openly, the first of them on the very day he became president.

A Mighty Job Creator

Donald Trump campaigned on a promise of jobs, jobs, and more jobs. He said businesses would create jobs galore during his presidency, especially manufacturing jobs. All he had to do was apply his negotiating skills while quickly dispatching 75 percent of "job-killing" federal regulations. With these rules dead, Trump said companies would rapidly and happily bring back all the jobs they had shipped overseas and create even more back home in America. Companies that persisted in manufacturing beyond America's borders would get hit with stiff levies when their goods reached American ports, he said. And for good measure he made clear that any company whose executives and directors were so foolish as to defy him would get tongue-lashings that would make their brand names mud.

The promise of a manufacturing revival resonated in the Rust Belt states, especially Michigan and Wisconsin. Along with Pennsylvania, the Wolverine and Badger states gave Trump his Electoral College victory despite his losing the popular vote nationwide by 2 percentage points and 2.9 million ballots.

Factory workers in these states had suffered through slowly worsening times as companies moved good-paying jobs making cars, cheese, and cleansers to the American South, often lured not just by cheap labor but fat subsidies that helped pay for whole new factories. Many jobs left the Midwest heartland for Mexico and China, where workers could be had for mere pennies on the dollar previously paid to Americans. The loss of these jobs radiated through the economies of places like Flint, Lansing, and Saginaw, where homes became like the cars once made there—depreciating assets whose value declined with time. The real value of homes in these once prosperous manufacturing communities was lower in 2016 than it had been four or five decades earlier. These economic hardships were the product of changes in the government rule book instituted by both political parties and taken advantage of by many employers, including the hotel and other businesses of Donald J. Trump, that last a fact he never brought up.

Six weeks before Election Day Trump gave a major address on jobs. "We're going to have job growth like you've never seen," he told the Polish American Congress meeting in Chicago. "I'm very good for jobs. In fact, I will be the greatest president for jobs that God ever created. That I can tell you."

As president, Trump promised "a bold plan to create 25 million new American jobs in the next decade."

Just four days after Trump took office he signed five executive orders that the White House said would create "massive" numbers of new jobs, especially by speeding completion of two controversial oil pipelines across the Upper Midwest. The Keystone Pipeline to move Canadian tar sands oil to Gulf Coast refineries would create "a lot of jobs, 28,000 jobs, great construction jobs," Trump said as he signed one executive order.

Covering all sides of the story, journalists quickly found official data, reports, and sources that knocked down the massive job creation Trump boasted would flow from his pen. Government reports showed that on average the construction jobs would last less than five months. Counting them as full-time equivalents, a standard measure used by business and government, the most generous estimates from Keystone's own reports put the figure at the equivalent of 3,900 full-time jobs lasting no more than two years. In addition, the State Department estimated 12,000 new long-term jobs related to the expanded extraction of tar sands oils in Canada, transporting the heavy oil and using it after refining in the American South, much of it to make a solid dry fuel for electric power plants, known as petroleum coke or petcoke, which pollutes the air much more than coal. Altogether those job count measures came to not much more than half of what Trump said in the Oval Office.

Further reducing Trump's 28,000 jobs figure was that much of the work making steel pipe, compressors, and other pipeline equipment had already been done. And a fair amount of that work employed people not in America, but in Canada, India, and Italy. Glenn Kessler, the *Washing-*

ton Post "Fact Checker" columnist, awarded Trump's Keystone jobs announcement three Pinocchios, rating Trump's words mostly false.

Interpreted generously, this was yet another example of Trump's explanation in *The Art of the Deal* for making stuff up, as when he said over and over that Trump Tower was sixty-eight stories even though it was only fifty-eight. Whether applied to how many apartments he sold at what prices, how much gamblers lost in his casinos, or his claims that his cheaply built concrete structures were the very best, Trump reveled in what he called "truthful hyperbole." While a real estate promoter may find commercial gain in such lies, when presidents speak, their words get scrutinized.

Trump disliked being held as president to a higher standard of accuracy than when he was in business boasting about how great his golf courses were, how fine his neckties were, and how everything with his name on it was the most beautiful, the best, the most desired. Trump and his surrogates complained that he was being held to a different standard than other politicians, being scrutinized more and more thoroughly just because he was Trump, and journalists who didn't like him were picking on him.

The fact-checking by many news organizations of his Keystone Pipeline jobs claims did not just wash over Trump. Instead it boiled inside until his first presidential press conference four weeks after he entered the Oval Office.

Straightaway Trump made clear what was on his mind. He was not being hailed as the greatest problem solver ever in the White House, the greatest jobs creator of all time. Only by going directly to the public, he said, would the American people ever know the truth about his mighty achievements. "We have made incredible progress," he said. "I don't think there's ever been a president elected who in this short period of time has done what we've done." The problem, Trump said, was that journalists refused to report these great achievements. "The dishonest press," he said in a hectoring tone. "The press honestly is out of control. The level of dishonesty is out of control."

Among his unheralded achievements was fundamentally changing the way business leaders thought about hiring, or so Trump insisted. The important story that no one knew, he complained, was that "there has been a tremendous surge of optimism in the business world, which to me means something much different than it used to. It used to mean, 'Oh, that's good.' Now it means, 'That's good for jobs.' Very different. Plants and factories are already starting to move back into the United States, and big league—Ford, General Motors, so many of them. I'm making this presentation directly to the American people, with the media present . . . because many of our nation's reporters and folks will not tell you the truth."

There were of course many front-page and network news stories at the time citing improved business confidence and how the stock market surged in expectation of a Trump tax cut and at least some regulations being shredded. But Trump was blind to these facts.

Continuing to let out the emotional steam inside, he said, "I'm here again, to take my message straight to the people. As you know, our administration inherited many problems across government and across the economy. To be honest, I inherited a mess. It's a mess—at home and abroad, a mess. Jobs are pouring out of the country; you see what's going on with all of the companies leaving our country, going to Mexico and other places, low pay, low wages." He then moved on to talk about the Middle East and other issues.

Reminders of his extraordinary prowess, his unappreciated greatness, in job creation became a recurring theme of Trump talks. The very next week, in his address to a joint session of Congress that new presidents give instead of a State of the Union address, Trump expanded on his self-proclaimed achievements in job creation.

"Since my election," Trump declared, "Ford, Fiat Chrysler, General Motors, Sprint, SoftBank, Lockheed, Intel, Walmart, and many others have announced that they will invest billions and billions of dollars in the United States and create tens of thousands of new American jobs."

In other settings, he took credit for tens of thousands of new jobs and many tens of billions of dollars of investment by such firms as cable television provider Charter Communications and oil giant ExxonMobil. He was still on this theme six months later, when job growth was slowing markedly, telling a Phoenix rally for the far distant 2020 campaign about even more jobs that came from Trump's leadership skills. "Struggling American workers are now beginning to see the light because plants are coming pouring back into our country and, by the way, we are doing a lot of good work on that front. A lot of good people are coming in. We have Foxconn, they make the iPhones for Apple, and so many companies are building now in our country, including the auto companies that are coming back."

There were problems with all of these statements. None of the claims of credit for bringing jobs back was true, according to the companies and others involved. None of the new investments were because of Trump, according to the carefully worded statements of the companies and the observations of stock market and industry analysts who followed the companies. Some of the deals had been negotiated as far back as 2011.

Five times, for example, Trump tweeted about ExxonMobil investing $20 billion and creating 45,000 Texas jobs over ten years along the Gulf of Mexico. The sum was not especially large given the company's annual revenues and the fact that it budgets over a ten-year period around $200 billion for capital expenditures worldwide. Trump claimed that the investment was "to a large extent because of our policies and the policies of this new administration." The company said the investments began in 2013 and were needed to process oil and gas made available by fracking technology, especially in Texas.

Then there was Intel, the leading maker of computer microchips. Trump announced that Intel "will move ahead with a new plant in Arizona that it was probably never going to move ahead with, and that will result in at least 10,000 American jobs." Intel had announced the deal in 2011, but soon after putting up the factory walls Intel decided to hold off on buying the very expensive gear for making computer chips because of soft demand from buyers.

Trump's tweet two days before crowed that Lockheed Martin would hire 1,800 people in Texas, saying the defense contractor "came back because of me!" Federal laws and regulations require most work on defense equipment to be done by Americans in American factories. In addition, the company gently noted, its hiring reflected a ramping up of F-35 fighter jet production from 36 warplanes in 2014 to an expected 150 or more by 2019.

One of the most interesting Trump claims, one that showed what thin reeds of fact he rested his job claims on, involved Foxconn. That is the brand name of the Taiwanese company Hon Hai Precision Industry Company, Ltd. Foxconn has a long history of promising to build plants in

America and then not following through. Its supposed $10 billion Wisconsin deal turned out to be nothing more than a single sheet of paper obtained by reporter Jason Stein of the *Milwaukee Journal Sentinel*.

The handwritten record of the negotiations, if they can be called that, showed Governor Scott Walker giving Foxconn an initial large taxpayer subsidy that kept getting bigger and bigger as negotiations continued so the company would announce plans for a new factory in America's Dairyland. That was itself strange because Walker holds himself out as a staunch fiscal conservative, as much a guardian of taxpayer money as Trump says he is the champion job creator. Yet Walker agreed to ever larger subsidies for Foxconn until the taxpayer gifts reached $3 billion. Beyond that, there was no solid evidence that Foxconn was serious this time about building, especially building a sophisticated electronics operation in a state not known as a high-tech center.

What Foxconn is well known for is pushing its Chinese employees to work such long hours under tight supervision while living in company-owned dorms that many workers have committed suicide. Numerous reports documented how the Apple contractor rigidly enforces a "forced labor" system, including workers who under Chinese law are children. To characterize the brutal conditions at Foxconn's China factories where Apple iPhones and other Apple consumer products are assembled, critics invoke the Mandarin word *guolaosi*. It means "worked to death."

Trump never mentioned these fatal working conditions, even though as far back as 2010 a newspaper he loves to see his name in, *The New York Times,* was reporting that Foxconn workers were taking their own lives. But if Foxconn ever does build a Wisconsin factory, one thing is clear— under Trump the number of American job safety inspectors will be much smaller than the already shrunken staff he inherited, because of Trump's budget cuts. When Trump took office, the Labor Department already had fewer inspectors than in 1940, when America's workforce was less than a third the size it is in 2017. And the requirements Foxconn will have to meet for keeping records of worker injuries and deaths will be much looser, part of that reduction in regulations that Trump said would mean so many more American jobs.

*   *   *

Many times Trump made claims that, because of him, before long many more Americans would have jobs making Ford cars and trucks, Lincolns, and other vehicles. These claims were gently shot down by company spokesmen, though they trod very carefully lest Trump's ire and presidential powers be aimed at the financially strongest of the American carmakers. Mark Fields, the Ford Motor chief executive, said Ford did indeed plan to build a new plant in Flat Rock, a half hour from its world headquarters outside Detroit, but purely for business reasons. The new plant would manufacture electric-powered cars and trucks the company was developing.

Ford also planned to experiment in Flat Rock with new manufacturing techniques to cut costs. The Michigan site was expected to help in developing Ford's first self-driving cars, technology that would require intense and expensive inputs from engineers, computer scientists, and materials experts. One auto analyst noted that "keeping a new technology near the engineers is an important thing, at least in the first generation" of vehicles. Another auto industry watcher pointed out that Mexico, where Ford said it would continue to make its inexpensive gasoline-powered Focus models, offered a "just good enough" workforce while Michigan had an abundance of much more skilled manufacturing workers. Ford later said Focus assembly was moving to China.

Curiously, Trump said very little critical of General Motors, which was laying off workers in Michigan and Ohio in 2016 while expanding production in China, including a plant to build sport utility vehicles for sale in the United States. Trump, like his father, Fred, is a lifelong Cadillac fan, having been driven in the family limousine on his morning newspaper route in Queens when it rained or snowed and going off to college in the maroon Cadillac his parents gave him as a gift. When he was in the gambling business in 1988, Trump licensed the sale of Trump-branded Cadillac limousines, each with two telephones, a videocassette player, a fax machine, rosewood cabinets, and Trumpian stemware to go with the alcohol dispensers. The two men Trump licensed to fabricate the Trump Executive and Golden series limousines were a convicted extortionist and a wealthy dealer of Japanese-built cars who also happened to be a convicted thief and was identified in law enforcement reports as associated with the Colombo crime family.

But while Trump made all these fantastical claims about his skill at creating jobs, other events were under way that challenged his whole claim to be the greatest job creator of all time. Job growth in America began slowing down after he took office. Companies were not honoring Trump's demands that they buy American. Some industries were eager to get apprentices to learn job skills, something voters no doubt thought Trump knew something about given his former job hosting two reality television shows in which contestants vied to be his apprentice. And the one small-bore effort Trump had made to save some jobs, garnering enormous favorable news coverage, was turning out to be smoke and mirrors.

Forgetting the Forgotten Man

In 2010, the United States Department of Labor created a website to honor workers who died on the job. "More than 4,500 workers lose their lives on the job every year. Below are the names of just a few who have died in recent months. OSHA's mission is to prevent workplace injuries, illnesses and deaths."

That Occupational Safety and Health Administration webpage was intended to highlight and humanize workplace deaths, to insure awareness of tragedies, especially those that could have been avoided, according to Jordan Barab, an assistant secretary of labor during the Obama administration.

"Without information like this, fatality statistics are just raw, sterile numbers," Barab explained. "The purpose of adding names and circumstances was to impress people with the tragedy that workers and their families face every day."

In August 2017 Trump's Labor Department quietly removed the preamble and the names when it killed the webpage. It also took down, without public announcement, the Fatality Inspection Data for all years prior to 2017.

Those were just two of many other Trump administration actions inimical to worker safety. Others included no longer posting press releases about deaths resulting from unsafe working conditions, delaying rules to reduce sickness and death from inhaling silica and beryllium at work, delaying rules to lower the risk of railroad engineers and truck drivers falling asleep at the switch or wheel because of untreated sleep apnea, and the appointment to the Supreme Court of a judge who held that a company had the right to fire a worker who chose not to freeze to death on the job.

A reasonable person listening to Donald Trump's inaugural address would never have expected these and other actions, assuming he believed what Trump said.

"The forgotten men and women of our country will be forgotten no longer," Trump declared. "You came by the tens of millions to become part of a historic movement the likes of which the world has never seen before. At the center of this movement is a crucial conviction—that a nation exists to serve its citizens."

Those men and women were forgotten again the following week. And it was not just workers whose interests were forgotten, not to mention who were put in danger. By deciding not to implement a rule to reduce the chances of truck drivers and train operators falling asleep at the wheel, Trump put at risk the lives of families driving along the highway, people riding on passenger trains, and many others.

The White House called it "President Trump's War on Regulation." In his weekly radio address in early May, he declared that "We have removed one job-killing regulation after another—they're not pretty and they're going. And believe me, we are just getting started on regulations. They're gone."

Removal of data on workplace deaths, which average thirteen per day, infuriated Jordan Barab, who was Obama's No. 2 at the Occupational Safety and Health Administration. As a private citizen Barab created a webpage to keep track of the names of the dead and the reasons they were killed on the job. He called it "OSHA Won't Tell You Who Died In the Workplace. We Will."

After the election, Barab's concerns that the Trump administration would be bad for workers increased when he asked where the Trump beachhead team was and learned that none was coming. Each incoming administrator sends people to scope out federal agencies, learn who does what, and get a feel for the place in advance. Then the incoming administration sends its landing team, the people who will initially implement its policies at each agency.

When no beachhead team came, Barab figured it meant worker safety simply was not a priority for Trump. He hoped that was the worst of it, nothing more than apathy about worker safety. But when the landing team arrived, Barab realized trouble was coming for American workers, and it was not official apathy but the start of assaults on workers' rights and safety. "Most of them had no idea they were going to Labor and had no interest in worker issues, either," Barab said.

What they did have was a mandate to delay, repeal, or weaken regulations that protected workers as part of Trump's plan to eliminate "any regulation that is outdated, unnecessary, bad for workers, or contrary to the national interest."

The first sign came when Trump nominated Judge Neil Gorsuch to the Supreme Court. Gorsuch was an acolyte of Antonin Scalia, whose seat he would be taking. Like Scalia, he said statutes should be read literally and if that made no sense, well, that was a problem for Congress. Also like Scalia, he had a habit of consulting dictionaries, often following Scalia's practice of relying on the third, fourth, fifth, or even lesser definition of a word when it supported his jurisprudence.

Trump's nomination alarmed unions. Jody Calemine, a Communications Workers of America lawyer, told Gorsuch's Senate confirmation hearing that Gorsuch "is a threat to working people's health and safety." Calemine cited Gorsuch's dissent in a 2016 case to make his point. "That dissent reveals an anti-worker bias and features a judicial activism that will ultimately put workers' lives at risk."

Those are unusually strong words about a Supreme Court nominee, but a review of the case shows Gorsuch has little regard for human life, at least when it comes to employers' power over their workers. He considers a rigid interpretation of the law more important.

The case was about a law Congress passed giving workers the right to refuse dangerous tasks.

Truck driver Alphonse Maddin was nearly out of fuel one January night in 2009. Temperatures had plunged to 14 degrees below zero. Maddin pulled over on an Illinois roadway to figure out where to get fuel. Ten minutes later he tried to drive off, but the rig wouldn't budge. The trailer's brakes had frozen. A dispatcher told Maddin to sit tight until a repair truck arrived. Maddin fell asleep in the unheated truck for two hours, awakened by a cousin's cell phone call. Maddin's torso was numb, his speech slurred, cousin Gregory Nelson testified, describing classic signs of hypothermia. Maddin radioed his dispatcher, who told him "Hang in there" until help arrived.

A half hour later, certain he was on the verge of freezing to death, Maddin disconnected the trailer and drove to warmth.

TransAm Trucking fired him for not following orders. The Olathe, Kansas, company calls itself "the premier carrier in the temperature-controlled freight industry by providing its customers with superior service that exceeds their expectations."

Congress subsequently passed a law that protects a worker by making it unlawful for an employer to discharge an employee who "refused to operate a vehicle because . . . the employee has a reasonable apprehension of serious injury to the employee or the public because of the vehicle's hazardous safety or security condition."

The worker bears the burden of showing that a reasonable individual in such circumstances "would conclude that the hazardous safety or security condition establishes a real danger of accident, injury, or serious impairment to health."

Maddin filed a complaint with the Labor Department. An administrative law judge and a review board both found the firing violated federal law protecting workers who refuse unsafe work orders. TransAm, ordered to reinstate Maddin with back pay, took the case to the Tenth Circuit Court of Appeals. It argued that the law protected only workers who refused to operate unsafe equipment, while Maddin drove the truck after being instructed to "stay put."

Two of the three judges hearing the case concluded that the Labor Department had reasonably interpreted the word "operate," and upheld the reinstatement with back pay.

The third judge, Neil Gorsuch, didn't see it that way.

The law "only forbids employers from firing employees who 'refuse to operate a vehicle' out of safety concerns," he wrote in dissent, adding that "nothing like that happened here. The trucker in this case wasn't fired for *refusing* to operate his vehicle. Indeed, his employer gave him the very option the statute says it must: once he voiced safety concerns, TransAm expressly . . . permitted him to sit and remain where he was and wait for help. The trucker was fired only after he declined the statutorily protected option (refuse to operate) and chose instead to *operate* his vehicle in a manner he thought wise but his employer did not. And there's simply no law anyone has pointed us to giving employees the right to operate their vehicles in ways their employers forbid . . . The law before us protects only employees who refuse to operate vehicles, *period*."

Gorsuch said Maddin had two choices if he wanted to keep his job. He could drag the truck with the frozen brakes locking its wheels, which Gorsuch said would be illegal. Or, Gorsuch wrote, "he could sit and wait for help to arrive (a legal if unpleasant option)."

"Unpleasant" is an interesting word for choosing to die, as Maddin was certain he would have within minutes had he decided to "sit and wait for help to arrive."

At Gorsuch's confirmation hearing, Senator Dick Durbin, an Illinois Democrat, said that 14 degrees below zero was very "cold, but not as cold as your dissent, Judge Gorsuch."

People who voted for Trump believing he was their economic savior and political champion could hardly have expected that his first Supreme Court nominee would have a man choose between his life and his job.

Calemine, the lawyer for the Communications Workers union, told the Senate Judiciary Committee hearing that he expects Gorsuch to take "a sledgehammer to workers' explicit statutory rights. . . . More workers will die on the job. . . . Our health and safety worker safety laws are written in the blood of working people, please do not allow Judge Gorsuch to repeal these laws" with "his brand of judicial activism."

Trump's nominee had a history of "judicial activism," a phrase most often used by conservative witnesses before Congress to criticize centrist and liberal judges.

Gorsuch was sworn in as the Trump administration took numerous actions inimical to worker safety, including veterans and defense industry workers.

A rule went into effect in Obama's last days to protect 62,000 workers from beryllium dust. Beryllium, a metal lighter than aluminum and more rigid than steel, is used in military and other applications, including making nuclear bombs. Obama updated a rule from the 1940s that was much weaker.

Under Trump's executive order to freeze regulations, the Labor Department also put off a rule to protect workers from silica dust. That silica dust can cause fatal lung disease was known since the Romans, who recognized the lethal effects, though not the cause. The rule that the Obama administration put into place was meant to protect about two million workers, in construction, dental labs, and other places where silica is used. The rule was expected to generate benefits of $7.7 billion greater than costs while preventing nine hundred new cases of silicosis annually and avoiding six hundred agonizingly slow deaths from the lung disease.

Trump's Labor Department also moved to revoke a rule requiring most employers with more than ten employees to keep a record of serious work-related injuries and illnesses. The U.S. Chamber of Commerce, the top business lobby in Washington, had called the rule onerous.

Most ominous for workers is the Chamber's support for the Trump plan to reduce records of injuries and protections against retaliation when workers report injuries. The Chamber also supports the Trump agenda of not making such data readily available to the public. "Posting safety records online" should be prohibited, Neil Bradley, the Chamber's chief policy officer wrote, because that "will provide unions and trial attorneys with information that can be taken out of context and used in organizing campaigns, or form the basis of lawsuits."

Meike Patten, a corporate safety officer in Minnesota, wrote that experience has shown her—sadly—"that unless 'OSHA says so,' it is often very difficult and time consuming to improve" workplace safety. "Production is usually more important than safety and despite the fact that catch phrases are being thrown out like 'Safety is number one' or 'Safety is a priority,' management quite often puts the employee's health and safety on the back burner. That's why we need OSHA so badly."

Patten also mused about "which other rules and achievements will be repealed over the next years and throw us back? We need someone in Washington who works FOR the people."

Barab summed up these and other Trump actions this way: "This is not a pro-worker administration, and workers will pay the price for rolling back these hard-earned protections—in injury, illness, and death."

Workers are not the only ones affected by workplace safety regulations. Rules affecting bus, truck, and train operators also affect passengers and motorists. Deaths and injuries from transportation accidents have been on the rise in recent years, a trend influenced by transportation safety rules.

Driver fatigue factors into nearly a third of truck crashes, noted Joan Claybrook. Claybrook has spent half her life trying to improve transportation safety as director of the National Highway Safety Administration under Jimmy Carter and later as president of Public Citizen, the liberal consumer advocacy organization in Washington.

She noted that the Federal Aviation Administration has rules that ground pilots with sleep apnea unless they are treated. Those rules save lives and prevent plane crashes.

"In 2015 truck crashes killed 4,067 people and injured 116,000 more, a 45 percent increase since 2009," Claybrook said. "For trains, several recent horrific crashes in New York and Missouri resulted in four deaths, over 60 injuries and millions in property damage because crew members fell asleep or were highly fatigued from obstructive sleep apnea. The facts demand a federal public safety rule."

The Obama administration did just that in March 2016, after a series of high-profile train and truck crashes where the operators suffered from sleep apnea, which can cause people to momentarily fall asleep with no warning. The rule required testing of bus, truck, and train operators and treatment for those found to suffer from the condition.

The Trump administration announced in August 2017 that it was withdrawing the rule.

A notice in the Federal Register said the administration described the rule as neither effective nor worth the cost of testing. Instead, the administration said it would "continue to recommend that drivers and their employers use the North American Fatigue Management Program . . . a voluntary, fully interactive web-based educational and training program developed to provide both truck and bus commercial vehicle drivers and carriers and others in the supply chain with an awareness of the factors contributing to fatigue."

Killing the sleep apnea testing rule infuriated Claybrook. She saw it as the opposite of Trump's forgotten man promise and the embodiment of wealthy privilege.

"President Trump's only focus is whether he or his family could be harmed, the public be damned," Claybrook said. The president "travels by private jet and police protected and Secret Service–driven vehicles. He doesn't care a whit about thousands of families each year losing loved ones to rolling time bombs—large trucks and trains barreling along at high speed driven by workers suffering from deadly serious sleep apnea."

The justification for delaying, withdrawing, or killing these and many other rules is fostering faster economic growth. In that regard, Trump's move to reduce significantly the number of workers eligible for overtime pay would have a dampening effect on economic growth. Many other Trump administration actions put downward pressure on wages.

Business ledgers record expenses and sales, profits and losses, but ignore costs that are shifted onto society at large. Every exhausted truck driver who falls asleep at the wheel, every worker whose lungs deteriorate because of silica dust or the much more dangerous beryllium dust, creates costs, but they are not recorded on corporate financial statements. The more that government rules allow companies to shift costs off their books and onto society, the more the corporations may profit, but the less well the nation will do economically and socially.

In the end, though, every cost must be accounted for on the universal ledger. There is no free lunch. The death of a worker may make a company money depending on its insurance coverage, but no record is made of the orphan crying for her daddy.

Rules that mean more death, more injury, more pollution favor those who shirk their responsibilities and force others to bear the costs. But do these Trump policies promote faster economic growth? Can they? Will they?

"There is no reason to believe that anyone is now expecting faster economic growth than before the election," observed Dean Baker, a liberal economist and press critic with the Center for Economic and Policy Research.

Rather than speeding economic growth, Trump's actions and inactions were slowing it. That was not Baker's assessment, but that of the International Monetary Fund in its World Economic Outlook. It said global growth in 2017 and 2018 would run about 3.5 percent, but that the outlook for U.S. growth was less rosy because of "difficult-to-predict U.S. regulatory and fiscal policies" and geopolitical risks.

So how to explain rising stock prices since the November presidential election? In theory stock prices represent current estimates of future corporate profits.

Baker noted two of many ways that Trumpian policies could boost corporate profits and thus raise stock prices while damaging the overall economy.

One would be "facilitating rip-offs of consumers," Baker said. Financial crimes make banks more profitable so long as they are not stopped by regulators. William K. Black discovered this when he was the key regulator exposing the savings and loan scandals of a quarter century earlier. After getting more than three thousand cases brought, and sending almost nine hundred high-level bankers to jail, Black earned a doctorate in criminology by developing a new theory of white-collar crime. When executives run a bank for their own benefit, looting it through bad loans, fat fees, and manipulating the stock price, Black calls that "control fraud." That's because the executives in control run the fraud.

Control frauds not only hurt shareholders, borrowers, employees, and taxpayers, they also impose costs on honest banks because they cannot compete in the short run with crooks who manipulate prices and values that cannot be sustained for more than a few years.

Black also showed how regulations can identify and stop control fraud without interfering in legitimate banking, not that anyone in the Trump (or Obama) administrations wants to listen to him.

Baker pointed to the Consumer Financial Protection Bureau, created at the urging of Elizabeth Warren before she became a senator from Massachusetts, as an example of good regulation. "It was set up in large part to prevent predatory practices by the financial industry. For example, it has sought to make it more difficult for financial firms to slip conditions into contracts that no one would ever agree to if they understood them."

Since its launching in 2011, the consumer bureau has recovered almost

$12 billion for people, more than four times its budget. The Trump administration wants to abolish the agency and, failing that, hobble it.

Another technique Baker cited to boost corporate profits was for a president to stop enforcing environmental laws. "Corporate profits can be increased by letting them destroy the environment at zero cost," Baker noted. The point of the Clean Water Act and related laws is to make companies that cause pollution clean up after themselves instead of dumping their toxic wastes on everyone else. Regulations requiring firms to clean up these wastes create jobs, encourage innovation, and improve lives.

To Baker a prime example of bad regulation is the Trump administration reversal of an Obama administration executive order that required mining companies to restore hilltops after they removed them. "By allowing these companies to mine areas without repairing the damage, the Trump administration is saving them money. The people in the communities will suffer the consequences in the form of polluted streams and ruined forests, but this is still good news for corporate profits," Baker observed.

Ignoring or repealing environmental laws would not be good news for life insurers who would have to pay out earlier for deaths caused by pollution, nor would it be good news for families whose breadwinners become sick from pollutants or whose children develop asthma and other conditions that limit their economic futures. And, of course, it would not be good news for those who get sick or die. Most of those people are, as Trump put it in his inaugural address, the forgotten men and women.

Apprenticeship programs could help many of the forgotten. Next up, the strange way President Trump embraced them.

Washington Apprentice

Donald Trump made his way to the White House not by putting up gaudy buildings, which got him noticed, often unfavorably, in New York City. Nor was it his casinos, which got him attention mostly along the East Coast. It wasn't golf or hotels that made him a household name, either. It was by association with would-be apprentices of an entertaining kind on his NBC television shows *The Apprentice* and *The Celebrity Apprentice*, where his signature line was "You're fired."

As a candidate and president, Trump made good use of the word *apprentice*, invoking it often to promote himself as the greatest job-creating president ever.

Apprenticeship programs can be excellent investments, paying back as much as $27 for each dollar spent on practical on-the-job training under experienced hands, according to one Canadian study. Based on Trump's statements, that estimate may be very conservative. In America, unions have run pay-as-you-learn apprenticeship programs going back many decades that economic studies showed were sound investments in job training. But those apprenticeship programs have suffered as more construction companies cut costs by hiring nonunion labor, softening demand for people who learned in apprentice programs how to become expert carpenters, electricians, glaziers, heavy equipment operators, masons, and plumbers.

The need for more apprenticeships was brought up by various labor economists and industrial expansion interests. The big accounting firm Deloitte, which audits the books of many manufacturers, estimated that America should expect to create 3.4 million additional manufacturing jobs over ten years, but was on a path to produce only about 1.4 million qualified applicants. And it noted that from 2003 to 2013, apprenticeship programs that combine on-the-job learning with mentorships and classroom education fell 40 percent even though manufacturing jobs paid 20 percent more wages than other industries on average. Give that demand for skilled workers and the high pay, apprenticeships ought to be growing, not shrinking.

During the campaign, and later as president, Trump said he wanted many more apprenticeships. In the White House a spur-of-the-moment suggestion became a proposal to create five million apprenticeships, ten times the existing number in 2017.

The idea arose during a March meeting Trump hosted for German chancellor Angela Merkel and business leaders from their two countries. Marc Benioff, the CEO of Salesforce, which helps clients manage their interactions with customers, said his firm expected to help create two million jobs using software that he said was 90 percent American-written computer code. More apprentices would be good, Benioff said, adding "We would encourage you to take a moonshot goal to create five million apprenticeships in the next five years."

Trump responded with his usual vague flattery—no specifics, but "nice" and "incredible" and "amazing." Then Trump said, "Let's do that. Let's go for that five million. OK? [Laughter.] Very good."

Soon Trump was talking apprenticeships everywhere he went. That made sense because as a candidate he vowed that his presidency would be all about jobs and that voters should choose him because he was such a successful businessman that he could make good deals that the existing political leadership could not even imagine. In his inaugural address, Trump promised that "every decision . . . will be made to benefit American workers and American families. . . . I will fight for you with every breath in my body—and I will never, ever let you down. America will start winning again, winning like never before. We will bring back our jobs."

In June he flew to Wisconsin with his daughter Ivanka and Labor Secretary Alexander Acosta to talk apprenticeships. He proposed apprenticeship programs at every American high school, saying, "I love the name apprentice." And just in case no one knew what being an apprentice means, Trump told his audience at Wisconsin's Waukesha County Technical College, "It's called earn while you learn."

He also made an astonishing claim. While in college—Trump enrolled at Fordham in New York City for two years and the University of Pennsylvania in Philadelphia for two more—he observed college classmates who "didn't have a great ability or frankly didn't have a great liking for what they were doing or what they were studying. But they could take apart an engine blindfolded." There was no way to tell if this observation had substance or was just another of his made-up stories.

Two days later Trump surrounded himself with apprentices in the Cabinet Room of the White House. They were props for the signing of an executive order on apprenticeships, part of Trump's effort to show that he really was the mightiest job creator of all time.

"Each of the apprentices here today has their own story and their own dreams—that's what they are—dreams. Apprenticeships teach striving Americans the skills they need to operate incredible machines. And some of these machines are so intricate, so powerful, and, really—the word is— they are incredible," Trump said.

He singled out Charles Robel, a combat veteran from Wisconsin. Upon completing an apprenticeship program, Robel would earn a starting wage of $60,000 "and going up much higher than that."

If five million apprentices each started out making the same wages as Robel, their combined first-year pay would be an eye-popping $300 billion. That is so much money that based on 2015 wage data it would mean a 4 percent increase in all the wages earned in America, a huge boost to economic growth. That also would be a big step toward realizing Trump's dream of doubling economic growth from about 2 percent annually to 4 percent or more.

So how much would a tenfold increase in federally supported apprenticeships cost? The federal government, in Obama's last budget, put $90 million of taxpayer money into apprenticeships. That clearly covered just a portion of the costs, but Benioff had called not for a program entirely funded by taxpayers, but for partnerships between business, government, and others.

"The key," Benioff said, would be "all these great companies doing workforce development. But if we all came together, if we all unified and created a great program with your leadership, I think we could create five million extra jobs in the U.S. And you know, our companies are some of the greatest universities in the world. We shape these employees, we train them, we educate them, we bring them in, and I think we can do this."

Anyone with a head for business could quickly calculate that if the current programs worked, then building up the capacity from five hundred thousand to five million people at the same cost per apprentice would mean spending another $810 million of taxpayer money. Based on Trump's example of Charles Robel making $60,000 his first year, that would produce an immediate return of $333 in increased wages for each dollar spent on apprenticeship programs for all five million people. Just the taxes on all those wages would pay for the program many times over.

Even at ten times the cost per apprentice in the last Obama budget, this would still be a very good deal. And because it's a one-time investment, the results when measured by lifetimes of work would be enormous, stupendous, mind-bogglingly large. The taxes that would roll in might even make it possible for Trump to show that the economists and government policy wonks were all wrong and that he really could sharply lower tax rates without adding to the federal debt.

Apprenticeships are a one-time cost, while the benefits of higher wages go on and on. Let's assume all five million apprentices made the amount Trump cited in his example, $60,000, and never got those big pay raises Trump characterized as virtually certain. Over thirty-five years, the standard the Social Security Administration uses in calculating retirement benefits, the total wages earned by those apprentices would come to $10.5 trillion. And how much is that? It equals all the money that all 161 million Americans with any paid work earned in 2015 plus everything they made in the first five months of 2016. It's a bonanza.

So what did Trump do?

Trump told the television camera "in just a few moments, I'll be signing an executive order to expand apprenticeships and vocational training to help all Americans find a rewarding career, earn a great living, and support themselves and their families, and love going to work in the morning. We will be removing federal restrictions that have prevented many different industries from creating apprenticeship programs. We have regulations on top of regulations. And in history, nobody has gotten rid of so many regulations as the Trump administration. And that's one of the reasons that you see the jobs and the companies all kicking in so strongly. I think some very good numbers are going to be announced, by the way, in the very near future as to GDP," referring to Gross Domestic Product, the country's entire economic output.

Asked what regulations the administration had gotten rid of, government spokespeople had a hard time coming up with answers. That doesn't mean there aren't any such terminated regulations, only that Trump spoke without staff work to back him up or, possibly, staff work to find if there were any such apprenticeship-blocking regulations.

The executive order declared, "It shall be the policy of the Federal Government to provide more affordable pathways to secure, high paying jobs by promoting apprenticeships and effective workforce development programs." Trump also directed government to review and streamline some forty-three workforce programs at thirteen agencies to find ways to spend less and do more, but without identifying any of them.

Trump's order also instructed Labor Secretary Acosta that he "shall use available funding to promote apprenticeships."

This was not an exercise in investing in the future of America and in better jobs, but in robbing Peter to pay Paul. Just where the money would come from Trump did not specify. Government officials told reporters they had no idea—and asked not to be quoted by name about that.

Perhaps the Labor Department could further reduce the number of job safety inspectors. Maybe there could be fewer investigations of labor racketeering, something Trump benefited from when he was constructing his New York apartments and Atlantic City casinos, as federal and state law enforcement records and testimony in a federal racketeering trial showed. Maybe less money could be spent protecting pensions and retirement savings from the small minority of dishonest employers.

Cutting job safety inspections would almost certainly come at a cost of more lives lost at work. The Labor Department inspector general's latest report in 2017 found that oversight of emergency plans for underground mines, for example, was woefully inadequate. When employers were cited for hazardous work conditions, one in six cases received no follow-up to see if the hazardous conditions were remedied. Trump inherited that mess, but his budget aimed not to fix it, but to make it worse.

The inspector general also scrutinized the Labor Department office charged with making sure workers receive their health benefits. That office "did not have the ability to protect the estimated 79 million plan participants in self-insured health plans from improper denials of health claims, due to a lack of knowledge of claim denials." Again, this was a problem Trump inherited. But both his campaign rhetoric and inaugural address committed him to solving such problems, not worsening them.

Senator Tammy Baldwin, a Wisconsin Democrat, called Trump out during his visit to her state for talking big on apprenticeships while putting deep cuts in his federal budget plan. The "rhetoric doesn't match the reality," she said, pointing to a $900 million cut in job training.

Trump ignored criticism from Baldwin and many others. Instead, the president smiled at the television cameras, surrounded by Robel and the other apprentices, and said, "We want to keep jobs in America, and we want to train people and hire American workers to fill those jobs. And that's exactly what we're doing."

Creating jobs was far from the only subject in which Trump claimed to be an expert, but which in fact, showed otherwise. Another is taxes.

PART III

TAXES

The Tax Expert

*"I think nobody knows more about taxes
than I do, maybe in the history of the world.
Nobody knows more about taxes."*

Donald Trump, May 13, 2016

Trump's short attention span, combined with his lack of knowledge about world history and events, clouds his actions in Washington. The intelligence officials who deliver the world's most expensive news report, the President's Daily Brief, have learned to keep it very short, to include Trump's name frequently to keep him interested, and to eschew nuance. When Trump talks publicly about issues, he uses what some scholars say is a sixth-grade grammar rich with words like "beautiful" and "terrific," but not much substance. Nothing he has ever said publicly demonstrates any substantial knowledge of taxes.

The public record shows something about Trump and taxes that is deeply troubling. Public records reveal that he is an income tax cheat. Trump's 1984 income tax returns were examined in two administrative trials held by New York state and city officials. No journalist reported on the proceedings until I found the decisions against him in 2016.

Trump's 1984 tax returns included what is known as a Schedule C. That is a tax form filed annually by about 27 million sole proprietors of unincorporated businesses like myself. To simplify coordination between federal and state income tax returns, New York State adheres strictly to the concepts and data required on the federal tax return.

Trump listed himself as a business consultant. He put down $626,264 in tax-deductible business expenses and zero income on his state return.

His city tax return also showed no income, but slightly less in business expenses for his consulting services.

Both state and city tax auditors examined the return. They asked for receipts and other business records establishing that the deductions were reasonable and necessary costs of doing business. When Trump did not produce any, the deductions were disallowed and Trump was sent notices to pay more tax as well as penalties and interest. He appealed.

The only witness at the tax trials was Jack Mitnick, the lawyer and accountant who had prepared Trump's tax returns for more than two decades and his father, Fred Trump's, returns before that. Mitnick testified that he was "thoroughly familiar" not only with Trump's tax returns, but all aspects of Trump's finances. At one trial Mitnick was shown a photocopy of Trump's tax return, the only version anyone could produce. The photocopy, evidently, was mailed to the tax authorities instead of the original.

Mitnick, under oath, examined the document. He confirmed that it bore his photocopied signature. But then Mitnick declared that "we did not" prepare the tax return, referring to both himself and his firm. That was strong evidence of income tax fraud, which can be a civil issue or a criminal offense. Had the federal, state, or city government investigated the tax return Mitnick testified about, Trump would have been at serious risk of indictment—and of losing his lucrative casino licenses.

H. Gregory Tillman, the administrative law judge who heard the city case in 1992, noted the strange circumstance of no original tax return being on file with the city, only the photocopy. In his written decision, Judge Tillman noted that Trump complained of double taxation, but he found that claim baseless. Taking the unusual step in a judicial opinion of using boldface to emphasize his point, Judge Tillman wrote, "The problem at issue is not one of **double taxation**, but of **no taxation**."

Tillman ruled against Trump, but did not impose penalties because the original tax return was never found.

State tax auditors also denied Trump's unexplained deductions. Judge Frank W. Barrie imposed the maximum civil penalties and included a note in his opinion indicating that Trump paid zero taxes on his entire income.

Mitnick, semiretired and living in Florida, told me he did not recall either tax trial. What he did recall in two interviews with me was that

Trump played no role in designing and executing tax strategies. "I did that—all of that," Mitnick said. "Donald just signed."

During the campaign, no journalist even attempted to pin down Trump on his claims of world-class mastery of the tax code. Few even noted that he usually speaks of taxes in slogans and vagaries, not the wonky and de-tail-laced argot of tax specialists. With a few questions, any well-prepared journalist could have exposed Trump's claims of expertise as nonsense. Nothing Trump said indicated an awareness of the hellish complexity of the American tax code, which runs to nearly 6,500 pages and includes a 1998 tax simplification provision that ironically appears in the tax code as Section 7803(c)(2)(B)(ii)(IX).

Early in the campaign there was a clear indication that Trump was not comfortable with tax policy, not even when reading from a script. Trump's announcement of his tax plan, such as it was, in September 2015 con-trasted with the launch of his campaign three months earlier in the same place, the lobby of Trump Tower.

In announcing his latest presidential run, Trump arranged for live national television coverage. He denounced China for not acting as he wished, accused the Mexican government of sending rapists and mur-derers across the border illegally, and promised to make Mexico pay for a wall on America's southern border. He mangled many facts, most bi-zarrely when he declared that in the first three months of 2015, America's Gross Domestic Product—the value of all economic activity—"was below zero. Whoever heard of this? It's never below zero." No one had heard of such a thing because it has never happened. Instead of all economic ac-tivity stopping, the American economy grew, albeit at the very slow rate of a fifth of one percent. What made Trump's statement astonishing was that he earned a bachelor's degree in economics from the University of Pennsylvania. Trump often claims he was a top student there, though no record of any academic honors being conferred on Trump has ever been found.

Wild claims, nonsense facts and all, were less significant than the image Trump projected when he announced his campaign for the presi-dency in June 2015. His speech and body language showed how years as host of a reality television show and performing promotional work for himself and his businesses made for a polished performance. His words flowed with easy cadence, the movements of his hands and body coordinated to project the image of a formidable power.

To the national television audience, it also seemed that Trump's racist, anti-immigrant speech had found an adoring audience right in the liberal heart of America's biggest city. Vigorous applause interrupted his remarks forty-three times, but not once was Trump knocked off his rhythm. The ovations, it came out the next day, did not come from ardent fans, however. Midtown Manhattan had not suddenly become a mecca for racists, white supremacists, and xenophobes. A help-wanted ad revealed that the seemingly adoring audience was salted with actors paid fifty bucks each to clap on cue.

Three months later when Trump announced his first tax plan, in the familiar Trump Tower lobby, the delivery was quite different, the polish and his customary bravado absent.

Trump read uneasily from a statement, looking down at the text on a lectern and then lifting his head as he haltingly repeated brief snippets of the words he had just seen. His cadence suggested that many of the words, as well as the concepts behind them, were unfamiliar. Only when he was slinging slogans was the delivery closer to the forceful and animated Trump that audiences were getting to know.

"I think you will see we have an amazing code," Trump said, implying that, as with George W. Bush in the year 2000, he already had a fully developed tax plan even if, like Bush, he would not show it to anyone until after Election Day. Trump even let slip with his choice of verb tense that he didn't yet have a tax plan written down. "It would be simple," he said using a conditional verb and then quickly adding, "it will be easy, it will be fair."

Speaking somewhat bumpily and dropping words, Trump continued. "It's graduated as you get up in income, you pay a little more. Some of the very unfair deductions that certain people have been given who make a lot of money will not [be] available any longer, but I believe they'll do better because I think the economy will grow. It will grow rapidly and [we] will have something very special. . . .

"I did the [tax] plan with some of the leading scholars and economists and tax experts that there are in this country," Trump boasted. "They love it. They say, why hasn't this been done before? And this is my wheelhouse, that's what I do well. The economy is what I do well."

There was no panel of experts standing behind or beside him, however. There were no economists and tax specialists waiting off camera to brief reporters and answer questions. There were no names made available to reporters so they could follow up with these experts.

Trump also promised huge tax cuts for big business, saying this would spur investment. He didn't mention that Bush's 2001 tax cuts failed to do that, nor did he point out that he would be a major beneficiary of such tax cuts.

Trump then ticked off numbers on tax rates. Partners in accounting, law, medical, and other firms and freelancers would pay a 15 percent rate on their profits, not up to 44.4 percent with the surtax for Obamacare. The 35 percent corporate tax rate also would be cut to 15 percent. Cutting tax rates is not tax reform, which in American politics has long meant eliminating loopholes and favors like letting real estate professionals live tax-free and other provisions that distort economic decisions.

Next, Trump said he would repeal the estate tax, which applied each year to fewer than five thousand very large fortunes. Out of every thousand Americans who die, just two owe any estate tax, and the average tax paid comes to 17 percent of the fortune, IRS data show. If Trump really had the fortune he claimed, a net worth of more than $10 billion, he stood to gain by eventually passing the full amount to his heirs instead of paying around $4 billion in estate tax, which would mean leaving his unfortunate heirs a paltry $6 billion or less. Only after the election would he reveal that his net worth was less than $2 billion and even that figure was likely significantly inflated.

The most tantalizing element, the one designed to win lots of votes, was Trump's promise to eliminate income taxes for half of those currently filing tax returns. Trump said he would exempt the first $50,000 for a married couple, half that for singles. Instead of filing a tax return these households would sign a "one page form to send the IRS saying, 'I win.'"

To millions of Americans that sounded wonderful, fantastically wonderful. For 90 percent of taxpayers, average income had been flat from 1967 through 2012. During the first eight years of the twenty-first century, the population grew five times faster than jobs. These two factors combined into a powerful incentive for many to vote Trump. The trick was to convince people he knew what he was talking about, that he really was a tax law expert. And, of course, he would need to persuade Congress to make his plan into law. He stoked the idea that he was such a skillful negotiator that Congress would do just as he asked—and pronto.

Trump's words provoked a very different response among the relatively small group of serious students of tax. They knew that those numbers could not possibly add up to anything but buckets of red ink spilling across federal ledgers, the federal debt rapidly expanding. Maya Mac-Guineas, president of the Committee for a Responsible Federal Budget, a bipartisan Washington nonprofit organization that wants to scale back federal spending, especially spending that benefits the middle class, said that at first glance "this looks like a tax cut of a magnitude of about $5 trillion" in the first ten years.

To get an idea of how much $5 trillion is, consider this: it's more than all the individual income taxes the federal government expects to collect from everyone in the next three years. MacGuineas called such a large reduction in federal revenues "simply unimaginable." She suggested this was a cynical ploy to win votes by selling voters a bill of goods. "Who doesn't love a tax cut, especially if no one has to pay for it? This is a free-lunch mentality."

The conservative and antitax Tax Foundation ran the numbers. It estimated that Trump's proposal was far costlier than MacGuineas imagined. Trump's plan would add at least $10 trillion to the federal debt over ten years, the Tax Foundation estimated. This undercut Trump's claims that as president he would reduce the federal government debt that he called dangerously high at $19 trillion.

The nonpartisan Tax Policy Center analyzed the Trump plan using its computer model, which for years had generated predictions that later events proved to have been remarkably accurate. It calculated Trump would add $12 trillion to the federal debt in just ten years. Both organizations cautioned that because of missing details, their estimates could significantly understate how much extra debt the Trump plan would require.

As the 2016 election drew near, Hillary Clinton challenged the believability of Trump's tax promises, saying they were so much pie in the sky. She proposed lowering taxes on the 99 percent, especially families with children, while paying for the cuts by raising taxes on the top one percent.

Trump ignored what she said and insisted that Clinton wanted to "double" income taxes. Clinton's message did not inspire people feeling economic desperation after fifteen years of flat wages the way Trump's did. And hers got little attention, in part because much as Trump stumbled in announcing his tax plan, she came across to many as offering so many specifics and qualifiers that to many voters it was just blah-blah-blah, her tax cut promise lost in a haystack of details.

Despite this, Clinton's comments and the calculations by experts in tax and economics had an impact on Trump. His promise of no income taxes on the first $50,000 for married couples was quietly reduced 40 percent to $30,000. Singles would get half that.

Trump also delivered an unwelcome surprise to widowed, divorced, and never married mothers and fathers with dependent children. Congress calls them heads of households and gives them them tax breaks halfway between being single and married. Trump wanted to tax them as singles. That message appealed to religious and social conservatives opposed to unwed parenthood and divorce. (These supporters generally ignore the plight of single mothers who were widowed.) Getting rid of head of household status would mean higher taxes for families raising about 20 million of the nation's 73 million minor children, my analysis of Census Bureau and IRS data found.

Trump's changes in his tax cut promises got little attention. They were seen as technical by the politics reporters who cover the horse race, not policy. Few reported that the reduced promise of tax-free earnings at $30,000 for married couples and half that for singles was not much of a change from existing law. Married couples already earned their first $20,800 income tax-free, singles half that. Trump successfully baited voters with a big promise, then switched to a much smaller one that few noticed.

Reforming the tax system is not simple. Taxes at all levels are the single largest part of the American economy, more than a quarter of all economic activity. The thousands of favors Congress has bestowed, by its grace, on the political donor class add complexity. They also create concentrated economic interests vested in preserving their tax favors. Groups who are helped, or hurt, by changes end up in contention. That's good for politicians raising donations for their next campaign, but not for sound tax policy.

Changing the American tax system is somewhat like playing a game of pick-up sticks. The object is to remove one colorful stick at a time without any of the other sticks moving. Successfully removing a stick may win the game, but is just as likely to shift the dynamics of the whole pile with unpredictable results. Changing any one section of the tax code has similar interactions that may not be at all obvious, especially when made in haste. A poorly thought through plan to change the tax code could sink the economy. It could also open vast new opportunities for some of the richest Americans to escape income taxes, even if that was not the intention.

Taxes don't have to be as complicated as health care, the second largest part of the American economy. But until there is thoughtful and serious reform, that's the way it is. (My next book will propose a completely new tax system using existing law, following ancient principles and eliminating income tax returns.)

Trump counted on millions of voters not thinking about whether he actually had a tax plan or was blowing hot air. He counted on them only dreaming of a few more after-tax dollars in their paychecks. Then came the election results. Eight months after his inauguration, Trump had yet to deliver on his pledge to immediately introduce a comprehensive tax reform bill and get it signed into law within one hundred days.

A few obstacles stood in the way of fulfilling that pledge. Trump didn't have a bill. He did not even have a detailed memo that congressional aides could translate into legal language. His comments on tax policy were as fluid and changeable as those science fiction shape-shifters who assume whatever form advances their interests at the moment. Even Trump's closest allies did not know just what he wanted. Based on his limited knowledge of tax law and economics, Trump himself may not have known what he wanted except to become a hero by arranging for others to pay less.

Trump lacked estimates on how changes to tax law would affect government revenue. Indeed, he had no reliable estimates, just claims conjured from the ethers. Without such projections, practical and political problems stood in the way of tax legislation. Before taking up a bill, the tax writers on Capitol Hill should insist on analyses known as *distribution tables* showing how the tax savings pie would be divided among different income groups. Not knowing who would pay more and who would pay less made it hard for representatives and senators to decide where they stood. Any bill that increased revenue would be rejected out of hand by the anti-taxers among congressional Republicans. So would a bill that required more government debt, though the political red line there was much more flexible than on increasing government revenues as a share of the economy. Moderates in both parties would be troubled by a bill that gave little or nothing to the poor and middle class, as well as the prosperous upper-middle-class professionals whose labors earned them $100,000 to $400,000 a year. Liberals would fret over how big a slice of the tax-savings pie would go to the rich.

Alongside this was the tricky issue of how interactions among the various provisions of the tax code would, or could, create unexpected winners and losers. Without details, no one could create rules to mitigate unintended consequences, an issue the Reagan team carefully studied in writing the 1986 Tax Reform Act, the last real overhaul of the federal tax system.

Candidate Trump had simply evaded these serious issues by using slogans and grand claims and then deleting his tax plan from the campaign website. As they say of frauds posing as ranchers in Texas, Trump was all hat and no cattle. Like every con artist who sold people the earth, moon, and stars, when the time came to deliver the goods, he didn't have them. Unlike con artists who can skip town with money fleeced from fools, or tell unhappy victims to sue him as Trump routinely did in his businesses, Trump has nowhere to hide in the glare of the White House. He also has nothing to show in terms of tax legislation.

Trump had been in office more than five weeks when he spoke to a joint session of Congress. His remarks were delivered so smoothly and without the angry and negative bombast of his dreadful inauguration address that even some critics called the speech his finest hour and said that for the first time he seemed presidential. Like his campaign talks, though, Trump was long on promises and short on substance.

That night Trump made no attempt to sell the tax cuts that had been central to attracting voters. There was no soliloquy on the benefits of his tax plan, no marshaling of even a few powerful facts to build a case for lowering tax rates. No claims that lower taxes would mean more jobs and better pay. There was not even a reminder of the campaign declarations that combining universal tax cuts with simplification and fairness would double the rate of economic growth. Instead Trump said only this: "We will provide massive tax relief to the middle class."

Trump had not forgotten his campaign promises. Earlier that day on Fox News he was asked about lower tax rates generating less revenue. Trump, in full con artist mode, waved the problem away. "I think the money is going to come from a revved-up economy," he said. "I mean, you look at the kind of numbers we're doing—we were probably G.D.P. of a little more than 1 percent, and if I can get that up to 3 or maybe more, we have a whole different ballgame."

While he had no legislation, the number of tax policy specialists finding fault with his proposals continued growing. The idea that tax cuts produce faster economic growth was ridiculed so widely that it was even challenged on Fox News.

Then there was the fairness problem Trump created by promising explicitly and repeatedly that simplification and fairness went hand in hand. Trump promised to slash the top marginal income tax rate by as much as 62 percent, while the middle-class tax rate cuts would at best be slight trims. Today, some Americans earn annual incomes of a billion dollars or more and hundreds of thousands make a million dollars or more. But the top tax rate Trump proposed was expected to retain existing law, meaning it applied at less than a half million dollars of annual income. That meant a married couple who both worked all year to make $500,000 would be taxed on most of their income at 25 percent and on their last dollars at 35 percent, while those harvesting thousands of times that much income would pay just 15 percent on income from capital rather than labor. Since 15 percent is less than half of 35 percent, the difference between labor and capital income tax rates would create lucrative incentives for accountants and lawyers to devise ways to escape the higher tax rate. In the past this has been achieved by converting salaries taxed at higher rates into what would appear to IRS auditors to be capital gains taxed at much lower rates.

Some critics noted that the Trump-Pence campaign website materials on taxes, read literally, proposed raising the income tax rate of the working poor and marginal small businesses by half, from a 10 percent tax rate to 15 percent. That surely was not Trump's intent, but it showed that on tax policy, as well as facts and logic, Trump was anything but the world's greatest expert. (The campaign tax promise was deleted from the website after the election.)

On April 26, his ninety-sixth day in office, Trump had yet to introduce tax legislation. It was more than a week after the historic Tax Day when income tax returns came due. But that day America finally saw a Trump administration tax plan. Well, sort of. Treasury Secretary Steve Mnuchin and Gary Cohn, the White House economic policy director, delivered a one-page statement to reporters. The "plan" totaled one hundred words. Those words read more like a hastily compiled tax cut shopping list for clients of Goldman Sachs, where both Mnuchin and Cohn had worked for years, than what the 90 percent were promised.

Cohn, who had been No. 2 at Goldman Sachs, complained about questions reporters asked for which he had no answers. "We're holding a bunch of listening groups right now," Cohn said, indicating that rather than coming into office with a plan, Trump was trying to find support for some sort of plan.

"We are working very diligently with the House and the Senate on coming up with final details of the bill. You're going into very micro-details," he said. "We're holding a bunch of listening groups right now. We have outlines; we have a broad-brush view of where they're going to be. We're running an enormous amount of data on the proposals right now. We will be back to you with very firm details. We're very confident to where they're going to be, we just wanted to get out and give you a broad-brush overview where we are."

The hundred-word plan would change the amount of income people could earn before income taxes began. The threshold was set at $24,000, half that for singles. This was less than half the $50,000 Trump had initially promised married couples. This was hardly the big savings Trump used as bait to lure voters by promising to remove half of them from the income tax rolls.

That Trump had tricked voters about their individual taxes became clear as soon as the Tax Policy Center ran the proposal, such as it was, through its time-tested computer model.

Among those making $20,000 to $30,000 in 2018 when the plan would take effect, only one in six households would get any tax savings. Those who did would save on average $40. Half of households making $40,000 to $55,000 would get a tax cut. The lucky half would save $34. These minor tax savings are as different from the tax wizardry Trump promised as the mythical Emerald City of Oz is from dusty Kansas.

The one percent, with annual incomes starting at about $600,000 in 2018, could expect to collect about a fifth of all the income in America and pay about two fifths of the income taxes, the Tax Policy Center estimated. They would get much bigger tax savings, however, enjoying two thirds of all the reduced income taxes.

The story was even better for the thin slice of Americans who, like Trump, make more than a million dollars a year. Tax cuts would go to the vast majority of these very high-income households. Six of seven would pay $62,000 less annually, with benefits concentrated far up the income ladder among people making many millions and more. While the million-dollar-and-up club is a tiny slice of all households, about one in 365, Trump would give them 24 percent of all the tax savings, the Tax Policy Center estimated.

Later the administration offered a nine-page plan, if you counted the cover sheet, that was more white space than text. Analysis by the Institute on Taxation and Economic Policy showed that the first-year tax cut would total $191 billion. The best-off one percent, those making more than $616,000, would get two thirds of all the tax savings. The middle class, those making $41,000 to $66,000 in 2018, would get just 6.5 percent of all the tax savings. They would save on average $410, but one in seven among them would pay slightly more in income taxes. The next group, the fifth of Americans with incomes of $66,000 to $111,000, would save $530 per taxpayer. The poor, those making less than $24,000, would get a tax break, too—two bucks a week on average.

The numbers showed a tax plan not for the vast majority of the American people, the left-behinds who embraced Trump as their savior, but for the political donor class, a gift from Trump to his fellow plutocrats.

There were more Trump goodies for the already rich in the one-hundred-word plan. It called for eliminating the estate tax, which Trump had pledged to do in his campaign.

*   *   *

The most generous and highly concentrated Trump cuts were reserved for business—not all businesses, but big businesses. Again, Trump was with Wall Street, not Main Street, the exact opposite of his campaign theme.

Mnuchin emphasized that late April afternoon that the 35 percent corporate tax rate would be slashed to 15 percent. He also said it would apply only to domestic profits, exactly as Trump had promised in 2015. Profits earned outside the country would be subject to foreign taxes only. Depending on the rules, that could be a boon to American companies but it could also open to door to massive tax avoidance, worsening the federal debt Trump rails against.

The key question Mnuchin failed to address concerned profits earned in the United States and then siphoned out of the country as tax-deductible expenses. Through accounting tricks and a single line added to the tax code in 1986, multinational American companies could convert the burden of taxes into a profit center. Enron, the energy trading firm that collapsed in 2001, was a pioneer in these techniques with more than six hundred offshore entities created to put its profits beyond the reach of the tax collector.

One way companies do this is by paying fees to themselves. Many companies place their corporate logos, formulas for making drugs, and other valuable intellectual property in offshore subsidiaries. When they sell a pair of shoes or sell a pill, they pay the offshore subsidiary a royalty for the use of their own logo or formula. This converts what would otherwise be a dollar of American profit into a tax-deductible expense paid to a foreign corporation, even though the money stays inside the parent corporation. It is as if Congress gave you a tax deduction each time you took a dollar bill in your right pocket and moved it to your left pocket. It's also a deal that benefits only multinationals. Purely domestic American companies, which includes most family-owned businesses, are not eligible. Once the profits are transformed into expenses and moved offshore, the money can be invested. Over the years, thanks to the magic of compounding, the deferred taxes will earn so much interest that the company can pay the tax and still have more money than if there was no corporate income tax. It's eating your cake and having it, too, often with an extra slice.

Another aspect of the Trump tax plan would, read literally, raise the tax rate on profits of many small businesses by half. The White House announcement proposed a flat tax rate of 15 percent on business profits even though many family-owned enterprises make such a modest profit that they pay only 10 percent. Were Congress to move on Trump's plan, lawmakers would, no doubt, make sure that small businesses paying the 10 percent rate continued to do so. But the focus by the Trump administration on the top rate showed how little thought it gave to the millions of mom-and-pop businesses. Middle-income Americans would get scraps while the rich enjoyed tax savings each year larger than what middle-class families earned.

Owners of small businesses typically seek to report little or no profit, taking money out instead as salary for relatives, contributions to retirement plans, and expenses they can charge to the enterprise, which is known as "the benefits of ownership." Of the nearly six million American corporations operating in 2013, close to four million had assets of less than $500,000. Their average profit was $1,825. The average federal income tax was $357, or less than a dollar a day. Another 374,400 corporations were slightly larger, with assets of a half million dollars to a million dollars. Their average profit was less than $11,000 and their average tax was less than $2,800. In neither case were taxes a major constraint on success.

Another way to evaluate small businesses is to calculate how much revenue these businesses take in from customers that ends up paid as federal corporate income taxes. It was less than a dollar on each thousand dollars of revenue, hardly a crushing burden.

At the top, fewer than 3,300 corporations owned 81 percent of all corporate assets. They paid an average tax rate of 21 percent, far below the 35 percent rate set by Congress, many because of those rules favoring tax avoidance by multinationals. Cut their tax rate to 15 percent and these big businesses would enjoy a massive windfall worth several hundred billion dollars a year. As with people, the Trump plan aimed to help the biggest businesses, not the most.

In tax policy, especially with a rich man in the White House, a reasonable question to ask is how would Trump benefit. We'll examine that next.

Trump's Tax Return

Standing on a strip of white sand beach along the Intracoastal Waterway on March 13, 2017, I held my iPhone with outstretched arms to record a panoramic view of Mar-a-Lago and neighboring Florida mansions. Halfway through the panning, my phone vibrated. Amy, one of my five grown daughters, told me that among the day's mail delivered to my home in western New York State was a letter whose contents she had scanned and emailed.

"LOOK AT—tax document" the subject line read. When the attachment opened, I momentarily stopped breathing. On the tiny cell phone screen I could just make out two pages of Donald Trump's 2005 federal income tax return. Never before had the public seen a single page from a Trump federal tax return. And while as a candidate Trump pledged to make his tax returns public, once he became president he said no one would ever see them.

Two thoughts hit me.

Is this real?

Does anyone else have this?

Turning to my host, the storied criminal defense lawyer Glenn Zeitz, who had been showing me around Palm Beach, I said I had to drop everything to work on authenticating and analyzing the document. Zeitz had been regaling me with the story of how he had bested Trump in a lawsuit, saving the home of Vera Coking, an elderly Atlantic City woman who refused to sell Trump her home. (The casino mogul got government officials to try to seize her house for his benefit. Zeitz saved the day by winning a court ruling that Trump abused his position, preserving Coking's home.)

The next evening, after the White House authenticated the document, I broke the tax return story at DCReport.org, the website my friends and

I created to cover what Trump and future presidents do, as opposed to what he tweets. That night Rachel Maddow and Lawrence O'Donnell had me on their MSNBC shows, as did ABC's *Good Morning America*, CNN, *Democracy Now!*, and other shows the next day.

The Form 1040 was just a keyhole view into Trump's taxes. Luckily, I knew that a great deal could be distilled from these two pages because I have spent decades reporting on our tax system and was deep into drafting a proposed new federal tax code for the twenty-first-century economy.

The most important revelation came from Line 44. It showed that on the $152.7 million that flowed into Trump's pockets that year, his regular federal income tax was just $5.3 million. But for a stopgap in federal tax law, that was all he would have paid.

That meant Trump's regular income tax rate was less than 3.5 percent on this enormous income. That rate was less than the poorest half of American taxpayers paid that year. They paid a tad more than 3.5 percent on their average incomes of just $16,000, IRS data showed. In 2005, it took Trump less than fifty-five minutes to earn $16,000.

The second biggest issue his tax return raised was about how he would benefit from the big tax reform package that he promised but had yet to propose.

Before this document, all that the public knew about Trump's taxes came from two limited disclosures. His income and taxes for five years in the 1970s had been revealed when Trump obtained his Atlantic City casino license more than three decades earlier. It showed that in the last two years, 1978 and 1979, he paid no income taxes because he had paper losses on real estate he managed. Under special rules put into place by Congress that protect the political donor class, his taxable income was less than zero even as he lived a lavish lifestyle. In 1979, he reported an income of minus $3.4 million for tax purposes—resulting not only in a tax-free single year, but the ability to roll unused tax savings into future years.

The second insight came a few weeks before the election. The front pages of Trump's 1995 state tax returns filed in Connecticut, New Jersey, and New York had been sent anonymously to *The New York Times* and the New York *Daily News*. Susanne Craig of the *Times* said the plain brown envelope she found in her mail slot at work showed "Trump Tower" as the return address. Her reporting partner, David Barstow, sought my help on the story they wrote without telling me what they had.

The state tax documents revealed that at the end of 1995 Trump had $918 million of tax losses—negative income—that he could use to offset future income, a tax benefit that proved to be important to understanding the 2005 federal tax return.

How Trump obtained the $918 million is the story of a tax shelter so odious that when Republicans in Congress learned of it, it took them only a few weeks to pass a new law to demolish the tax shelter. However, as it usually does, Congress let those who had already bought this sham keep their ill-got savings.

The sheltering technique involves a lot of technical details. For tax wonks the short version is this: Trump's shelter combined tax benefits under section 1231 of the Internal Revenue Code with the exception provisions in section 108, a concoction that is now illegal.

The device involved Trump reporting a tax loss of a billion dollars. He did this by claiming as his personal business loss nearly a billion dollars he had borrowed from the banks but never paid back. The banks had already deducted the loss on their corporate tax returns. What Trump did was to take that deduction again for himself.

Normally when people borrow money from banks and don't pay it back, they *owe* tax. Congress treats unpaid loans as income, which they are. Millions of Americans learned this the hard way when the housing market melted down in 2008 and banks lowered the balances on some mortgages so people would not abandon their homes. These homeowners then got IRS notices telling them they owed taxes on the amounts their mortgage lenders forgave.

The only way out of being taxed on loans not paid back is to get the debt discharged in federal Bankruptcy Court.

Trump had not filed personal bankruptcy when he got his relief in 1990 from roughly a billion of the more than $3 billion he had borrowed. Instead his lawyers negotiated a deal with the banks. Then they persuaded New Jersey casino regulators to take his side in the negotiations with bankers. For New Jersey politicians with pliable ethics, this was not an especially hard choice. Except for two small lenders, the bank headquarters were in New York and more distant jurisdictions. Trump was a major employer with thousands of people working at his three Atlantic City casinos.

Once the casino regulators pointed out to the banks that if they foreclosed on Trump, they would be the owners of seaside hotels without gambling licenses—meaning vastly less resale value than licensed casinos—the banks surrendered. This was not how the casino law was supposed to work. A trustee was supposed to keep the casinos open if the owner was unable to pay his debts as they came due. But Trump's political influence won out over integrity in New Jersey government.

Because this was a private deal done outside of bankruptcy court, Trump faced a tax bill of about a third of a billion dollars. That's where the tax shelter came into play.

In step one, Trump essentially gave up his right to future real estate paper losses on his casinos. Instead he used the remaining value of the buildings to offset immediately the income he got from not paying his loans back in full. In step two, five years later he put the casino hotels, their value as real estate tax shelters now eliminated, into a publicly traded Trump casino hotel company. It never made a penny of profit, losing more than $1.3 billion before shutting down after thirteen years, the investors wiped out. Meanwhile, Trump paid himself $82 million in cash for heading the company. Step three was buying the tax shelter Congress later shut down. The shelter was based on the faulty economic premise that the losses the banks took were really Trump's because of the change in the value of his assets.

The 2005 federal income tax summary pages showed what was left of the shelter.

Adding up the wages, rents, profits, and other income on the 2005 federal tax return revealed that Trump enjoyed $152.7 million of income flowing into his pockets. But the last line on the front page of the return showed that his adjusted gross income was only $49.6 million.

The huge difference came from $103.2 million of negative income.

That indicated that Trump had by 2005 used up $815 million of negative income from the tax shelter and in 2005 took the last $103.2 million to lower his taxable income. In turn, that revealed that Trump's annual income for the previous ten years averaged at least $81.5 million. If Trump found new ways to generate negative income, he may have enjoyed even more money without sharing in the burden of supporting the federal government that weighed on everyone else.

So long as he had unused value in the tax shelter, Trump would be able to offset dollars he earned with dollars from the tax shelter, paying little or no tax. "Little" is a qualifier because of complex interactions among the tax rules governing deductions; some taxes may have come due despite his big-bucks tax shelter, but vastly less than his income would normally warrant.

During the September 2016 presidential debates, Hillary Clinton said Trump "doesn't want the American people, all of you watching tonight, to know that he's paid nothing in federal taxes" in at least some years.

Trump did not argue the point. Instead, he interrupted Clinton. "That makes me smart," he said.

There was another important element to his 2005 income tax return. In addition to the relatively tiny regular federal income tax, Trump had to pay $31.6 million of Alternative Minimum Tax or AMT. That brought his total tax bill to almost $36.6 million.

The White House issued a statement saying that despite "substantial income figure and tax paid . . . the dishonest media can continue to make this part of their agenda, while the President will focus on his, which includes tax reform that will benefit all Americans."

The official White House announcement falsely stated that Trump paid $38.4 million of income tax, improperly counting the payroll taxes Trump paid as a self-employed individual. Most news organizations went with press secretary Sean Spicer's inflated number instead of checking his words against the document that they had while preparing their own stories on my scoop, a reminder of how much American journalists rely on official statements regardless of their accuracy rather than documented facts.

The next day Trump went on Tucker Carlson's Fox show and inflated the numbers far more than Spicer had. "The income was actually $250 million for the year and if you notice there was about $100 million in tax deductions and depreciation and various other charges so actually the income was at the 250 level," Trump said.

Watching the show, I burst out laughing. What Trump told Carlson indicated that the self-proclaimed greatest expert in the world on taxes did not understand his own tax return or he had inflated his reported income by two thirds.

"Fake news!" I shouted at my television, startling my wife.

What hardly anyone, except financial columnist Allan Sloan, reported was that Trump could recoup the Alternative Minimum Tax paid in 2005 in future years. That's because of a special rule for real estate investors that lets them get AMT refunds for years when the rules limit their ability to use their tax favors.

That rule does not apply to the vast majority of Americans who are forced to pay the AMT ever since Ronald Reagan signed it into law for the 1987 tax year. Most of the AMT is paid by married couples with more than two children who own their homes and live in high-tax states, which also happen to be the states that tend to have the most good-paying jobs. Under the AMT people cannot take personal exemptions for themselves and their children; they lose the standard deduction; they cannot deduct state income and local property taxes; cannot deduct miscellaneous items such as union dues or cleaning official uniforms; and they get to deduct fewer catastrophic medical bills. A family can be hit with the AMT just because they have seven or more children. Running up big medical bills saving the life of a child with cancer can result in a higher tax bill because of the AMT, and no family in this situation can do anything but pay. Congress, however, by its grace lets Trump and other real estate investors recoup in subsequent years most or all the AMT they pay in one year.

Whether Trump scrupulously followed the law in his tax returns cannot be determined without seeing his other returns, including all the schedules and attachments. What we do know is that Trump has publicly warned Robert Mueller, the special counsel looking into Russian efforts to help Trump win the election, to stay away from his tax returns and business deals. The documents Mueller subpoenaed and witnesses he called before a grand jury make clear, however, that Mueller was not deterred by Trump's threats. This raises the question, what does Trump have to hide?

Mueller's inquiry is focused on Russian interference in the presidential campaign, including a June 2016 email to Donald Trump Jr. that suggests the Trumps knew the Kremlin was already working behind the scenes to elect Trump. The email states that as "part of Russia and its government's support for Mr. Trump" the crown prosecutor (Russia's attorney general) wanted to deliver damaging documents about Hillary Clinton. President Trump and his namesake son, who got the email and said he "loved" the offer of sub rosa assistance, have told at least six different stories about the email and subsequent events, all proved to be false.

But even if Mueller's team finds tax fraud, the federal tax system is so riven with favors and court rulings on behalf of aggressive tax avoidance by the rich that Trump might be able in civil or criminal court to defend them.

While the integrity of Trump's tax returns is unknown, other public documents show that he has cheated on his income taxes and that he has officially acknowledged sales tax fraud.

Without a thorough audit of Trump's tax returns back to 1990 there is no way to know if he cheated on his taxes in the last thirty-six years. And there is no way to know if any cheating was civil, which means the punishment would be financial penalties and interest charges, or criminal. We also cannot get a sound idea of whether his tax returns were meticulously prepared to survive the most rigorous IRS audit with no change or even the government refunding money to him, as it does in about a sixth of audits.

His tax returns, even with all the attached schedules that for Trump no doubt run to more than a thousand pages a year because he owns more than five hundred businesses, are only the starting point. It is the books and records that Congress requires businesses to keep that matter. And for wisenheimers who think that the absence of records will protect them, the law sets a simple standard: no documentation, no deductions for business and other expenses.

What we do know is that Trump has in fact manipulated financial records to cheat on his obligations to government. New York City auditors proved that after being forced into a long fight just to get access to Trump's books and records for the Grand Hyatt Hotel, his first big project.

Trump and some of his enterprises have been the subject of multiple criminal investigations into financial transactions, some with American and Russian crime figures, that make no obvious economic sense. In the mid-1980s he retained Joseph Weichselbaum, a mob associate with two felony convictions, to supply helicopters for high rollers and to manage his personal helicopter under unusual financial arrangements. After federal agents arrested Weichselbaum as a major international drug trafficker in 1985, he confessed.

Trump continued to retain Weichselbaum and even risked his casino license by writing a letter—a letter he initially denied existed—pleading for a light sentence, calling Weichselbaum "a credit to the community." Weichselbaum asked that his case be moved to Florida or Manhattan, but instead it was mysteriously moved to the New Jersey court of Judge Mary-anne Trump Barry, Donald's older sister. She later recused herself, but her brother's pleas for mercy worked. While the mules who drove cocaine and marijuana from Miami to Ohio got up to twenty years, Weichselbaum served just eighteen months. To qualify for parole, he said he had a job as Trump's helicopter consultant. While he paid only $600 of his $30,000 in fines, saying he was a pauper, Weichselbaum moved into a multi-million-dollar Trump Tower apartment bought by his girlfriend. Trump has declined to answer my questions about this relationship, including the obvious one: Did he finance Weichselbaum's drug business?

Hiding the records and manipulating financial figures for his benefit and to the detriment of his legal obligations was bad enough when Trump was merely a businessman short on integrity. But after he became president, Trump continued these vile practices, as shown in the earlier chapter on his continuing refusals to pay. Trump made another promise to voters, that he would build a wall and make Mexico pay for it. But would Mexicans pay for it? Or Americans?

Trump's Wall

When Donald Trump launched his campaign in 2015, he asked people to trust him on many things, none more than his plan to wall off America from the south and stick Mexico with the bill.

"I would build a great wall, and nobody builds walls better than me, believe me," Trump said in kicking off his campaign at Trump Tower. "And I'll build them very inexpensively. I will build a great, great wall on our southern border and I will have Mexico pay for that wall, mark my words."

Two weeks later, in the wake of intense criticism of his initial remarks, he tweeted a stance both softer and more aggressive. "I love the Mexican people, but Mexico is not our friend. They're killing us at the border and they're killing us on jobs and trade. FIGHT!"

Soon a standard feature of Trump rallies was his calling out to the crowd with the question "Who is going to pay for the wall?" The crowd would shout back "Mexico!"

Trump would not reveal his financing plan, just as he would not reveal what he said were his plans to replace Obamacare with something better and cheaper, or to lower taxes without increasing the federal debt, or extinguish "radical Islamic terrorism," or destroy the Islamic State in Syria and the Levant (ISIL, or as he called it, ISIS), or many other policies. When pressed for answers, his mantras were "trust me" and "believe me" and "I'm not going to give away my negotiating strategy."

He told supporters and skeptics alike to remember that he was a great negotiator, so not to worry because he would make it happen.

At the end of August 2016, with questions mounting about how he would get Mexico to pay for the wall, Trump made an unscheduled trip to Mexico City in his personal Boeing 757 jet. Mexican President Enrique Peña Nieto agreed to receive him. The trip's purpose, the campaign said, was to deal with financing the wall.

Going to the Mexican president would be seen, in most sophisticated negotiations, as a sign of weakness on Trump's part. Besides, he held no office, so why would Mexico negotiate with him? And Trump evidently paid no heed to the Logan Act, a law Congress passed in 1799 that makes it a felony to negotiate in any dispute between a foreign power on behalf of the United States without authorization, which Trump obviously did not have. Then again, no one has ever been prosecuted under the Logan Act, though it has caused some lawmakers serious political problems.

What happened in that meeting would become the first of many diplomatic matters involving Trump that would tarnish the reputation of the United States both before he took office and after.

Trump's version when asked at a press conference afterward who would pay for the wall: "Who pays for the wall? We didn't discuss. We did discuss the wall. We didn't discuss payment of the wall. That'll be for a later date."

He also said, "Mexico will work with us and especially after meeting with their wonderful, wonderful president today they want to solve this problem along with us and I am sure they will."

It turned out that Trump, the self-proclaimed master negotiator, had not worked out an agreement with the Mexican president or even a joint statement on their talks. He also had not told President Peña Nieto in advance what he would be saying, an amateur mistake in high-level diplomatic talks that anyone worthy of calling himself the world's greatest negotiator would never make.

Just hours after Trump spoke, the Mexican president used his Twitter account to give his version of events. Translated from Spanish, he tweeted, "At the start of the conversation with Donald Trump, I made it clear that Mexico will not pay for the wall."

Team Trump scrambled to respond. The campaign issued a statement suggesting that they also had become aware of the Logan Act. The statement said that the Mexico City meeting was merely "the first part of the discussion and a relationship builder. . . . It was not a negotiation, and that would have been inappropriate. It is unsurprising that they hold two different views on this issue, and we look forward to continuing the conversation."

Peña Nieto did not stop with his tweet.

"I let him know that the people of Mexico felt wronged," he told a television interviewer. Trump's positions constituted "a threat to Mexico," he said, adding, "I am not prepared to keep my arms crossed and do nothing."

Peña Nieto also lectured Trump on negotiating style. He made no mention of the lack of advance preparation for the trip, or the lack of an agreed-upon statement at the end. Instead, appearing on a Spanish-language television program associated with CNN, Peña Nieto said, "That threat must be confronted. I told him that is not the way to build a mutually beneficial relationship for both nations."

What happened when Trump returned from Mexico would become an early indicator of how Trump would behave as president, disregarding facts he did not like and relying heavily on the "best" advisers, those experts he has said reside in his own head.

Speaking to a rally in Phoenix the night of his meeting in Mexico City, Trump upped his rhetoric about the wall, knowing he had annoyed and perhaps angered the Mexican president.

"On day one we will begin working on an impenetrable, physical, tall, powerful, beautiful southern border wall," Trump announced. "We will use the best technology including above- and below-ground sensors—that's the tunnels. Remember that, above and below." The crowd went wild.

Trump said that in addition the wall would have towers, which implied federal agents with guns who could look into Mexico as well as America He also promised aerial surveillance and more federal agents, all to "supplement the wall, find and dislocate tunnels and keep out criminal cartels and Mexico—you know that—will work with us. Mexico will work with us, I absolutely believe it," repeating that phrase.

Based on what Peña Nieto had said, however, Trump had no factual basis to support what he himself said.

Throughout the campaign, bankers, diplomats, government finance authorities, journalists, and many others all scratched their heads trying to figure out how a sovereign nation could be forced by another sovereign nation to pay for a wall that would offend its own citizens. Peña Nieto had made it clear the wall offended Mexicans, as did many of Trump's other remarks, especially launching his campaign with a declaration that the government Peña Nieto headed was sending rapists and murders, mixed in perhaps with a few good people, north to the United States.

After winning the election, Trump had to come up with some plausible plan to fulfill his absolute and never qualified promise that Mexico would pay for the wall. His first response was to attack journalists as dishonest.

Then he said that the United States would front the money for the wall and get it back later from Mexico, still without saying how the reimbursement would be done. That tectonic shift from "Mexico pays" to "America pays first" received extensive news coverage. Trump evidently didn't see any of it. Two weeks before taking office he tweeted, "The dishonest media does not report that any money spent on building the Great Wall (for sake of speed), will be paid back by Mexico later."

Journalists reporting what he tweeted noted that in seeking votes Trump never said Americans would pay and Mexico would pay back, which in commerce would be considered a bait-and-switch scam.

Finally, six days after Trump assumed office, the White House spoke of Trump's plan to make Mexico pay for the wall. It was not in a document thick with policy points or an economic analysis. There were no written statements. No flock of friendly experts stood at the ready to answer questions. Instead, Sean Spicer, the White House press secretary, casually informed reporters on Air Force One. They were flying back following a Trump talk at a closed Republican congressional retreat in Philadelphia.

The president was considering a comprehensive tax plan that could include imposing a 20 percent tariff on Mexican imports, Spicer said.

Spicer's exact words sowed some confusion about just how a tariff works. But he eventually made clear that the tariff, which he called a tax, would be 20 percent. A tax on "$50 billion at 20 percent of imports . . . that way we can do $10 billion a year and easily pay for the wall just through that mechanism alone."

Spicer's remarks made clear that the tariff would apply to everything coming from Mexico. Fresh winter tomatoes, automobiles and car parts, oil, and beer would all be levied until the cost of the wall was covered.

Another remark by Spicer showed how ill-prepared the White House staff was. Spicer, who faithfully expressed Trump's wishes from his first appearance when he insisted the inaugural crowds were the biggest ever, said, "Right now our country's policy is to tax exports."

Taxes on exports are prohibited by the Constitution. Article I, Section 9, states: "No Tax or Duty shall be laid on Articles exported from any State."

What Spicer could have said, had he known or been briefed by someone with knowledge, is that the corporate income tax is baked into the price of American-made exports. That tax cost could be eliminated by replacing the corporate income tax with a value-added tax or VAT, which can be applied to domestic buyers only. But Trump was not calling for repeal of the corporate income tax, only lower tax rates. There is no indication Trump was planning as part of the Mexico wall scheme to make such a substantial change in tax policy, leaving White House ignorance about the Constitution as the only logical explanation for Spicer's comment.

There was a big problem with the plan to slap a tariff on Mexican goods, a surprising problem given Trump's assertions about his world-class expertise in economics and taxes.

A tariff on Mexican imports meant that Americans, not Mexicans, would be paying for the wall.

A tariff is a form of tax, and it would increase prices on goods subject to the tariff, though not with the transparency of a sales tax paid at the cash register. Instead the tariff would be built into the price ultimately paid by consumers, hiding it from those not familiar with how tariffs work or who don't ask why a car made in Mexico suddenly costs more than a comparable one made in Canada or Brazil or Kentucky.

A 20 percent tariff on imports from Mexico would mean that tomatoes from south of the border that cost $1 at the supermarket would rise to $1.20 to cover the tariff. An automobile made in Mexico and sold in Iowa that had cost $10,000 would now cost the buyer $12,000 because of the tariff.

Sales of Mexican tomatoes and cars built in Mexico might dip a bit because the tariff would make them too costly for some consumers. For Mexicans that would mean less income. Viewed that way, the tariff could be seen as a plan to punish Mexico. Certainly Mexicans would see it that way. Still, the tariff would not make Mexico pay for the wall except in the sense of economic punishment.

To avoid losing customers, some American business owners might cover the tariff's cost by trimming their payroll, perhaps holding down wages or shedding some workers. Or they could take part of the hit themselves. Greengrocers and car dealers might decide to absorb part of the tariff. Those tomatoes might then sell for $1.16 and that car for $11,200 with the four cents per tomato or $800 per car reducing profits.

The tariff might also cause some tomato growing to move back to the United States, but that, too, would come at a cost. Because of the tariff, the costs would still be paid by American consumers because the tariff would put upward pressure on the prices of all tomatoes.

In the early days of the American Republic, as the country transformed from an eighteenth-century agricultural nation into the world's leading manufacturer in the late 1800s, tariffs on imported goods financed the government. Those tariffs also helped domestic manufacturers grow by enabling them to charge higher prices than in a theoretically free market. But those higher prices came at a cost: they generated extra-large profits, but the higher prices paid by consumers left them worse off because they could buy fewer goods.

No matter how the cost of the wall was paid, Americans would pay the price in dollars. Clearly, a tariff would not be the America First policy that Trump promised workers and businesses.

The tariff trial balloon was informative for another reason. Trump said he knew more about taxes than anyone else in the world, yet his plan showed no awareness whatsoever of the history of American tariffs. Popular dislike for tariffs was a major reason the individual income tax was adopted a century ago. The burden of tariffs fell heavily on the poor and emerging middle class at the start of the twentieth century century, while the super-rich enjoyed their profits and salaries free of a levy on their enormous—for the time—incomes.

The Smoot-Hawley Tariff Act enacted in 1930 at the start of the Great Depression made that economic downturn worse. The act provoked retaliatory protectionist measures by other countries. American exports and imports fell by about half during the Depression, much of which mainstream economists blame on the trade conflict the Smoot-Hawley Tariff initiated.

The vulnerability of American exporters to a protective tariff like Smoot-Hawley also escaped Trump and his staff. After years of importing oil from Mexico, in late 2015 the U.S. became a net exporter of petroleum to Mexico, selling that country about 211,000 barrels of oil per day, worth about $4 billion per year. The Trump tariff plan might, however, prompt Mexico to rely on its own oil or perhaps buy from Venezuela or some other country hostile to the United States. That would cost America in lost export revenue and run counter to Trump's plan for America to acquire global "energy dominance."

That Trump obviously did not know that with a tariff Americans, not Mexicans, would pay for the wall tells us two things. One is that Trump is no expert on taxes.

The other goes to his frequent statements that "I'm really, really smart" and "I'm like a smart person." However smart he is or is not, the tariff plan and many other actions show that he did not pay attention when he was a student or forgot what he was taught at Penn, an Ivy League school, about economics.

That Trump doesn't know the economics of finance became clear in lawsuit testimony from a decade earlier. He said he did not understand accounting. That Trump doesn't know the economics of finance became clear in lawsuit testimony from a decade earlier. He said he did not under-stand accounting:

> The concept of net present value to me would be the value of the land currently after debt. Well, to me, the word "net" is an interest-ing word. It's really—the word "value" is the important word. If you have an asset that you can do other things with but you don't choose to do them—I haven't chosen to do that.

Like his plan to make Mexico pay for his wall, that's gibberish. Net present value is simply the cost of acquiring and supporting an investment over the years measured against the expected money it will bring in and then reduced to the equivalent of a financial exchange made today.

The tariff balloon popped quickly, but Trump continued with his fan-tastical comments about the wall. At a February 17 press conference the president said,

> We've undertaken the most substantial border security measures in a generation to keep our nation and our tax dollars safe. And

are now in the process of beginning to build a promised wall on
the southern border, met with general—now Secretary—Kelly yesterday and we're starting that process. And the wall is going to be
a great wall and it's going to be a wall negotiated by me. The price
is going to come down just like it has on everything else I've negotiated for the government. And we are going to have a wall that
works, not gonna have a wall like they have now which is either
non-existent or a joke.

He threw in a gratuitous slap at Mexico and other countries south of the
border, too, saying a new office would deal with "the many forgotten victims of illegal immigrant violence."

Trump called the Mexican president on his eighth day in office to talk
about his wall. Again, he was told Mexico had no interest in any wall.

"Mr. President, this is not a personal difference. It has nothing to do
with you personally, Mr. President," Peña Nieto said, his tone cordial
throughout. However, he added, "I cannot ignore this because we find
this completely unacceptable for Mexicans to pay for the wall that you are
thinking of building."

He expressed sympathy for Trump, too. "I understand, Mr. President,
the small political margin that you have now in terms of everything you
said that you established throughout your campaign. But I would also like
to make you understand, President Trump, the lack of margin I have as
President of Mexico to accept this situation."

Trying to find a mutual way out of the issue, Peña Nieto said the wall
was "the critical point that has not allowed us to move forward in the building of the relationship between our two countries. I propose, Mr. President,
for you to allow us to look for ways" to resolve the differences because "for
both our governments, this could constitute a win-win situation."

Trump's responses were all about his situation. "I was voted on the
basis that we are losing so much money to Mexico in terms of jobs, factories, and plants moving to Mexico. We cannot do this anymore and I
have to tell you it is not sustainable," he said, adding, "I won with a large
percentage of Hispanic voters." (Trump got a third of those voters.)

Again, Peña Nieto sought a different approach, suggesting they "find a
route towards the dialogue to find a balance in our trade . . . the best vir-

tual wall that I think we can build between our two countries is to make sure that both countries have economic development. And it is exactly on this issue that we have been talking about a more fair trade relationship between our two countries, so we can build this type of framework for that relationship. I leave this for your consideration, Mr. President. The will of my government is not to have points of difference with you, but rather points of agreement."

Trump then turned to pleading. "We are both in a little bit of a political bind because I have to have Mexico pay for the wall—I have to. I have been talking about it for a two-year period, and the reason I say they are going to pay for the wall is because Mexico has made a fortune out of the stupidity of U.S. trade representatives."

Trump's mind may have drifted as he spoke his next words, because in addressing his counterpart, he used the third person. "They are beating us at trade and they are beating us at the border, and they are killing us with drugs."

Peña Nieto then suggested, "Let us stop talking about the wall." He said all governments have a right to protect their borders, adding, "My position has been and will continue to be very firm saying that Mexico cannot pay for that wall."

Trump's tone shifted. Instead of talking trade deficits, he spoke of himself. Addressing Peña Nieto as if he were a subordinate, or even a servant, Trump issued an order: "You cannot say that to the press. The press is going to go with that, and I cannot live with that."

Later in the call Trump said, "If you're not going to say that Mexico is going to pay for the wall, then I do not want to meet with you guys anymore because I cannot live with that."

Trump's final negotiating position was exactly what I warned voters about during the campaign. Trump had spent his whole life in business deals that often benefited him and hurt others, ending their relationship on an acrimonious note. But as president, Trump would have to deal with people in positions of power he could neither fire like his faux apprentices nor ignore. The dictator in North Korea, the Senate majority leader, the judges hearing cases brought against his executive orders, and the president of Mexico were not going to go away, and as president, Trump would not be able to ignore them.

Trump's style as president continued his lifelong pattern of ignoring facts, ignoring realities he wished did not exist. Three months after the conversation with the Mexican president—a conversation the contents of which would not become known for another three months—Trump gave an interview to CBS. Appearing on *Face the Nation*, a Sunday morning politics show, Trump told host John Dickerson that Mexico would pay all the costs. And then he added a Trumpian fact-free flourish: "They're going to be happy with it. They'll be very happy to pay."

Attorney General Jeff Sessions, appearing on ABC News about the same time, seemed a little more convinced that money would be found. He told George Stephanopoulos, "I don't expect the Mexican government to appropriate money for it. But there are ways that we can deal with our trade situation to create the revenue for it. No doubt about it."

Sessions said, "We're going to get paid for it one way or the other. I know there's $4 billion a year in excess payments" to people illegally in the United States—"tax credits that they shouldn't get."

There was some basis for his comment, but it was also Trumpian exaggeration. The $4 billion referred to child tax credits paid to undocumented immigrants for their children sixteen and younger. Over ten years, the total came to $7.6 billion. That number, far below what Sessions said, came from the nonpartisan staff of the congressional Joint Committee on Taxation.

Trump's wall will cost $21.6 billion, according to an internal report by Homeland Security, so taking away the tax credits Sessions cited would pay for only roughly one third of the wall.

But Sessions's comment also had the economics wrong. Again, this would not be Mexico paying for the wall, but Americans. Stopping child tax credits to people inside the United States who do not qualify because they entered the country without permission would save taxpayers and follow the law. It would stop errors and, mostly, tax fraud, but it still would not result in Mexico paying for the wall.

But Trump continued to insist that he would make Mexico pay for the wall. Not even the disclosure of his exchange with the president of Mexico, who flatly rejected paying for the wall, seemed to have any effect on Trump's grasp of the situation.

At a White House press briefing in August with the president of Finland, Trump was asked if Mexico would pay for the wall.

"Yes, it will," Trump said. "One way or another Mexico is going to pay for the wall. It may be through reimbursement. But one way or the other Mexico will pay for the wall. We're right now negotiating NAFTA. In my opinion Mexico's been very difficult. Why wouldn't they be. They had a sweetheart deal for many years. It's one of the great deals of all time for them, one of the worst trade deals ever signed" by the United States.

Trump may have stumbled on a truth. Despite all his hard-line talk, and America becoming a net supplier of oil to Mexico, the deficit in goods traded with Mexico soared after Trump took office. The net balance of trade increased in Mexico's favor by more than a third in the first half of 2017 compared to a year earlier, Census Bureau data showed.

PART IV

FOSSIL FUELS AND CLIMATE AND SCIENCE DENIAL

Polluters' Paradise

During the administrations of George W. Bush and Barack Obama, Betsy Southerland grew accustomed to speaking directly with the dozen administrators and acting administrators they had appointed to run the Environmental Protection Agency. As director of the Office of Science and Technology working on the Clean Water Act that Richard Nixon had signed into law, it was routine for Southerland to have Christine Todd Whitman, Lisa Jackson, Gina McCarthy, and other administrators pop into her office or ask her to come over to chat.

To address the complex and subtle issues of how to fulfill the Clean Water Act requirement to "restore and maintain the chemical, physical, and biological integrity of the Nation's waters," Southerland often assembled teams to assess the science needed to implement the act.

"With Gina McCarthy and Christine Todd Whitman and Lisa Jackson and all the others, they would normally take notes. They would debate with us. They would say what they had been hearing from industry and the critiques they had heard" of EPA policies and practices. "They let us know what was on their minds," said Southerland. And they were open to persuasion and paid attention to the findings of scientists inside and outside EPA, she added.

That all ended when Donald Trump named Scott Pruitt the administrator of the EPA, an agency Trump had promised he would smash into "tidbits." Pruitt seemed just the politician to do that. As Oklahoma attorney general, he sued the EPA fourteen times, taking up the cause of energy companies whose suggestions his office sometimes cut-and-pasted into official documents. In his LinkedIn profile, he described himself as "a leading advocate against the EPA's activist agenda." Pruitt never stopped by Southerland's office or summoned her over for a chat. Others who were called in said they usually had to wait because doors to the administrator's section were locked. Some said they were required to surrender their smartphones, which could record conversations. Sometimes they were told to not take any notes.

This was not the first time the EPA operated under a president who favored industry over the environment. Ronald Reagan had been a vigorous advocate for reining in the EPA through his administrator, Anne Burford, mother of the conservative, if not reactionary, lawyer and judge whom Trump would name to the Supreme Court, Neil Gorsuch.

But Reagan was not antagonistic to science, just friendly to industry. Trump was dismissive of science. He called climate change a "Chinese hoax."

Pruitt introduced himself to EPA staff by video over the agency's computer network. He said he wanted to "dig down deep with respect to how we're going to do business in the future, and get to know you personally and how I can be a resource to you as you do your work." But he went on to declare that "regulators exist to give certainty to those that they regulate. Those that we regulate ought to know what's expected of them so they can plan and allocate resources to comply; that's really the job of a regulator. And—in the process that we engage in, in adopting regulations, is very, very important because it sends a message . . . on how it's going to impact those in the marketplace."

EPA would be "open and transparent and objective in how we do rule-making and make sure that we follow the letter of the law as we do so because that will send, I think, a great message to those that are regulated, but more importantly, they will know what's expected of them and they can act accordingly."

Pruitt's framing of the issues revealed his one-sided approach to EPA's mandate. His only stated concerns were those of industries EPA regulates.

Pruitt did not talk about why environmental regulations exist: to protect human health and safety, to make sure children are not drinking water laced with lead as happened in Flint, Michigan; to minimize the damage from industrial processes, such as ensuring that fumes from electric power plant smokestacks are not so toxic that they turn the rain falling on northeastern forests acid, killing trees and trout; to make sure that a century of the Cuyahoga River in Cleveland catching fire because of chemical dumping remains history; to ensure that fish caught in the Great Lakes and the Hudson River and the coastal seas are not laced with man-made chemicals that cause cancer in humans who eat those fish; to protect the wildlife and plant life that create enormous amounts of economic value for mankind all on their own.

Trump called global warming "a con" in 2010. Two years later he tweeted "the concept of global warming was created by and for the Chinese in order to make U.S. manufacturing non-competitive." Since then in tweets and speeches he has repeated the charge many times and has cited cold weather and snowfall as evidence that climate change and global warming are hoaxes.

In these remarks, Trump demonstrated that he does not understand simple terminology, much less atmospheric science. Weather refers to temporary atmospheric conditions like hail, rain, or partial cloud cover; climate refers to long-term weather conditions such as the permanent cold air over Greenland, the dry Sahara winds, or the daily rain high up the mountain on the Hawaiian island of Kauai.

Three months after launching the campaign, Trump told Hugh Hewitt, a smart right-wing radio talk show host, "I'm not a believer in man-made global warming. It could be warming, and it's going to start to cool at some point. And you know, in the early, in the 1920s, people talked about global cooling. . . .They thought the Earth was cooling. Now, it's global warming. . . . But the problem we have, and if you look at our energy costs, and all of the things that we're doing to solve a problem that I don't think in any major fashion exists."

Trump is entitled to his own opinion, but not, as Senator Daniel Patrick Moynihan used to say, to his own facts. Among scientists whose work appears in top journals, the opinion is near unanimous that climate change is under way and that human activity, primarily burning carbon, is driving that change or at least accelerating it.

We know how much it costs to clean discharges into the air from automobile and truck fumes, smokestacks, and other human activity. We also know how much cleaning up saves. That's because Congress has required the EPA to periodically justify the costs of the 1990 amendments it made to the Clean Air Act. Viewed the way a businessman would a potential in-vestment—and Trump boasts that he is a super-successful businessman—the returns are astounding.

For the three decades from 1990 to 2020, the EPA calculated, the direct costs of the 1990 Clean Air Act amendments will come to $380 billion. The benefits, depending on assumptions, range between $1 trillion and $35 trillion. The central estimate was $12 trillion.

Those figures are in 2006 dollars.

That is a return of $35 of benefits for each dollar spent on compli-ance, using the middle estimate. Who wouldn't buy an investment with those kinds of returns? The answer would be Trump and Pruitt. Viewed from the narrow perspective of a corporate financial statement, any cost reduces profits as measured by generally accepted accounting principles.

Those financial accounting principles don't count asthma, lung can-cer, heart disease, and premature death caused by pollution. All costs, however, must be accounted for on the universal ledger. Someone pays, because all costs, as well as benefits, must be accounted for somewhere, somehow. There is no free lunch, especially not for a society that lets pol-luters have their way with our air and water.

What research shows is that costs go up a little and benefits go up a lot more when polluters must clean up after themselves as best as current technology allows.

Many EPA career officials would have been happy to explain this and much more to Pruitt and his team of politicals, but that was not how they operated. Pruitt did not come by to introduce himself to Betsy South-erland and her staff. Pruitt worked through the political appointees he brought along, whose numbers the career staff believed were larger than in previous administrations, not that anyone in the headquarters suite was sharing such information with them.

Career employees soon realized that on the rare occasions when the political appointees working under Pruitt wanted to speak with them, the sessions had a fixed formula. The appointees always came in pairs or larger groups; they did not take notes; they asked questions only to clar-ify the meaning of technical terms in engineering and biosciences. They never said what was motivating the meetings and especially not what the industries regulated by EPA were discussing with Pruitt and his staff.

Southerland was in the same room with Pruitt only twice, on July 14 and 21 of 2017. She had a half-dozen staff people with her and Pruitt had almost as many politicals.

For weeks Southerland's staff of environmental engineers and scientists had prepared exhaustive reports requested by Pruitt's team detailing the damage done by toxic waste from coal-fired power plants and how EPA could address remediation.

For more than a century, electric utilities had used a simple and low-cost technique to dispose of the ash left behind after burning coal, a toxic mix laced with arsenic, lead, mercury, selenium, and other metals and chemicals that no one wants in their drinking water. They soaked the ash until it became a liquid and let the slurry flow downhill to ponds, many of them built on or near riverbanks. Continual flows of new slurry resulted in pools of toxic liquid that, should a dike or pipe break, could flow into streams and rivers, as happened with Duke Energy.

A Duke Energy slurry pond failed in 2014, sending thirty thousand tons of toxic sludge down the Dan River that separates North Carolina and Virginia, killing fish and other wildlife and rendering the river water unsafe to drink even after treatment. Duke had thirty-two other coal ash ponds, every one of which would cause the same problems if its dikes failed. And Duke was just one company in a vast industry of coal-burning power plants across the nation that did not clean up its toxic waste, billing electricity customers for the cost of cleaning up but instead storing the waste.

Duke paid a fine of $6 million, but penalties never come close to covering the costs of spills, including any lives shortened of people who develop cancer or other illnesses as a result. Paying the fines is a lot cheaper than covering the costs of drying out the toxic waste, which would eliminate most of the risk of damage to human health and the environment from coal ash sludge getting into drinking water, groundwater, and surface water.

Six years earlier, a similar toxic spill occurred at a federal government–owned Tennessee Valley Authority coal ash pond near the Emory River at Kingston, Tennessee. The six years of cleanup cost almost $1.2 billion.

Southerland and her team set out to protect people from similar incidents, which research showed would be likely since the ponds were aging. "These ponds were a technology available in the early 1900s," Southerland said. "We now live in the 21st century and we told the utilities you can definitely afford to treat those wastes."

And, after all, the way utility regulation works, the companies would just ask state utility rate boards to let them add those costs to the monthly bills sent customers, either by including them in the total cost of supplying power or adding a surcharge specifying the cost. The shareholders would pay nothing. Indeed, for utilities whose rates are set based on a financial return on the amount of money they have invested, cleaning up polluted ponds adds to profits.

To prevent more slurry pond disasters a rule was formally put in place in the fall of 2016 directing the cleanup of these toxic wastes over eight years. But shortly after taking office Trump said he would end the rule, and in fall 2017 the EPA was in the formal process of repealing it.

In her farewell address to about 120 EPA clean water staff, Southerland expressed her frustration at Pruitt's actions to undo various regulations, including the slurry pond rules, and her fear of what they will mean for public health and safety and the environment. She was especially troubled that Pruitt showed no balance, always taking the side of polluters.

Southerland worried that the costs of cleaning up toxic messes would continue to be shifted from those who make them to everyone else, creating not just environmental pollution, but economic pollution as well. That concern grew out of Pruitt's efforts to get rid of the rule that puts the legal duty on polluters to pay for the damage they cause.

"Abandonment of the polluter-pays principle that underlies all environmental statutes and regulations," she said, will mean polluters must contend not with the federal government, but also "the states, tribes and local government." They are much more likely to fall sway to corporate influence than Washington, at least before Trump.

"The best case for our children and grandchildren is that they will pay the polluters' bills through increased state taxes, new user fees, and higher water and sewer bills," Southerland warned. "The worst case is that they will have to live with increased public health and safety risks and a degraded environment."

She pointed out how cost cutting on the margin often leads to much greater costs later. She cited New Orleans's concrete water barrier walls that were not sunk deeply enough into the Louisiana mud to withstand the pressure of rising water. When they tilted in 2005, the waters from Hurricane Katrina flooded the lower parts of the city.

"Today the environmental field is suffering from the temporary triumph of myth over truth," Southerland said. She added that there is no war on coal, no economic crisis caused by environmental regulations, and no doubt that human activities were causing climate change.

Southerland ended her farewell on an optimistic note. She said in years to come she fully expected that Congress and the courts would "eventually restore all the environmental protections repealed by this administration because the majority of the American people recognize that this protection of public health and safety is right and it is just."

For that to happen, however, voters would need to elect lawmakers and presidents who share her concerns and are not, like Pruitt, determined to act solely in the interests of the energy industries and other polluters.

Go FOIA Yourself

The EPA, like other administrative agencies reporting to the Trump White House, has shut off informal and much formal communications with journalists who are the primary means by which most people learn information. Even scientists are alerted to new and significant developments from news reports more than from technical journals—or were, until the Trump administration began stopping the flow of information.

Dan Ross, a racehorse jockey before he took up the much less dangerous trade of reporting on the environment and worker safety, noticed a change soon after Trump took office. Like other journalists, Ross had found the Obama era agencies cautious in dealing with journalists. But as a Los Angeles–based writer for the website FairWarning, which tracks safety issues, Ross said he managed to arrange background interviews when needed.

"Before Trump, the EPA people were kind of helpful and they would respond to emails and I could reach out to have a tentative relationship— because they wanted accurate information in news articles they would reach out directly and be helpful," Ross told me. "Since Trump has come to power sometimes the press office won't even respond when asked for comments. Sometimes they come up with a stock answer. . . . If I reach out to any officials in the agency I get sent straight back to a media spokesperson. It just feels like there are a lot of frightened rabbits in there."

That concern grew when Ross started asking the EPA about tons of rubbish riddled with PCBs burning in Tennessee. There are more than a hundred types of PCBs, short for chemicals known as polychlorinated biphenyls.

PCBs were once widely used as insulators by electric utilities. PCBs cause skin eruptions called chloracne, but they can also cause liver and nervous system damage, lesions in the eyes, damage to sex organs, and when ingested by pregnant women can result in babies with reduced intelligence and health problems that may not be immediately obvious. PCBs are also carcinogens, chemicals believed to cause cancers. They have strong similarities to dioxins, a group of toxic compounds used in the Vietnam War era as jungle defoliants and commonly called Agent Orange.

Ross had two simple questions for the EPA. Did its Region 4 have responsibility for the rubbish and its PCB-laced smoke? And what was being done? Not only did Ross learn nothing, but he said the EPA "spokesperson seemed terrified. He won't even say if there is a case ongoing or not. That's absolutely ludicrous."

Ludicrous it is, but it is also the norm for many journalists trying to get answers out of federal agency spokespeople in the Trump era. Some agencies are more cooperative than others, with EPA among those that hold the tightest grip on information. Canned emailed responses that avoid the core question, or anodyne answers that say nothing instead of giving details and policy positions, have become the new EPA standard under Administrator Scott Pruitt.

There has been another benefit to polluters since Trump took office. New criminal investigations of polluters have dropped sharply. The Obama administration initiated on average 254 criminal cases per year in its last five years. That rate dropped to 170 new investigations in Obama's last year because he bought into an industry plan that was supposed to persuade polluters to self-report the way airlines and pilots do. Under Trump, the rate at which new cases were opened indicates that just 80 cases will be initiated in Fiscal 2017, less than a third of Obama's five-year average.

Fewer new cases mean that in the years ahead, convictions will fall sharply. And that in turns means a likely increase in flagrant violation of clean air, water, and other antipollution laws because of the principle on which most federal law enforcement is based. Local police declare that they intend to catch every bandit, drug dealer, killer, and rapist they can. This is known as *specific deterrence*. Their aim is to catch the perpetrators and lock them up. Uncle Sam follows a different approach, known as *general deterrence*. The idea is that pursuing and punishing a few high-profile cases scares many people who might otherwise break the law into behaving. The theory is of no value when it comes to crimes of passion, but general deterrence can be effective in calculated crimes, especially pollution cases, where the underlying offense is based on polluting for profit.

An essential element of general deterrence is prison time. Those corporate executives willing to flout the law will do so if the only penalty is monetary since their employers generally cough up the cash. But the prospect of ten years in prison, even at a minimum security prison with dormitory-like accommodations, introduces a different calculus.

For general deterrence to work, though, there must be enough criminal investigators, enough cases initiated, enough indictments returned, and enough convictions resulting in lengthy prison sentences to create a culture of compliance. General deterrence is based on fear, and that requires an expectation that if you do the crime you will do the time.

By summer 2017, EPA was down to only 147 criminal investigators, far below the 200 positions Congress required in the 1990 Pollution Prosecution Act. Buyouts were being offered to experienced agents, whose practical knowledge of the law, policy, and standards of proof required to win convictions generally makes them the most effective in developing cases for prosecutors.

To Jeff Ruch, a former prosecutor and whistle-blower attorney who runs Public Employees for Environmental Responsibility, the concern was not so much with today as with the long run. "This evaporation of criminal enforcement is snowballing in that fewer agents generate fewer cases leading to ever-fewer convictions down the road. The spigot sustaining complex corporate anti-pollution prosecutions—which take years from genesis to fruition—is being turned off at the source."

While Ruch saw general deterrence failing and Ross got nowhere in his reporting, a host on Fox did somewhat better. Pruitt avoided reporters, especially those known to ask hard questions. But in April 2017 he agreed to appear on Trump-friendly Fox News. Host Chris Wallace got right down to it, noting that Trump had just signed an executive order aimed at undoing the Clean Power Plan put in place in the last year of the Obama administration. Because of the Clean Power Plan, Wallace noted, by the year 2030, Americans could expect 90,000 fewer asthma attacks a year, 300,000 fewer missed work or school days, and 3,600 fewer premature deaths each year.

"Without the Clean Power Plan, how are you going to prevent those terrible things?" Wallace asked.

Not expecting a hardball question on Fox, Pruitt tried to evade it. "The president's keeping his promise to deal with that overreach," he said. "It doesn't mean that clean air and clear water is not going to be the focus in the future. We're just going to do it right within the consistency of the framework that Congress has passed."

Wallace was not having it. "But sir, you're giving me a regulatory answer, a political answer. You're not giving me health answer," he said, dragging Pruitt back to the health issue.

Wallace kept at Pruitt throughout the live television interview. What about the 166 million Americans, half the population, who breathe unclean air? The thousands of children who develop asthma? The many who die prematurely because of pollutants such as micro dust particles from coal-burning electric power plants?

Pruitt stuck to his rhetorical safe zone of alleged "regulatory overreach," noting that American emissions of carbon dioxide were back at pre-1994 levels. Pruitt did not mention that the major reason for this was Obama era regulations that he had just characterized as "regulatory overreach." Nor did Pruitt mention that as Oklahoma's attorney general he filed lawsuits to block those regulations.

Pruitt defended Trump's withdrawal from the Paris climate accord, which set voluntary standards for reducing greenhouse gases, with an argument based on geopolitical boundaries, something Mother Earth pays no attention to as her breezy outer layer warms. "Paris represents a bad deal for this country," Pruitt said. "We frontloaded our costs. China and India backloaded theirs. That caused a contraction in our economy."

That last point is a Trumpian alternative fact, in Trump adviser Kellyanne Conway's memorable phrase. The U.S. economy last contracted in June 2009. At the time Pruitt spoke, the economy had been expanding for almost eight years, the stock market had more than tripled, and millions of jobs had been added, many in energy industries.

Pruitt's responses show how Trump and the energy industries seek to frame the debate about the environment and regulating polluters to minimize the damage from industrial processes. Pruitt talked in abstract terms. He employed fifty-cent words and ideas that policy wonks debate among themselves, not the nickel words and ideas that resonate with most people. "Regulatory overreach" and "frontloaded costs" and "contraction in our economy" cloud the issues in abstract obfuscation.

Framing questions as Wallace did clears the rhetorical air.

Avoiding the word *health* at the Environmental Protection Agency has been a hallmark of the Trump administration. When it comes to the EPA, the administration also treads lightly with the words *benefits* and *economics*. There are sound reasons in propaganda and rhetoric to avoid these words and focus on alleged "regulatory overreach."

Legal scholars have noted that in trials, the advocates who define the terms and take the lead in educating the jury or the judge usually win because they focus the arguments in a way favorable to their interests. The same holds true in civic debate.

If pollution is discussed in terms of sickening and killing people for profit, public opinion will sway in the direction of requiring companies to clean up after their operations rather than dumping toxins into the air and water. But if the discussion is framed in terms of bureaucracies handicapping enterprise, especially with claims that the jobs of honest hardworking people like coal miners are being needlessly destroyed, it becomes much easier to give aid and comfort to the polluters because people do not recognize them as an enemy of their well-being and that of their children, grandchildren, and other loved ones.

Similarly, the Trump White House referred to the effects of carbon dioxide from burning coal, the dirtiest of all fossil fuels, as "social costs."

Framing environmental issues in terms of people's health changes the debate. Make the debate about children sickened for life by water in the schoolyard fountain, adults gasping for air, and people dying sooner than they otherwise would, and regulation becomes an issue of the quality of life and of premature death. Framing regulation of energy companies in terms of corporations taking responsibility for cleaning up the messes they make resonates with most people. Then throwing in the economics, especially when environmental regulations show huge benefits that far outweigh the costs, adds sensible logic.

Pruitt's reluctance to go anywhere near health issues is not surprising. He has awards aplenty from groups like the Oklahoma Well Strippers Association. On the taxpayer dime he flew back and forth from the nation's capital to his Oklahoma home, throwing in the cost of a side trip to attend a Colorado gathering of the Heritage Foundation, long a foe of fossil fuel industry regulations. Pruitt's predecessor, Gina McCarthy, also flew to her home in Massachusetts. But unlike Pruitt, McCarthy paid her own way.

At his Senate confirmation hearing, Pruitt could not recall ever receiving an award from an environmental or public health group. Senator Sheldon Whitehouse, a Rhode Island Democrat, said Pruitt may also be the only prosecutor in America who does not keep a record of successful cases, his official website as Oklahoma attorney general showing not a single case brought against a polluter. Pruitt said he hadn't checked his official website so he couldn't say.

Asked about his contacts with energy industry sources, Pruitt was evasive at his confirmation hearing. He said as Oklahoma attorney general he taught government officials how to comply with requests for records. Whitehouse repeatedly tried to get Pruitt to explain why his office had not responded after two years to requests for the emails and other public documents.

"I actually have a general counsel and an administrator in my office that are dedicated to performing or providing responses to Open Records requests," Pruitt said.

Whitehouse was not buying that, saying snidely, "Not very dedicated, if it takes 740 days." Pruitt then changed his tack, absolving himself of responsibility because "I'm not involved in that process. That is handled independently by the administrator and that general counsel in responding. So I can't speak to the timeline and why it is taking that length of time." He said he couldn't provide the documents to the senators, either.

It would come out later that Pruitt had exchanged more than three thousand emails with oil companies, industry groups, affiliates of the Koch brothers, and others from the fossil fuel industries. The Center for Media and Democracy, a liberal nonprofit media watchdog, and lawyers from the American Civil Liberties Union fought for more than two years to get these emails, which were not available until after Pruitt got his expedited Senate confirmation hearing. No emails meant no hard questions about Pruitt's conduct as Oklahoma's top law enforcement official.

Those emails, released after Pruitt was sworn in, show that he worked hand in glove with fossil fuel companies as Oklahoma attorney general. Nothing in the emails suggested any regard for public health, the focus being on maximizing fossil fuel industry profits by allowing the industry to shift the costs of pollution onto the society at large instead of taking responsibility to clean up.

Interior Purging

The attacks on science that advanced the interests of fossil fuel industries were not limited to the Environmental Protection Agency. Donald Trump's political appointees also went after scientists who worked at the National Oceanic and Atmospheric Administration at the Commerce Department run by Secretary Wilbur Ross, at the National Aeronautics and Space Administration, and at the Interior Department. Managers and policy experts whose work touched on climate issues were purged. People whose job was to manage federal properties and wildlife in an era of rising temperatures, severe storms, and raging fires were also singled out in a drive to get them to quit.

The purge at Interior began on Thursday evening June 15. At about 8 p.m. some fifty managers and senior executives received emails giving them new job assignments.

Federal executives and managers get reassigned as the government's needs change, but this was not like any previous redeployment. People whose skills the federal government had spent years or decades developing were not being moved into positions of greater or parallel responsibility. Instead they were reassigned to jobs well below their skill levels, often to jobs not connected with their education or work experience.

Joel Clement was a senior federal executive, director of Interior's Office of Policy Analysis. His work included advising the Interior Department about management of its assets. One of his areas involved rising sea levels in the American Arctic, where a half dozen small coastal villages were being battered by winter waves, their land in danger of being permanently underwater. Relocating the Native American residents to other federal lands was part of Clement's portfolio.

Knowledge gleaned from these North Bering Sea communities could be used to develop strategies to deal with rising ocean levels predicted for highly populated areas of America including Florida, the Gulf Coast, and the barrier islands on the eastern seaboard.

Another part of his duties included working closely with the Denali Commission, created by Congress in 1998. In some years it spent as much as $150 million building health clinics, roads, oil and other fuel storage facilities, community electric power plants, and houses for teachers in some of the most remote areas of Alaska where extreme weather is the norm. Its budget when Trump took office was just $15 million. Trump's first budget, the so-called skinny budget, cut that to zero.

The White House also ended a long-term goal of Native Americans in Alaska to have representation on the Denali Commission board, which they finally were about to get when Trump became president. But with no commission there would be no seats at the government table, no opportunity for Native peoples to have a larger say in their relations with the federal government.

In one of his executive orders, Trump included a clause rescinding an Obama executive order from December 2016 dealing with climate change in the North Bering Sea.

"We don't work on greenhouse gas stuff, we work on stuff already baked into the system," Clement explained to my reporter Jill Ambroz. "We have equities and assets to manage—wildlife assets, American Indians and Alaska natives, and how they are being affected by climate change."

Clement's reassignment email came from James Cason, a Trump political appointee with the title of associate deputy secretary at Interior. Cason had also been a political during the George W. Bush administration.

Clement was moved to the Office of Natural Resources Revenue, which is responsible for collecting, disbursing, and monitoring oil and gas royalty checks on federal and tribal lands. "It's not my skill set and they've had to completely retrain me, reprogram me," Clement said.

Because his new post has nothing to do with his areas of knowledge, Clement figures he was expected to quit. The signal he got was clear: "The new administration wants to cut loose anyone doing stuff they don't want to do."

Instead, he took a hundred hours of training in accounting at taxpayer expense. To his delight, others in his new office "are bending over backwards to help me in my new position. They had a stack of fan mail waiting for me!"

He has also taken the new work seriously so as not to give any excuse for firing him while a whistle-blower complaint that he filed is reviewed as he tries to get his old job back. "I'm not just phoning it in. I have to be a Boy Scout because I have a pending complaint," he said.

While Clement was pondering what to do, his telephone began to ring. Fifty other Interior executives and managers were reaching out to one another trying to figure out why they were being reassigned to positions for which they were unsuited.

To Clement it was clear that the incoming interior secretary, Ryan Zinke, who had not yet been confirmed by the Senate, "was going to use reassignments to trim personnel. I spoke to some others that night who had been reassigned. Dozens were. It's never been done before and it could be unlawful. They did this to clear out people."

Zinke had been a one-term congressman, the only one representing Montana, after a career as a Navy SEAL followed by becoming a developer and serving on the board of an oil pipeline company.

What struck Clement and others was that neither he nor his colleagues were climate scientists. They were administrators for the most part whose jobs included managing federal government assets. "We didn't understand why they were targeting work that was essential to our mission," he said.

One of Clement's duties was to be Interior's representative to the U.S. Global Change Research Program. There were representatives from thirteen federal agencies as well as state, county, and city officials. Congress mandated that the program produce a National Climate Assessment every four years.

The final report was under review at the Trump White House. Clement and the many others who had some role in writing or reviewing it heard nothing back. "The concern is that it's in review and it contradicts everything the White House is saying about climate change," he said.

The White House could have buried that report, but a copy had been provided to a nonprofit Internet library, and in August it was found by reporters at *The New York Times*, which published the 673-page document.

The draft report noted that 2014 was the hottest year since records began being kept. It was succeeded by record warmth in 2015 and then again in 2016. Of the prior seventeen years, sixteen were the warmest on record for the planet. The report said that in recent decades temperatures rose more than at any time in the previous 1,700 years. It also said that human activity, notably burning carbon fuels that increase carbon dioxide in the atmosphere, explained the rising temperatures. Much of the report detailed how rising temperatures were adversely affecting the United States and what could be expected as the trend continued.

During the transition, it became clear that a purge of those who worked on climate change and fossil fuels issues was being contemplated. The Energy Department received a list of seventy-four questions that included a demand for the names of every federal civil servant or contractor who had attended meetings on ways to reduce burning of carbon fuels and any who worked on the Obama administration's climate change action plan. The Obama administration rejected the request.

The questionnaire evoked a much stronger response from Senator Edward Markey, a Massachusetts Democrat who has long been critical of fossil fuel industry practices.

"Any politically motivated inquisition against federal civil servants who, under the direction of a previous administration, carried out policies that you now oppose, would call into question your commitment to the rule of law and the peaceful transition of power," Markey wrote. "Civil servants should never be punished for having executed policies with which a new administration disagrees."

Markey also warned that if any information gleaned from the questionnaire "is used to demote, sideline, terminate, or otherwise discriminate against federal civil servants whose only 'crime' was to execute the lawful policy directors of their supervisors, then your administration would violate U.S. law that protects employees against such wrongful acts of retaliation. Politically motivated employment decisions will erode the foundation of apolitical civil service and run counter to federal law."

It was civil service and whistle-blower laws that Clement and others cited in seeking to get back their executive, managerial, and professional positions at Interior and other agencies after the Trump administration began its purges.

Clement says he and others misunderstood what Trump meant when he spoke of draining the swamp in Washington. "When they were talking about draining the swamp, we thought they were talking about lobbyists, but they meant civil servants . . . the civil servants were the swamp.

"When your entire workforce is described as the swamp, morale is done," he said. "People are walking around feeling devalued, targeted, like a group of people with Stockholm Syndrome. Trump's cabinet and high-level office nominations demonstrate the desire to tear down the executive branch. They are making it impossible to implement the laws of Congress. They'll be swimming in litigation. They won't get much else done. They have tossed every guideline from ethics to personnel management.

"When," Clement asked, "will they be held accountable?"

Stripping Science

Scientists across the country and around the world were aghast at what they saw in Donald Trump's first federal budget. It cut billions of dollars of spending, especially basic research and biomedicine, where huge advances in the last two decades have created vibrant economic growth. These cuts came as China, India, and other countries have been increasing their investments in scientific research and luring some American scientists to leave the United States by giving them well-funded laboratories and a free hand to hire their research staffs.

John Holdren, a plasma physicist and 1981 MacArthur Genius Award winner who was President Obama's science adviser, said there was much more at stake than the work of this or that scientist whose project would not be funded because of the proposed budget cuts. "The partial budget blueprint released by the White House will put U.S. leadership in science and technology at serious risk if Congress goes along," Holdren warned.

For America to lose its more than century-long leadership in science and technology would be a stunning blow to the economy and America's influence and reputation. And yet Holdren was just one of many leading science policy experts who saw long-term disaster for the country in the Trump science and technology budget.

Cutting spending on scientific research runs directly counter to Trump's claim that he will create a robust economy with growth rates unseen in decades. The opening of one coal mine or even a hundred cannot come close to matching the economic benefits that can flow from a single research project. For example, federal spending to sequence the human genome has returned at least $140 for every dollar spent. That figure is conservative, Holdren said, and in any event will continue to grow as genomics produces more lifesaving medical advances, more techniques to improve the quality of life, and new insights that no one could imagine before the sequencing project.

How, Holdren asked, does anyone look at the return on the genomics project and not propose greater spending or at least continued spending at existing levels? Beyond the economic growth benefits, what of the benefits of improved well-being and relief of suffering?

Science gets little attention in the Trump administration, other than the ferreting out of scientists whose work offends Trump's love of coal and steam, combined with his frequently expressed hostility to all things digital. Anything digital, he says, requires the brain of an Einstein, a curious remark for a man who has claimed to be one of the smartest human beings, to be "like a smart person," and to possess the world's greatest memory. Of course, that may explain his disdain for science. A man who has asserted that he is the world's leading authority on more than a score of topics from taxes to ISIS and negotiating to nuclear missiles would not have much need for others to advise on science. And, on top of that, during a telephone call with the the prime minister of Australia, Trump described himself as "the world's greatest person."

Whatever his expertise in science, Trump has little interest in spreading scientific knowledge. In its first eight months, the Trump administration did not release a single report or study by the White House Office of Science and Technology Policy. It also did not post any science news or announcements at the policy office webpage. The Obama White House, which embraced science, issued 125 reports and studies in eight years, nine of them in the first year, on a wide array of urgent scientific and technological issues.

There was not much interest in hiring scientists to top policy posts, either. Of forty-six science positions requiring Senate confirmation, only sixteen were filled by summer's end. Seven of those involved the military or nuclear energy. There were no nominees in environmental areas such as atmospheric, oceanic, and food safety science.

Basic research has no obvious commercial applications, which is why government funds the work. But the reason America is rich is due in very large part to basic scientific research. Despite this and despite the rapid pace of expanding knowledge in other countries, basic science received a lower priority in the Trump administration budget than developing deadlier military weapons, devising new techniques for national security, and helping companies develop profitable products and services.

The American Association for the Advancement of Science gives an annual Golden Goose Award to encourage public understanding of basic research and how it can have big economic benefits. The 2016 award honored scientists who spent years studying the sexual activity of the screwworm fly. Now, there's an easy area of science for know-nothing politicians and pundits to mock, and many did. The research results got a lot less attention. The scientists learned how to eradicate the pests, which can otherwise kill an otherwise healthy cow in two weeks. Today the price of beef is about 5 percent lower than if the little parasites were still infesting cattle herds.

Discoveries made through fundamental research in biology, chemistry, genetics, mathematics, and physics have opened vast new areas of knowledge that enabled entrepreneurs to develop valuable commercial goods and services. More than a century of taxpayer-funded basic research made possible everything from jet engines that run for years without an overhaul to lithium batteries that power automobiles, from algorithms streaming movies on smartphones to the smartphones themselves. Advances in genomics and other biological sciences are beginning to deliver individually tailored cancer treatments. Take away those investments by taxpayers and most of the conveniences, tools, and lifesaving technologies of the twenty-first century would exist only in the pages of science fiction magazines.

Trump's first budget proposed lopping a fifth off the National Institutes of Health's budget, a $6 billion reduction. Holdren said the budget should go up, not down. "In recent time a lot of economic growth has been driven by investments in a lot of the big advances in science, in biotech, genomics, and so on," Holdren said.

Many medical researchers complain that tight budgets hold back scientific advances because only safe projects get funded, not the moonshot gambles that when they work change the world. The National Institutes of Health in recent years has funded only about 16 percent of the projects that review panels of experts said are top-notch. With only one project in six getting any funding from the NIH, the incentive for researchers is to have their labs work on incremental advances of existing knowledge, not the foundations of medical knowledge.

Trump's insistence that he can learn any subject in minutes and that the best advisers reside in his head stands in contrast to Obama's approach. Obama often told Holdren that the memos he received about science issues should be longer and include more details. "Obama had a solid understanding of science and he asked questions that reflected his deep knowledge."

The Trump administration asserts that science budgets are rife with what it calls "duplication and inefficiencies" that supposedly would not exist in corporate labs. Mick Mulvaney, Trump's budget director, ordered federal agencies to identify research and development "programs that could progress more efficiently through private sector R&D, and consider their modification or elimination where Federal involvement is no longer needed or appropriate."

Generations of politicians have relied on the budgetary unicorns of duplication, waste, and inefficiency. The Trump administration is notable for its zeal in promising more results from much less money so long as the tax dollars are spent by business, not government, or not spent at all. There is evidence aplenty that business is often as inefficient as or more inefficient than government.

In proposing sharp reductions in spending on science, Trump is trying yet again to get a free lunch. Indirect costs are things like administration, building space, utilities, and insurance in case the building catches fire or floods. In other words, they are part of the cost of scientific research. How much universities charge for overhead is a legitimate issue, but it is closer to a paper cut on a finger than the sort of budget-devouring waste that Trump imagines.

Nuclear physicist Rush Holt sees both contradiction and irony in the Trump approach to science, especially climate change and global warming. Holt holds a 1979 patent for an efficient solar heat system using salty water. He was a professor at Swarthmore before serving sixteen years in Congress as a representative from New Jersey and then, in 2015, becoming president of the American Association for the Advancement of Science. The association has been America's leading organization promoting scientific research and defending freedom of scientific inquiry since 1848.

The Trump administration budget, combined with all the vacant science positions in government and the dismissal of expertise, vexes Holt.

"It appears that much of the federal agency work on climate change is being slowed down or stopped, even as you have Scott Pruitt from EPA and others saying, 'climate science is so uncertain we don't know enough to take economic actions,'" Holt said.

The logical response to such uncertainty would be more scientific research. Much of the research in climate science is done through two federal scientific agencies, the National Oceanic and Atmospheric Administration and the National Aeronautics and Space Administration. "And yet they are cutting the very research programs that might tell us even more," Holt said in an interview.

"The silence from the Trump administration on science is ominous. It's not just that he has not gotten around to appointing people to many science posts," Holt added, but that Trump "doesn't seem to have any sense that people from science can help him with what he is trying to do."

Doubling the economic growth rate from around 2 percent to 4 percent or more was a key promise that candidate Trump made to voters. More than 80 percent of American economic growth in the four decades ending in 1949 came from technological innovation, economist Robert Solow of the Massachusetts Institute of Technology showed in 1956, work that won him a Nobel Prize three decades later. Other research shows that at least half of American economic growth since World War II stems from advances in science and technology.

Knowledge-based industries refers to the eighty-one American industries that generate the most patents and trademarks. They accounted for 45.5 million American jobs in 2014, roughly 30 percent of all jobs. Those jobs paid on average almost half again more than all other jobs. That margin of extra pay has been growing, from an extra 22 percent pay in 1990 to an extra 46 percent 2014, according to the Commerce Department.

The share of national economic output, the Gross Domestic Product, by these knowledge-based industries is growing. They accounted for 38.2 percent of the economy in 2014, up from 34.8 percent in 2010. Most significantly for Trump's plan to expand American exports, these knowledge-based industries accounted for 61 percent of American goods exported in 2014.

There is one piece of knowledge we can deduce from the Trump budget cuts. Spending less on scientific research is not a policy to make or keep America great and it certainly is not a policy to put American workers first. Neither is raising the price of electricity, the most ubiquitous product of the modern age, yet that is what Trump set out to do immediately upon taking office.

Stocking the Swamp

Donald Trump handed out an important promotion on his first work-ing day as president. It appeared to be a routine appointment, curi-ous only because the official being promoted was a Democrat, a holdover from the Obama administration. The promotion didn't garner a single line in *The New York Times, The Washington Post,* or *The Wall Street Journal.*

Understood in context, however, this promotion was a key to under-standing how Trump would address his pledge to "drain the swamp" in Washington, block the revolving door between industry and government boards, as well as fulfill the core promise of his inaugural address, to act on behalf of forgotten Americans struggling to get by.

"We are transferring power from Washington, D.C., and giving it back to you, the American People," Trump said moments after swearing to faithfully execute his duties.

> For too long, a small group in our nation's capital has reaped the re-wards of government while the people have borne the cost. Wash-ington flourished—but the people did not share in its wealth . . . the establishment protected itself, but not the citizens of our country. Their victories have not been your victories; their triumphs have not been your triumphs; and while they celebrated in our nation's capital, there was little to celebrate for struggling families all across our land. That all changes—starting right here, and right now, be-cause this moment is your moment: it belongs to you. . . . January 20th, 2017, will be remembered as the day the people became the rulers of this nation again. The forgotten men and women of our country will be forgotten no longer.

It took Trump three days to forget the American people and their struggles. The promotion letter he signed was among the first of many actions showing that rather than draining the swamp, Trump was turning America's capital into a lucrative paradise for the greediest predators on Wall Street and their clients. And rather than blocking the revolving door, this promotion and subsequent actions greased its pivot.

The promotion went to Cheryl LaFleur, who was elevated from member to chair of the Federal Energy Regulatory Commission, known as FERC. While it is a tiny agency with fewer than two thousand employees, FERC wields enormous power. How much you pay each month for electricity, part of the cost of the natural gas you use to boil water, and part of what you pay to fuel your car is determined by this agency. FERC licenses hydroelectric dams and determines the level of water behind them. It decides who can build oil and natural gas pipelines as well as high-voltage electric transmission lines. It sets the prices customers pay these monopolies and the profits the owners earn. And it oversees a growing and complex system of wholesale electricity markets that operate in more than half the states, a system Wall Street easily manipulates to jack power prices and generate colossal profits.

FERC's financing is unusual. It is a federal agency, yet taxpayers do not cover its budget. The money comes from fees paid by the electric utilities, fossil fuel pipelines, and other energy interests it is supposed to regulate in the public interest. This financing arrangement is one reason the agency is often cited as the prime example of a regulatory agency that acts more like a handmaiden servicing the companies it regulates than a guardian of the interests of customers, or what economists call *regulatory capture*.

By law the commissioners are supposed to make sure that both the prices paid by consumers and the profits earned by utility owners are fair. The legal standard for this is called *just and reasonable*. Often, though, FERC puts its thumb on the scales. For example, FERC allows oil pipelines to charge 54 percent more than their net profits to cover the federal corporate income tax. That would be entirely appropriate except for one crucial fact: Congress exempted most pipelines from this levy in 1986. Similarly, when interest rates fell in the twenty-first century, the commission maintained monopoly profit margins that ignored the cheaper cost of borrowed capital, another policy favoring the industry that finances the commission. And the commission approved electricity auctions under rules that by their very design tend to raise prices and are built on the assumption that electric-generating companies would follow textbook economics rather than find ways to further manipulate these markets to earn unjust and unreasonable profits.

A president who wanted Washington to act in the interests of forgotten Americans could find no better agency than FERC to reform as a demonstration of resolve to drain the swamp. For starters, just appointing one commissioner with a résumé as a consumer advocate would help. LaFleur, like all the other commissioners, came from an industry FERC regulates. She had been CEO of National Grid USA, an electricity monopoly in the Northeast owned by British investors. Her votes and written opinions had long established her as a guardian of industry. When presented with complaints, backed up by strong evidence, that Wall Street traders had manipulated the New England electricity auctions, LaFleur proved to be a sightless sheriff, blind to the evidence of price manipulations that cost consumers dearly.

In promoting LaFleur, Trump also forced the resignation of Norman C. Bay, who was the chairman. Bay was the only commissioner with a bent toward enforcement of the just and reasonable rules, as might be expected of the former chief federal prosecutor for New Mexico.

With Bay out, the commission had only two members, not the three required for a quorum. It was the first time in the four decades since Congress created FERC, or in the decades-long history of its predecessor agency, the Federal Power Commission, that it lacked the quorum necessary to make decisions.

The lack of a quorum blocked the planned Nexus Pipeline, a $2 billion project to build a 256-mile high-pressure natural gas pipeline in Ohio and Michigan, including a compressor station with a whopping 130,000-horsepower engine to squeeze natural gas into the pipeline. For comparison, each engine on a Boeing 777 generates only 110,000 horsepower.

Also stopped were eight proposed liquefied natural gas terminals to export the relatively clean fossil fuel found in abundance using modern fracking technology. Seven of the projects are on the Gulf Coast, the other at Jacksonville on Florida's Atlantic coast. Delays in approving those projects hurt American construction workers, but benefited Australia, Qatar, and other countries that were signing long-term contracts to export boat-loads of liquefied natural gas.

These delays in energy projects did not square with Trump's America First strategy, his promise to focus on creating jobs, or his declared support for fossil fuel industries. The damage could have been stopped by simply naming new commissioners and getting them swiftly confirmed by the Senate. Instead, the Trump administration dawdled. Soon $50 billion worth of energy projects stalled because of Trump's laxity.

More than a hundred days after he took office, Trump finally got around to making two nominations. His appointees were classic revolving door.

The first was Rob Powelson, a member of the Pennsylvania board that regulated utilities in the Keystone State. He was considered a nasty foe by consumer and environmental groups. Powelson openly expressed contempt for farmers, environmentalists, and just average Joes and Joans who complained that virtually unregulated fracking for oil and natural gas in Pennsylvania fouled water supplies, stank up the air, and pulverized paving, burdening taxpayers with the costs of mitigating damage to water supplies and replacing roadways. Powelson, speaking at a pipeline industry conference, brought up protesters at FERC who had accused it of bias in favor of pipeline owners. Said Powelson: "The jihad has begun."

The other appointee was Neil Chatterjee, the top energy adviser to Mitch McConnell of Kentucky, the Senate majority leader. Having worked for the energy industry, Chatterjee was just the kind of revolving door veteran Trump promised to drain from the swamp. Chatterjee was also a cheerleader for the burn-drill-frack school of fossil fuel management that loves Kentucky coal and detests environmental regulations, the attitude that has diminished the quality of life in parts of Pennsylvania and other states where fracking abounds.

While the Powelson and Chatterjee nominations were pending before the Senate, Trump nominated a new FERC chairman, with LaFleur expected to stay on as a member until her term expires. This time Trump chose Kevin McIntyre, an energy industry lawyer known for pursuing the interests of energy producers against consumers. McIntyre was co-chief of the worldwide energy law practice at the law firm Jones Day. His clients, the White House said, come from every area FERC regulates—electric power, hydropower, natural gas, and oil.

The choice of McIntyre disturbed Daniel Sponseller, a Pittsburgh regulatory lawyer whose clients are consumer organizations and unions that assert that the electricity auctions are rigged to favor power plant owners. Sponseller was litigating electricity price manipulation claims that FERC refused to investigate, a refusal that surely would continue under McIntyre. "You can't find a law firm more oriented to the energy industry and to electricity-generating companies than Jones Day," Sponseller said, with its "massive District of Columbia and nationwide energy practice representing the big corporations and always litigating against consumers and energy-purchasers. Drain the swamp, indeed."

With these nominations, there was no chance that the Trump administration would relieve struggling Americans of the rule that forces them to pay for a corporate profits tax on pipelines that the pipelines are exempt from. This fake tax, by the way, results from a rule adopted by the commission after close and secret coordination with the pipeline industry. After I exposed this fake tax charge and estimated the cost to consumers at about $3 billion per year, Congress ordered a study. The official estimate for Congress put the cost at nearly $2 billion. Either way, customers are being forced to pay a tax that the pipelines do not owe. The extra money inflates their profits, already at bounteous levels FERC sets, by 54 percent. To paraphrase Mel Brooks, it's nice to be a pipeline owner.

Any president worried about struggling Americans could end this unjust and unreasonable expense and at the same time make a powerful point about draining the swamp. All it would take is naming FERC commissioners who insist that monopoly utilities charge customers only their actual costs plus a reasonable profit without any charge for fake taxes. Another approach would be to send a bill to Congress requiring pipelines to refund, with interest, all the taxes collected but not turned over to the Treasury.

Likewise, a president concerned with forgotten Americans struggling to pay their bills would have a keen interest in holding down electricity prices, which are crucial to the profit margins and investment decisions of many businesses that use juice in vast quantities. Consider the New England electricity market after four energy traders from Goldman Sachs and one from Deutsche Bank got together as Energy Capital Partners. The partners bought a fleet of seventeen electric power plants. Just five weeks later they announced plans to shutter their biggest electric power plant, Brayton Point in Massachusetts. Buying an expensive facility just to close it would not make sense in industries like manufacturing, but under the electricity market rules approved by LaFleur and other FERC commissioners, it was an exceptionally lucrative move.

The market in which utilities buy electricity to distribute to their customers operates under the aegis of FERC. These auctions, in periods from a few minutes up to a year, are what economists call *single price* or *clearing price* auctions. All the power plants in a market, hundreds of them, file bids to sell electricity. Assume the average cost of generating power is $10 per unit and the average bid is $12, which would make for a handsome profit for winning bidders. But there's a wrinkle in the auction rules. The bids are arrayed from lowest to highest. Every bid is accepted in order of rising price until all the needed electricity is supplied. Those whose bids are too high get nothing. The wrinkle is in what happens to the successful bidders: every power plant gets the highest price, the price set by the last successful bidder. So imagine that the average cost of producing power is $10, the average bid is a very profitable $12, while the last winning bid is $2,000. Under the *single price* or *clearing price* auction every successful bidder gets $2,000.

There are also *capacity auctions*, which operate under the same rules. Owners of electric power plants promise to make their electric-generating stations available in the event they are needed to supply an extra or unexpected customer demand for juice. These capacity auctions are like paying car dealers to keep a pink car of every model on their lots just in case someday a customer wants one without delay.

In theory, such super-high prices encourage investors to build new power plants. The idea is that investors will look at the prospect of getting two hundred times the cost of generating electricity, even if it is for a short period of time, and decide to build new power plants. That the prospect of super-large profits will attract new investment is textbook economics. But there is a fundamental problem with this theory. It assumes Wall Street traders and power plant owners behave like the elegant mathematical models of Chicago School economics professors, not like greedy individuals out to make every buck they can. In practice, these single price auctions create a powerful incentive to restrict the supply of electricity. If each investor was limited to one power plant, the concept might work. But when investors own fleets of power plants, the incentives change. If they close one power plant, or schedule it for maintenance so it is not available when demand for electricity is greatest, the clearance price can be pushed higher. The incentive is to withhold, not expand, the supply of electricity.

FERC has rules to prevent such manipulations. Without enforcement, though, rules are meaningless.

Sponseller, the Pittsburgh utility lawyer, filed a lawsuit challenging three years of New England auctions as illegal because they violated the fairness rule, the *just and reasonable* standard. The evidence showed that New England electricity customers paid an extra $3.8 billion because a single power plant was not in the capacity auction bidding. Those former Goldman Sachs and Deutsche Bank traders, the very kind of people Trump promised to drain from the swamp, made an extra $225 million in profits, federal court papers state.

LaFleur's response? Nothing to see, folks, so move along.

Her position is that once FERC declares that a market exists, any price the market auction sets is the market price. That circular argument ignores an underlying problem. If the rules themselves are flawed, if the rules enable price gouging, the results cannot be just and reasonable. And as with the fake pipeline tax, ripping millions of people off for a few extra dollars each month concentrates billions of dollars in the hands of the very few who own power plants. And that upward redistribution of money occurs thanks to the federal government adopting unfair rules, rules that few people know about. Stopping electricity price gouging would seem to be exactly what Trump was talking about in his inaugural address when he said Washington made the few prosper while "the people did not share in its wealth."

Trump's first federal budget also included a proposal to sell various federal electricity assets, including the Bonneville Power Administration's electricity transmission network in the Pacific Northwest. Robert Mc-Cullough, a utility economist known for exposing regulatory games and artificially inflated electricity prices, told me he was struck by the proposed sale terms. Private ownership would require profits and within a few years would almost certainly mean high costs for consumers, not at all what Trump had promised voters. But it was the proposed selling price that startled McCullough. Trump offered the grid at 75 cents on the dollar taxpayers had invested. "This is a new way to sell a car," McCullough said, "start the bidding significantly below the sticker price."

Congress created FERC and its predecessor agency the Federal Power Commission to protect families, small-business owners, and industry from monopolists and pricing schemes that jack up prices while at the same time ensuring an abundant supply of electricity. Unregulated, electricity prices can cause economic and political turmoil. Enron, the energy trading firm that collapsed in 2001, took power plants offline and used other manipulations to make West Coast electricity prices soar, devouring the profits of electric-intensive businesses from ice-skating rinks and grocers with freezer cabinets to metal-bending factories. That issue prompted California voters to recall Governor Gray Davis and replace him with Arnold Schwarzenegger—like Trump, a novice politician who was a household name only because he was an entertainer.

Trump's letter promoting LaFleur and forcing out Bay, along with the three long-delayed appointments of new commissioners, was also an early indicator of the quality of the Trump White House team. Historically the people fortunate enough to have the once-in-a-lifetime opportunity to work in the White House exercise extreme diligence to get every detail right, from how names of appointees are rendered to references to historical events. Trump's letter to LaFleur was late arriving. The address on the envelope was wrong, the letter mailed to a location that FERC had moved out of more than a decade before.

PART V

GLOBAL AFFAIRS

Diplomacy

Four months after taking office, Donald Trump flew to Saudi Arabia, where he lavished praise on a family-run country that makes sure its people learn only the official version of events, not unlike the regimes in Russia and North Korea.

The extended family that has run Saudi Arabia for nearly a century was not satisfied with controlling what its own people know. They were determined to make sure that people throughout the Middle East lacked access to independent news because it was a threat to their absolute rule.

Trump's visit helped that cause mightily while offending the government of Qatar, the Middle Eastern country that is home to the most important United States military base in that part of the world. Qatar runs Al Jazeera, a television news service that the Saudis and other dictatorial and monarchical regimes in the Middle East cannot block because it uses satellites to beam its reports directly to television sets.

The Saudis and their allies, after the Arab Spring uprisings in Algeria, Egypt, and Bahrain, wanted desperately to shutter Al Jazeera to ensure their iron grip would not be challenged. They saw an ally in Trump, who complains that news he does not agree with is fake news that should not be allowed.

It quickly became apparent that the Trump administration had no idea about the authoritarian nature of the Saudi regime, nor the competing interests and religious divisions in the Arab world. This was especially true when it came to the official form of Islam in Saudi Arabia, an extreme form of Sunni Islam called Wahhabism that had inspired many attacks on America, including those on 9/11.

Mieke Eoyang, a longtime Capitol Hill adviser on diplomatic, intelligence, and military matters, said Trump brought "bluff and bluster" to the Gulf Cooperation Council meeting in Riyadh. "He goes to Saudi Arabia, gives a speech he thinks makes him popular with the host country, but masks a much more complicated situation as he steps into this fight between the monarchist-based Wahhabist-friendly Gulf States and those who say the Saudis shouldn't have a lock on religion within the Sunni branch of Islam."

Eoyang said Trump's speech and actions in Riyadh showed that "he really doesn't get what the issues are and he won't pay attention to those who try to explain it to him. He speaks without thinking about other people, other interests. Below-the-radar people are turning away from the U.S. in ways Trump does not see."

Trump acted against America's traditional role as a beacon of liberty and a promoter of freedom. And he did so while swaddled in what by his own account was a major conflict of interest that raised questions about what motivated his actions. (More on that later.) Those actions were inconsistent with those of any previous administration. His moves made no obvious sense in the three-dimensional game of global geopolitical chess, especially his attack on America's militarily important ally Qatar.

The clearest example of Trump administration know-nothingism in world affairs emerged on the final day of the visit to Riyadh. Wilbur Ross, the richest member of the Trump cabinet, appeared on the CNBC business channel, where he unintentionally revealed his ignorance about how rare the freedoms Americans enjoy are and why petition and protest are constitutional rights. Ross had made his money as a vulture capitalist, buying cheaply the distressed bonds of companies headed toward bankruptcy. He reorganized their finances to make himself a pot of money. The companies, infused with cash from new loans, became corporate zombies stumbling toward collapse again in the future. That was how he met Trump more than a quarter century earlier when Trump's companies could not pay their debts.

CNBC wanted Ross to tell its audience of investors about how newly announced arms sales to the Saudi regime would affect the stock of American weapons makers like United Technologies and Lockheed Martin. The White House announced that it had made deals worth $110 billion in immediate sales of weaponry. In time, it said, the total value was expected to reach $350 billion.

That was not true. Not a single deal was signed during Trump's May 20 to 22 visit to Saudi Arabia. Instead the official-looking documents in large portfolios that Trump and Saudi officials signed with flourishes before cameras in a great hall were nothing more than preliminary memoranda about deals that might be made. The $110 billion of arms sales that Trump claimed credit for turned out to include $26 billion of deals made by the Obama administration.

Ross repeated the official version of events. Then he volunteered that beyond the speed with which deals were made he had something else to share with the CNBC audience.

"The other thing that was fascinating to me," Ross said, "was there was not a single hint of a protester anywhere there during the whole time that we were there. Not one guy with a bad placard."

As Ross marveled at the lack of public dissent in Saudi Arabia, the CNBC host, Becky Quick, broke in. She pointed out that Saudi Arabia does not allow demonstrations. "They control people and do not let them express their feelings," she explained.

This prompted a Trumpian response by Ross, who neither acknowledged facts he was not aware of nor recognized his misunderstanding. "In theory, that could be true," Ross replied. "But, boy, there was certainly no sign of it. There was not a single effort at any incursion. There wasn't anything. The mood was a genuinely good mood."

Had Ross read the State Department's latest annual report on human rights during his long flight on Air Force One, he would have known that the Saudi "government strictly monitored politically related activities and took punitive actions, including arrest and detention, against persons engaged in certain political activities, such as direct public criticism of senior members of the royal family by name, forming a political party, or organizing a demonstration." The report cited examples of arbitrary arrests lasting years without trial and long prison sentences for dissent, which explained the lack of protesters that had so impressed Ross.

Ross further demonstrated his naïveté by noting that as he departed, his Saudi security guards wanted to pose with him for photographs and then presented two gigantic bushels of dates, which he called not a diplomatic courtesy but "a genuine from the heart gesture that really touched me."

Ross also said he was impressed at how Saudi Arabia was liberalizing. The seventy-nine-year-old billionaire pointed out that a woman runs the Saudi stock exchange, gratuitously observing that she was young and beautiful.

Ross said nothing of laws that banned women from driving or even being in a car with a man unless he is a relative. He said nothing of the religious police using violence to enforce requirements that women wear abayas, an outer robe, lest men lose control of their lustful impulses. There are other such examples too numerous to mention. Then there were the Saudi beheadings, public executions that human rights groups say often are carried out based on dubious evidence.

During the presidential campaign, Trump stirred up crowds with lurid descriptions of ISIL's beheadings. ISIL sought to inflame Americans and Europeans with its atrocious acts. But they served another purpose as well—frightening people in areas ISIL controlled so they would submit to its authority lest their heads come off.

Trump said nothing about Saudi Arabia beheading people, which government executioners did on average three times per week in 2015 and 2016. Nor did he protest executions via public stonings, another Saudi government technique to frighten its 28 million people into submission to the monarchy's absolute rule. Burying people in the ground up to their necks so rocks could be thrown at their heads was both a brutal way to kill and a terrifying reminder of the regime's barbaric views on official violence.

Sometimes beheaded bodies are crucified in Saudi Arabia, all this done in public as crowds watch what journalist John R. Bradley describes as the "only form of public entertainment" in Saudi Arabia, aside from soccer matches.

Qatar, the country the Saudis wanted to bring to heel, does not stage beheadings. The last Qatari execution occurred in 2003 when a firing squad ended the life of a convicted murderer. But it was Qatar that Trump denounced while he was in the Saudi kingdom, shocking its emir and many American diplomatic and military leaders because Qatar is crucial to American interests in that part of the world.

More than 11,000 American military personnel work out of the twenty-square-mile Al Udeid Air Base south of Doha, the capital of Qatar.

From there the Air Force directs American bombers and jet fighter attacks on ISIL, the Taliban in Afghanistan, and Houthi rebels the Saudis want suppressed in Yemen. Americans at the airbase in Qatar also controlled drones used for surveillance of suspected Al Qaeda, Taliban, and other terrorist leaders, directing missile strikes at them and their entourages.

Trump's Riyadh speech praising the Saudis and their Middle Eastern allies while condemning Qatar drew firm lines in the sand. "With God's help, this summit will mark the beginning of the end for those who practice terror and spread its vile creed," Trump said, adding, "there can be no coexistence with this violence. There can be no tolerating it, no accepting it, no excusing it, and no ignoring it."

Those remarks indicate Trump was unaware, or did not care, that the Saudis are the world's largest sponsor of terrorism, far exceeding the Iranian government that Trump frequently denounces for its support for terrorism. The State Department lists sixty-one terrorist organizations, all but two of which are aligned with Sunnis and the extreme Wahhabi sect that is officially endorsed in Saudi Arabia. The Saudis fund fifty-seven of those terrorist groups. Qatar, the country that Trump joined the Saudis and their allies in denouncing, was also involved in funding terrorist groups, though they committed their acts of political violence mostly in the Middle East.

All American presidents before Trump had, in varying degrees, modulated their remarks to avoid exacerbating the centuries-old rivalries within Islamic countries. Their carefully scripted and nuanced public statements and official actions reflected the intelligence assessment that taxpayers paid for so our officials would understand the Middle East. Previous presidents took care not to excite a viper's nest of poisonous religious and political conflicts in that part of the world and to balance American interests among these contending factions.

Abandoning that history of thoughtful diplomacy, Trump went all in with the Saudis and their allies. He said he applauded the "Gulf Cooperation Council for blocking funders from using their countries as a financial base for terror, and designating Hezbollah as a terrorist organization last year. Saudi Arabia also joined us this week in placing sanctions on one of the most senior leaders of Hezbollah." While the designation did occur, it was likely window dressing to please Trump, not an actual severing of the

relationship between rich Saudis who depend on the Saud family government for their fortunes and Hezbollah.

The official White House version of the speech, including capital letters, declared:

> A better future is only possible if your nations drive out the ter-
> rorists and extremists. Drive. Them. Out. DRIVE THEM OUT of
> your places of worship. DRIVE THEM OUT of your communities.
> DRIVE THEM OUT of your holy land, and DRIVE THEM OUT
> OF THIS EARTH. For our part, America is committed to adjust-
> ing our strategies to meet evolving threats and new facts. We will
> discard those strategies that have not worked—and will apply new
> approaches informed by experience and judgment. We are adopt-
> ing a Principled Realism, rooted in common values and shared
> interests.

How attacking Qatar could be principled or realistic is something
people deeply versed in the Middle East could not understand. It did,
however, align with Trump's desire to make American news organizations
come to heel and present only news that in his opinion accurately reflects
his actions.

We cannot know what Trump was thinking as he read his speech. He
showed no sign then or later of realizing the irony of delivering these remarks to a room filled with religious authoritarians whose governments
and citizens finance terrorists, including the 9/11 hijackers. Nothing he
said suggested that he understood the disputes among the various countries controlled by Sunni potentates and dictators.

Trump's remarks also made no sense to those who know that Saudis
fund the Taliban, the Afghan forces that harbored Osama bin Laden at the
time of the 9/11 attack.

The Saudis surely have an interest in going after some terrorists. Their
interest is in stopping terrorism by Shia Muslims, the branch of Islam
dominant in Iran.

Trump had interests, too. At a 2015 rally in Mobile, Alabama, Trump
said Saudis "buy apartments from me. They spend $40 million, $50 million. Am I supposed to dislike them? I like them very much." Trump cre-

ated more than a half dozen companies in Saudi Arabia. All were inactive, but he suggested that he had plans to build a golf course, hotel, or other property there.

A month after the inauguration, his sons opened the Trump International Golf Club in Dubai. A few weeks before taking office, Trump said that his partner in that venture, Hussain Sajwani, offered him a $2 billion deal. Trump said he rejected the offer out of concern that people would think he would "take advantage" of the presidency to make money.

Trump said he would have a conflict of interest regarding Turkey if he became president. "I have a little conflict of interest 'cause I have a major, major building in Istanbul," he told Breitbart in 2015. "It's a tremendously successful job. It's called Trump Towers—two towers, instead of one, not the usual one, it's two." Ivanka Trump tweeted thanks to Turkish leader Recep Tayyip Erdoğan in 2012 for attending the launch of the Trump twin towers.

There was also a possible explanation for his attack on Qatar. Trump has a long history of being incredibly petty, his tweets showing his thin skin. Qatar Airways rented space in Trump Tower in 2008, but moved out in 2014, a slight Trump would likely not forget.

In Las Vegas, during the final presidential election debate, Trump had taken a very different tone about Saudi Arabia. Referring to gifts to the Clinton Global Initiative, a charity that helps poor people, Trump demanded that Hillary Clinton and her husband "give back the money you've taken from certain countries that treat certain groups of people so terrible."

Trump specified "Saudi Arabia giving $25 million, Qatar, all of these countries. You talk about women and women's rights? So these are people that push gays off . . . buildings. These are people that kill women and treat women horribly. And yet you take their money."

Trump's flip-flop on the Saudis after the election showed how little he understands the Middle East by comparison with Hillary Clinton. As secretary of state, Clinton had a nuanced and deep understanding of the complexities of the Middle East and how all the governments there in some way support terrorists. In an email from February 14 that was revealed by WikiLeaks, she wrote that "we need to use our diplomatic and more traditional intelligence assets to bring pressure on the governments of Qatar and Saudi Arabia, which are providing clandestine financial and logistic support to ISIL and other radical Sunni groups in the region."

Donald Trump proposed to cut more than $14 billion from the $50 billion State Department budget, a 29 percent reduction. Only the Environmental Protection Agency was to be cut more. The Trump budget would essentially end foreign aid, most of which benefits American companies by buying goods and services from them and giving them to poor countries. While Congress is unlikely to approve such cuts, their significance lies in showing where Trump would put federal money. He asked for $54 billion more for the military.

Trump's first budget proposed cutting by more than half the $3.1 billion the United States contributes to United Nations Peacekeeping operations. It eliminated all funding for the Africa Peacekeeping Rapid Response Partnership. The rise of Muslim extremism in Africa had been a concern of the Obama administration. It persuaded Congress to spend nearly $900 million between 2009 and 2014 to train and equip more than a quarter million African peacekeeping troops and police officers and some support personnel, including engineers. The program also provided medical care, aircraft maintenance training, and communications gear.

In 2014, the United States started providing $110 million annually to help Senegal, Ghana, Ethiopia, Rwanda, Tanzania, and Uganda maintain and quickly deploy peacekeepers in "response to emerging conflict, a concept that holds powerful life-saving potential."

This strategy helped locals counter African affiliates of Al Qaeda and Hezbollah, and to intercede in mass crimes like the 2014 kidnapping of 276 Nigerian schoolgirls by Boko Haram, which Trump called a "radical Islamic terrorist" organization.

A major benefit of this strategy was that it did not require the involvement of American or other Western troops, taking a propaganda tool away from radicals who preach hatred of America. Just five days after Trump took office, the State Department's Bureau of Political-Military Affairs issued a fact sheet detailing the benefits of helping poor African countries to develop trained forces to quell violence and equip them with transportation, without direct American involvement.

The Trump budget statement asserted that it was eliminating duplicative and wasteful diplomatic efforts. "Reform is needed to create not only more efficient and accountable peacekeeping operations but also ensure that each mission's mandate reflects realities on the ground and is supported by the necessary political will and structures to achieve its objectives."

An African rapid response team for peacekeeping, which would reduce the chance that American troops would have to become engaged at enormous cost, came to about a nickel a month per American.

The Trump administration's budget plan also proposed cutting support overall for United Nations Peacekeeping, which ran even bigger risks of increased American military involvement unless Washington withdrew from its role as the global police department. The administration said the budget "sets the expectation that the UN will rein in costs by reevaluating the design and implementation of peacekeeping missions and sharing the funding burden more fairly among members."

But what may matter most from Trump's first foreign trip was how his conduct helped Saudi efforts to suppress news that was not strictly controlled by its government and those of its allies.

Qatar is ruled by the Al-Thani family, put in full charge in 1972 when the British gave up their protectorate. The emir installed by the British, Khalifa bin Hamad, created a television channel, something of a breakthrough at the time that showed his bent toward the West. In 1995, his son deposed him. The new emir, Hamad bin Khalifa al-Thani, launched Al Jazeera, Arabic for "the Peninsula."

Using satellite technology, the cost of which was falling fast, it began beaming unofficial news into homes throughout the Middle East. It would develop into a sophisticated and remarkably professional worldwide news operation, including Al Jazeera America, for which I wrote a weekly column for two years until it was shut down in early 2016.

While Al Jazeera had plenty of critics, none was more vociferous than the Saud family. They blamed Al Jazeera for stirring up people through the Middle East and fostering the Arab Spring uprisings. For the Saud family, with 28 million people they must control or placate, the Arab Spring was a serious threat to their reign. One option would have been to embrace change and allow more freedom and steps toward an open society. Instead the Saud family organized the other Gulf Cooperation Council members to boycott Qatar. That Trump would be inclined to help these Gulf States in their demand that Al Jazeera's Arabic-language channel be shuttered was obvious. Trump admires Vladimir Putin's popularity in Russia, which is due in large part to his control of state media. He also admires Turkey's Erdoğan, who has moved to control news in that country.

Trump's remarks attacking Qatar and aligning himself with the Saudis touched off angry diplomatic complaints from a variety of countries. Rex Tillerson, the former ExxonMobil chief executive who had become secretary of state, and James Mattis, the general and military scholar who became defense secretary, had to get on the phone to calm anger over Trump's visit by other Middle East countries, especially Qatar.

The blundering in Riyadh came a month after Trump telephoned Erdoğan in Turkey to offer praise on his winning a referendum that vastly enhanced his powers. Trump was the only leader of a democratic nation who called Erdoğan with praise. The referendum passed by a slim margin, almost certainly because of fraud, according to international election monitors. The referendum gives Erdoğan powers to crack down on political opponents and close news organizations that do not genuflect to his rule.

Denunciations of Trump's call to Erdoğan were also widespread, especially since Erdoğan was moving to replace almost a century of secular democratic government in Ankara with an authoritarian Islamic regime.

Evan McMullin, a former CIA operations officer who ran against Trump as an independent, winning almost half as many votes in Utah as Trump, succinctly captured the criticisms in a tweet: "An American president should never support a foreign dictator's power grab. A simple gesture like this can weaken liberty here and abroad."

Gestures concerning trade have enormous impact, too.

Trade

One day before the G20 meeting of leaders of the world's largest econo-mies began in Germany in July 2017, Donald Trump stopped briefly in Warsaw. He delivered a speech to an enthusiastic crowd organized by Poland's ruling Law and Justice Party, a populist, nationalist, and rightist movement not unlike the one that had provided his margin of victory in America. The crowd was unified in its support of Trump. That was not because all Poles loved Trump, but because police kept protesters far away to foster the impression of solidarity between the new American president and people of Poland.

Poland was in fact torn by conflict because the Law and Justice Party was moving toward authoritarian rule. Jarosław Kaczyński, the party chief and the de facto leader of the government, made Trumpian calls to prose-cute political opposition leaders, though with more subtlety than the "lock her up" chants at Trump rallies. Kaczyński also spread wild conspiracy theories and attacked Muslims, saying they spread parasites and disease.

What television viewers saw was reality political television, not fair and balanced news.

Trump's speech served another purpose. It diverted the attention of American news organizations from something much more important, something of enduring economic significance, that was taking place the same day. Had that event been the focus of the news, it would have high-lighted the growing disconnect between Trump's inaugural promise to al-ways to act on behalf of the forgotten men and women who work and his conduct on trade.

Trump spoke of how beautiful Poland was, how beautiful his wife was, how beautiful Krasiński Square was. His speech even put the Warsaw Ghetto Uprising and *beautiful* in the same sentence. All this was prelude for a sudden turn into his dark view of the future, an extension of his in-augural remarks less than six months earlier about "carnage" in America and his promise to restore law and order and always to champion working people.

"The fundamental question of our time is whether the West has the will to survive," Trump declared.

That line came out of the blue with no context. It also dominated the news that day. It was not preceded as most grand pronouncements are by a buildup to prepare people for a jarring or monumental observation. Nor did it turn out to be the first step in a campaign to save Western Civiliza-tion from imminent or even possible extinction. That's because its pur-pose was something quite different, something that distracted from much more important business taking place that day eight hundred miles to the west in Brussels.

Trump ticked off a long and eclectic list of challenges. It began with a theme of aggression without reconciliation, a theme in many Trump speeches when it came to racial, ethnic, and religious matters: "We are fighting hard against radical Islamic terrorism, and we will prevail. We cannot accept those who reject our values."

To many people around the world the idea that Western Civilization faces extinction seemed not just surprising, but paranoid. But this speech was not aimed at people with a rational and fact-based view of the world. This speech was intended for the audience Trump counts on to maintain his power, an audience represented in the White House by his very close advisers the speechwriter Stephen Miller and, at the time, his chief adviser, Steve Bannon.

Trump's repeated references to "our civilization" and his ten references to "the West" were not about the West in any geographic or even cultural sense. They were subtext about religion and ethnicity.

He was assuring those who did not want to accept refugees from the Middle East, who did not want to have to look at a mosque or believers entering it, that he was one with them. He was speaking to those who feel aggrieved because they want to live only among neighbors who are white-skinned and at least nominally Christian with, perhaps, a tolerance for Jews.

But while Trump was doing his best in Poland to appeal to those who feel aggrieved and imagine acts of violence will make them feel good, the latest of his many appeals to the worst in people, he was not involved in a civilized event of lasting economic importance to American workers.

A new trade deal was being signed that day in Brussels. It lowered tariffs and other barriers to trade between the European Union and Japan. The twenty-eight European countries had a larger economy than America, and if this deal worked as planned the mutual exchanges between Europe and Japan stood to make both economies measurably larger.

Shinzo Abe, the Japanese prime minister, called what was created that day "the world's largest free, advanced, industrialized economic zone."

Japan anticipated a nearly 30 percent increase in exports to the European Union, principally Japanese-made cars. The EU, in turn, expected to sell far more food to Japan, a boon to Europe's farmers and ranchers, growing its total sales to Japan by a third. There also would be plenty of high-tech industrial and consumer equipment going both ways.

Jean-Claude Juncker, the president of the European Commission, the EU parliament, said the Euro-Japanese agreement "shows that closing ourselves off from the world is not good for business, nor for the global economy, nor for workers. As far as we are concerned, there is no protection in protectionism."

The president of a closely related organization, the European Council, Donald Tusk, could not resist getting in a dig at Trump. Just as Trump delivered his Warsaw message to those in the know, bewildering others, Tusk's statement assumed his audience would get the point without being jabbed. "Although some are saying that the time of isolationism and disintegration is coming again," Tusk said, "we are demonstrating that this is not the case. The world really doesn't need to go a hundred years back in time. Quite the opposite."

This was not the only major new trade deal in the works. Another was taking shape that would enhance the influence of China, the world's largest economy and a country that Trump told voters was responsible more than anything else for America's economic problems.

Days after taking office, Trump had killed the proposed Trans-Pacific Partnership, or TPP, which would have created a trading alliance among a dozen Pacific Rim countries but not China.

The Chinese, knowing on Election Day that Trump was likely to fulfill his promise to dump the TPP rather than present the treaty for Senate vote, got busy promoting their own trade deal. Their sixteen-nation Regional Comprehensive Economic Partnership left the United States out, but brought in India.

Chinese diplomats calmly and steadily worked to persuade Eastern Pacific governments that theirs was the country of the future, guided by serious people steeped in economics and history, and with a deep appreciation for science, unlike the erratic poseur that the Americans had made the head of their country. Stop operating in the shadow of Washington, China told the other fifteen governments. Turn toward the country of the future, not one whose leader keeps talking of restoring a mythical past.

With Trump giving speeches like the one in Warsaw, among other actions that the leaders of many countries found bizarre, the Chinese emissaries did not have a hard time selling the regional plan.

Trump's protectionist instincts, growing out of his dark vision of an America run by what he called stupid leaders, included at least two other actions that helped the Chinese in promoting their plan to dominate trade on the eastern rim of the Pacific Ocean.

Two months after the Warsaw speech, he tweeted that he might end the American–South Korean trade agreement that took full effect in 2012. He said its terms tilted toward Seoul. The pact indeed favors Seoul, as I reported after I went there to investigate in 2012. The deal was especially unfair regarding cars and helped explain how Hyundai and Kia were able to capture almost a tenth of the new car market in the United States while American car sales in South Korea could be counted in the hundreds per month.

But the damage done by that agreement occurred before Trump became president. Gutting the South Korea trade agreement in 2017 would only embolden the North Korean dictator, whose taunts got under Trump's skin and whose hills looking down on Seoul held an estimated 15,000 heavy cannons capable of quickly leveling that city of ten million.

Trump also said that said any new trade deals would be bilateral because he felt better deals were made between two countries than among a group of them.

One possible exception to this bilateral-deals-only policy was floated by Commerce Secretary Wilbur Ross. He said that the Trump administration might be open to the proposed Transatlantic Trade and Investment Partnership with Europe.

That would, of course, be an agreement with countries whose residents were mostly, like Trump and his fan base, white. The countries China was wooing to its trade pact hardly needed be reminded of this Trumpian tilt.

On trade matters, Trump was not entirely out of step or wrong in his concerns.

The canceled Trans-Pacific Partnership was deeply flawed. I was one of its most vigorous critics, partly because it was negotiated in such secrecy that even members of Congress could not see it unless they left their cell phone, pen or pencil, and paper outside when they entered a secure room. More significantly, the agreement granted even more power to corporations to raise prices, thwart competition, and use litigation rather than marketing skill to make money.

But the TPP, if modified through further negotiation, could have become an important tool to advance American influence in the Pacific Rim and blunt the transformative ambitions of Beijing. Seen in strategic geopolitical terms, even with its flaws the TPP was better than the void Trump created.

And while China was not included among the twelve nations in the TPP, it was America that was not included in China's Regional Comprehensive Economic Partnership. The net result of Trump's killing the TPP and not coming up with a new plan to counter China's was bad news, especially for American workers in exporting industries.

By abruptly withdrawing from the TPP with no plan for a better trade deal, Trump did more to help the Chinese fulfill their ambitions of becoming the twenty-first-century superpower than anyone else. Further, his attacks on Mexico for supposedly sending murders and rapists north created ill will not just in that country, but also in Chile and Peru, which were also part of the TPP.

The Regional Comprehensive Economic Partnership that China pushed would mean much more trade among economies on the rise. By the time Trump took office, China was the world's largest economy, according to the CIA's annual *World Factbook*. The European Union second, America third, and India fourth.

Japan was fifth, its economy stagnant for three decades because of a low birth rate, an aversion to immigrants even greater than Trump's, and a population aging faster than America's. But unlike America, Japan had in Shinzo Abe a leader who knew how to make trade deals. The one he signed with the European Union would mean growth for that nation in part at the expense of American workers, who would not share in the Euro-Japanese exchange.

Japan enjoyed some significant advantages over America. A big one was that 60 percent of working-age Japanese had a tertiary or college education, compared to only 48 percent of Americans. The share of the population with a four-year college degree or equivalent, a narrower measure of educational credentials, was more than a third higher in Japan, though Japan trailed America badly in people with doctoral degrees.

In a world of rapidly expanding knowledge, with science and technology the main drivers of economic growth, Trump was proposing major cuts to higher education, as detailed in another chapter.

An America that cuts its investment in its most valuable asset, young minds, combined with a president who pulls back from trade is an America that will have fewer jobs and especially fewer very good paying jobs in the future. That is even more true when comparing America to countries led by people with a forward-looking view and a desire to make the future better than the present, like Japan's Abe and China's Xi Jinping. They were busy making successful trade deals while Trump diverted attention with ominous talk of the pending doom of Western Civilization.

Unlike Trump, China acted not with an eye on tomorrow's television news, but with enduring improvements that would be of great economic value years, decades, and even centuries into the future.

China, roughly the same geographic size as the United States, was lacing its cities together with high-speed railroads while America's trains ran late and rough on tracks beaten down by freight trains. The Chinese built magnificent new airports with spacious terminals and plenty of wide runways for jumbo jets while America's airports were often overcrowded and sometimes crumbling.

China laid deeper beds for its expanding highways than the German Autobahn and especially America's Interstates, battered by heavy trucks above and supported by too little ballast below.

Not seeing global warming as a hoax, as Trump does, China built the

Three Gorges Dam project, which made it possible for cargo ships to go hundreds of miles upriver. Should Shanghai disappear one day beneath the liquid remains of ancient polar ice, the Chinese government was prepared to move millions of people inland while America was not even building adequate catch basins for torrential rainfalls in low-lying areas like Houston.

Donald Trump promised a massive American infrastructure renewal. But after eight months no one had seen a plan or how to pay for fixing the nation's multi-trillion-dollar deficits in roads, bridges, dams, and other infrastructure. And that was just for what was falling apart, not new needs for a growing population.

When hurricanes Harvey and Irma flooded Houston and Florida, Trump flew there, but he stayed so far from the flooding that his wife's white canvas shoes were still spotless when they flew home. Trump boasted about the size of the crowd that turned out to see him. And on another trip, he offered not a massive rebuilding program that would create jobs and reduce future flooding, only a smile and an admonition to those at one shelter to "have a good time."

When Trump got to Hamburg for the G20 meeting the day after his Warsaw speech, he was, other world leaders said later, standoffish.

He arrived having behaved like an oaf a month earlier at a meeting of North Atlantic Treaty Organization presidents and prime ministers. When the heads of government gathered for the obligatory photo, Trump pushed aside Prime Minister Duško Marković of Montenegro so he could be front and center for the cameras. With that shove, Trump made himself in the eyes of many Europeans a new version of the Ugly American.

The bad impression from Trump's barging was reinforced at the G20 when he left his chair during a meeting in which the world leaders sit at a table, their subordinates seated behind them. Ivanka took her father's chair. At the time, she was not even on the White House payroll. To the democratically elected leaders at the table, this was at best amateurish and at worst monarchist.

That and other breaches of protocol, along with Trump's solitary position on climate change, effectively turned the annual gathering into the G19 plus one.

The nineteen negotiated what became the G20 Climate and Energy Action Plan for Growth. The plan declared the Paris climate accord, which Trump had withdrawn America from, to be irreversible. The plan also called for something that would be anathema to the political termites Trump had placed into the structure of America's environmental, interior, energy, and other agencies to promote the interests of fossil fuel industries.

The plan statement urged "all G20 members that have not yet done so to initiate a peer review of inefficient fossil fuel subsidies that encourage wasteful consumption as soon as feasible."

Trump also talked often of imposing tariffs not just to pay for the wall with Mexico but also to discourage imports. In some speeches, he suggested tariffs as high as 45 percent. Tariffs, especially at such high rates, would surely touch off a trade war that would be bad for the world economy and that of every country, including the United States, with goods and services to trade.

Trump got some support for limited use of tariffs from the liberal economist Dean Baker, who writes about the follies of politicians and reporters who get textbook economics wrong. Used strategically, tariffs could be good for American workers and investors, Baker said. President Obama did just this with China several times to subtly coerce China into abandoning unfair trade practices.

"China almost certainly is violating trade rules in many areas, most obviously by subsidizing exports," Baker said. "Tariffs can be a way to force China to change the policy."

If Trump imposed tariffs on imported steel, that would force Americans to pay more for steel whether imported or made in America. That's because domestic makers would raise their prices to the amount of the tariff, or a bit less, to enhance their profits without losing sales. Using tariffs strategically for short periods could help steelmakers get through downturns in the economy or other turbulence beyond their control much the way the Obama stimulus package rescued the American auto industry, allowing it to revive and prosper.

The smart use of steel tariffs in the past, Baker said, "bought the American steel industry some breathing space at a time when most of the old-line producers were facing bankruptcy. As a result, the companies were able to reorganize and are now profitable. This has likely preserved tens of thousands of jobs in steel in Pennsylvania, Ohio, and other Rust Belt states."

Trump, by the way, had some experience with importing steel when tariffs were not an issue. For his high-rise hotel in Chicago and his hotel without a casino in Las Vegas, Trump imported cheap steel from China, costing American workers their jobs. He went to great lengths to hide where the steel came from.

The Chinese sourcing for the steel was "hidden within a chain of various corporate entities, including holding companies registered in the British Virgin Islands," investigative reporter Kurt Eichenwald wrote in *Newsweek*. Eichenwald detailed how Trump used "obscure off-shore entities that exist only on legal documents, limiting the potential liability of real businesses while obscuring their true owners" to make it hard for anyone to suss out where the steel was made.

America has run an overall trade deficit of 2 percent to 3 percent for years. Had it been whittled down to one percent, the country would have enjoyed near full employment some time ago instead of only in the last year of the Obama administration.

There's a better tool than tariffs for reducing America's chronic trade defecits. It's making the dollar worth less against the euro, China's renminbi, Canada's dollar, Mexico's peso and other currencies. Trump claimed China was artificially reducing the value of the renminbi against the dollar, but he never suggested the U.S. do the same to spur American exports and discourage imports.

"The normal mechanism for reducing a trade deficit is an adjustment in currency values," Dean Baker said. A so called strong dollar makes American exports expensive and imports cheap so Americans sell fewer Chevys abroad and buy more BMWs. But a so-called weak dollar would have the reverse effect: Americans would not import as much and other countries would buy more American products and services. The policy goal is to get a long-term balance between exports and imports.

"During the campaign, Trump pledged to declare China a currency manipulator," Baker observed. But after becoming president "Trump quickly abandoned doing anything on currency with China," a switch that occurred after he and his daughter got a basketful of trademarks on Trump-branded products that the family could sell in China.

Trump had one more not-ready-for-prime-time idea about trade policy. In September, after one of North Korea's missile launches, Trump tweeted, "The United States is considering, in addition to other options, stopping all trade with any country doing business with North Korea."

That would mean, of course, ending all trade with China, which imports from America as well as exports to it on a grand scale. And it would mean American companies would no longer be able to buy or sell goods and services to India, Pakistan, the Philippines, Russia, Thailand, and even Burkina Faso, because they also trade with Pyongyang.

David Frum, a conservative Republican who was a George W. Bush speechwriter before becoming a senior editor at *The Atlantic* magazine, had the smart response to Trump's less than half-baked tweet: "If you proudly publish unworkable options, you advertise your lack of better ones."

Digital Delusions

On his forty-second day in office, Trump stepped off the Marine One helicopter and onto the deck of the most expensive ship ever built, the *Gerald R. Ford,* the first in a new class of American aircraft carriers. The giant ship, eleven hundred feet long and twenty-five stories from keel to the top of its superstructure, served as a prop for Trump to promote his plan to add $54 billion in the coming year to what was already by far the world's largest military budget. Trump also asserted, yet again, that his prowess as a negotiator would drive down the costs of military equipment, which he promised soon would be bought with abundance.

The shipboard imagery was smart television. Even though it rehashed the dramatic landing fourteen years earlier of President George W. Bush on the deck of the aircraft carrier *Abraham Lincoln,* it helped Trump create the impression of a capable commander in chief.

The most important shipboard news from Trump's visit that second day of March would not emerge for more than two months. Trump broke that news in statements showing how he reacts instinctively, often without advice or knowing basic facts, and revealing how his ignorance of science and the technology of modern warfare blocks his ability to understand issues when they are explained to him.

Aboard the *Gerald R. Ford,* Trump began his remarks, as he often does, with self-centered comments. "They just gave me this beautiful jacket," he said, grinning, about a Navy flight jacket like the one that Bush wore in 2003 as a banner behind him declared, very prematurely as it turned out, "mission accomplished" in Iraq.

Trump, wearing his jacket, continued. "They said, here, Mr. President, please take this home. I said, let me wear it. [The sailors laughed.] And then they gave me the beautiful hat, and I said, you know, maybe I'll do that. We have a great Make America Great Again hat, but I said, this is a special day, we're wearing this. Right? [The sailors applauded as he put on the ship's baseball cap.] I have no idea how it looks, but I think it looks good. It's a great-looking hat—just like this is a great-looking ship. . . . What a place. It really feels like a place."

Trump told the sailors under his command that "we will give our military the tools you need to prevent war and if required, to fight war and only do one thing, you know what that is?"

"Win!" the sailors shouted as one.

"Win, Win. We're going to start winning again," Trump said, reiterating one of his themes.

As with Trump campaign rallies, this was an exercise with no substance, its purpose to work up the crowd and create images for television, a variation on the faux reality show that made Trump a household name. Then Trump turned to military spending, which he asserted must rise sharply to support warfighting capability.

"We are going to have very soon the finest equipment in the world," Trump declared. That did not square with numerous statements by Navy brass that the United States already had the best Navy with by far the best equipment.

Trump said the *Gerald R. Ford* "provides essential capabilities to keep us safe from terrorism and take the fight to the enemy for many years in the future." Aircraft carriers have little to do with combating terrorism, and some military strategists have argued that they are weapons from a bygone era. They are useful in positioning jet fighters and helicopters with limited range close to military targets, but acts of terrorism are often committed in places where dropping bombs or strafing the ground with cannon fire would kill and wound more civilians than combatants. Carriers are useless against many kinds of terrorist attacks such as those using backpack bombs or driving trucks and cars into crowds. Ships like the *Gerald R. Ford* are primarily weapons of conventional mechanized warfare, useless against small-bore attacks committed by small teams of suicidal ideologues and lone wolves.

Trump vowed to grow the Navy from ten aircraft carriers to twelve. That was, at best, misleading. Congress in 2006 required a minimum of eleven aircraft carriers, though the Navy had only ten in service at the time because the *Gerald R. Ford* had not yet been commissioned. Navy brass had long planned for twelve floating airports. Once again, Trump was taking credit where he deserved none.

Aircraft carriers may be outmoded in the modern world because of advances in torpedoes, missiles, and smart bombs, one of which could cripple and perhaps sink an aircraft carrier. Consider the firepower of relatively small South Korean attack ships, the *Sejong the Great*–class of guided missile destroyers. They displace about 11,000 tons of water, not much more than America's *Arleigh Burke*–class destroyers. The South Korean warships come with 128 missile silos (the *Burke*-class have 96), more than enough to rain down hell on an aircraft carrier and the small armada of support ships surrounding it for protection. That a million-dollar or less missile could disable or even sink the *Ford* is among the reasons that Chinese plan for only three aircraft carriers and the British, French, and Russians each own one. Keeping friends around the world who will allow land-based airports for fighter jets, bombers, refueling tankers, and other aircraft is an option.

Trump also implied that he was fighting for military spending increases in the face of shrinking Pentagon budgets. That's not true. The Pentagon calculated that Congress increased the basic military budget by 14.3 percent or $41 billion in 2002, by another 11.3 percent or $37 billion in 2003, and by 10.9 percent or $47 billion in 2008. Spending in 2015 and 2016 declined because the level of warfare in the Middle East declined. The Pentagon is just part of the national security budget. There is also the cost of the Central Intelligence Agency (human intelligence), the National Security Agency (telecommunications surveillance), and other security operations that add mightily to the total cost.

The $54 billion spending increase Trump proposed is, by itself, a meaningless figure to most people. One way to put it in perspective is to examine the cost per American worker at the median wage, the midpoint where half of the workers make more, half make less. Divvied up this way the annual cost of the proposed increase in spending equals more than half of a week's gross pay for the median wage worker.

America spent $611.2 billion on its military in 2016, the Stockholm International Peace Research Institute calculated, while the Trump White House cited a figure of $585 billion. The peace institute calculated that the United States spent 36 percent of all global military budgets. The American figure came to more than the spending of the next eight countries combined: China, Russia, Saudi Arabia, India, France, Britain, Japan, and Germany. Indeed, the proposed increase alone was equal to what Russia spends each year on its military from January to mid-September.

Those figures are not simple comparisons based on currency exchange rates. Rather they are what economists call purchasing power parity comparisons that consider such facts as the low cost of Chinese labor, and therefore Chinese soldiers and sailors, compared to the cost of military labor in America and Western Europe.

"Our Navy is now the smallest it's been since, believe it or not, World War I," Trump said. "Don't worry, it's going to soon be the largest it's been. Don't worry. [Applause.] Think of that. Think of that."

Indeed, the 2017 fleet of 274 ships was not much larger than the 245 at the end of World War I almost a century earlier. By 1930 the Navy floated just 130 ships, while to prosecute World War II America launched 6,768 fighting ships. Fulfilling Trump's promise of the largest fleet ever would require a 24-fold increase in the number of ships. No need for such a fleet exists. Even if a third mechanized global war, like the first two world wars, were to erupt, the weaponry needed to fight would be much different from that in the first half of the twentieth century. Advances in engineering, science, and technology reduce the need for both ships and sailors, just as tanks and armored personnel carriers mean the Army buys few of the horses and bayonets it relied on in the nineteenth century.

The costs of adding more than six thousand ships to create a naval force larger than in 1944 would cost many times the $54 billion of extra Pentagon spending Trump was pushing. The *Ford* alone cost $13 billion, with the next two aircraft carriers projected at about the same figure. And that huge sum does not count the ninety warplanes for each carrier or the battle carrier group—the surface ships plus submarines that must escort the carrier lest it be taken out with a missile or three that cost less than a million dollars each or even a modern torpedo costing much less than that.

John Richardson, the Navy's top admiral, had long promoted improved training and a change in the way of thinking about war rather than just throwing money at the Pentagon. "We will not be able to 'buy' our way out of the challenges that we face," he wrote in a 2016 plan for maintaining U.S. naval superiority. The admiral favored a larger Navy, but with 355 ships, not nearly 6,800.

The *Gerald R. Ford*, powered by two nuclear reactors, was designed to require seven hundred fewer sailors than the *Nimitz*-class aircraft carriers that will be replaced in the decades ahead. Among its increased efficiencies, the *Ford* uses two aircraft elevators instead of three to lift planes to the flight deck and return them to the interior hangars. The elevators are powered by electricity instead of steam, allowing them to move three times faster than on the older *Nimitz*-class carriers. Redesign of the superstructure and the flight decks allows the *Ford* to launch 270 flights a day, far more than its predecessors.

But the ship was also a financial disaster. The George W. Bush administration got Congress to order the keel laid before the ship was fully designed. Costs ballooned to $13 billion, roughly the cost of three of the Nimitz class of carriers. The *Ford* price tag alone equaled a quarter of the increase in military spending Trump wants. Construction began in late 2009. The ship was launched in November 2013, but not commissioned by the Navy until almost three months after Trump's visit. It is not expected to be operational until 2020.

Ray Mabus, the Obama administration's Navy secretary, called the *Gerald R. Ford* "a poster child for how you don't build a ship." Mabus said, "They were designing the *Ford* while they were building it—not a good way to—to build a ship. This is just a dumb way to build—to build any type of ship, but particularly something as big and as complicated as a carrier." Senator John McCain, a Navy fighter pilot denigrated by candidate Trump because he was captured when his plane was shot down over Vietnam, has also criticized the *Ford* costs and design during construction as an unnecessary fiasco.

But even with design before construction, the cost of ships as well as jet fighters has risen because of modern electronics, much more powerful engines, and advanced weaponry. These complex systems require highly trained personnel, who can command higher pay if they leave the military for civilian jobs. But even with increased skill requirements for sailors and others, the economics of war are shifting. What was for centuries a labor-intensive enterprise that relied on soldiers, who are relatively cheap meat machines, modern warfare is capital-intensive, requiring god-awful expensive ships and planes that use digital-era weaponry, nuclear power, and other sophisticated equipment and systems.

Two months later, in an interview with *Time* magazine, Trump broke the most significant news from his March 2 visit to the *Ford*. Keep in mind that Trump says that he does not use a computer, does not trust them, and has important messages hand-delivered—as he did when he fired James Comey, his bodyguard Keith Schiller delivering the note to FBI headquarters five blocks from the White House. Trump does not embrace new technology but tends to look backward.

What Trump told *Time* shows that he did not understand what he was told.

"You know the catapult is quite important," Trump said, bringing up the future of aircraft carriers and the systems used to fling military planes into the sky from short floating runways.

"So, I said 'what is this?'" Trump recounted to *Time*.

"'Sir, this is our digital catapult system,'" he quoted a sailor as responding. "He said, 'well, we're going to this because we wanted to keep up with modern [technology].'

"I said 'you don't use steam anymore for catapult?'

"'No sir.'

"I said, 'Ah, how is it working?'

"'Sir, not good. Not good. Doesn't have the power. You know the steam is just brutal. You see that sucker going and steam's going all over the place, there's planes thrown in the air.'

"It sounded bad to me," Trump said. "Digital. They have digital. What is digital? And it's very complicated, you have to be Albert Einstein to figure it out. And I said, 'and now they want to buy more aircraft carriers.' I said 'what system are you going to be—'

"'Sir, we're staying with digital.'

"I said, 'no you're not. You [*sic*] going to goddamned steam, the digital costs hundreds of millions of dollars more money and it's no good.'"

First off, the system is not digital, but electromechanical. It uses the same concept as the roller coasters that for nearly a century clicked and clanked as cars full of thrill seekers were pulled to the top of the first rise.

Modern roller coasters use series of magnets that, when turned on in rapid sequence, accelerate the cars much faster.

Second, it's unlikely that any Navy officer or enlisted personnel described the system the way Trump did. Rather, lacking knowledge of the principles of science and engineering, Trump converted what was said into something that made sense to him, including the word *digital*, which to Trump is a red flag for technology to be avoided at all costs. His remarks show that he did not listen, he just reacted, a trait described by many of his former top employees, casino regulators, and others who have dealt with him since he was a young man.

Third, while the Electromagnetic Aircraft Launch System, or EMALS, was born in trouble, delaying the formal acceptance of the ship by three years, it was reworked and refined until the technical problems were resolved. That's how progress works, by tinkering with new systems until the practical problems are overcome.

Fourth, the electromagnetic system enables launching much heavier planes and getting them into the air much faster. Not having to maintain high-pressure steam lines saves taxpayers several billion dollars in personnel costs over the life of each vessel.

In issuing his demand to return to steam, which will not happen because the ship is already built, Trump again demonstrated his backward-looking perspective on the world and his rejection of ideas, science, and technologies that move our species forward. Just as he promotes coal and rejects electricity made from wind, solar, and other renewable sources, Trump's vision is not about the future but about a mythical past, at best a romantic nostalgia.

Trump's limited capacity to understand complex issues prompted some of his advisers to find unusual ways to arouse his interest in policies they wanted, *Washington Post* reporters Philip Rucker and Robert Costa learned. Trump's hawkish national security adviser, three-star general H. R. McMaster, and other military leaders found it difficult to persuade Trump to renege on his campaign promises and his 2013 "Let's get out!" of Afghanistan tweet. Then McMaster and others told Trump that sending Americans into combat could revive an era when Afghanistan had been amenable to Western culture. What persuaded Trump to flip-flop, ordering more soldiers into combat seven months into his term? McMaster showed Trump a 1972 black-and-white photo of Afghan women in Kabul. They wore miniskirts.

In the *Time* interview, Trump also demonstrated, yet again, his ignorance of economics. Trump said that when Shinzo Abe arrived in Washington soon after the inauguration, the first thing the Japanese prime minister said was "Thank you, thank you."

"I said, 'For what?'" Trump said, again quoting himself.

"F-35," Abe supposedly replied. "You saved us one hundred million dollars" on the cost of the planes Japan was buying.

The lower cost means that the prime manufacturer, Lockheed Martin, collects less money from Japan. That's good for Japanese taxpayers, not so much for Lockheed Martin, its subcontractors, or the American economy. And it's certainly not "putting America first."

Blithely unaware of how his own words undercut his America First promises, Trump continued boasting. "I saved Japan a hundred million bucks!" he proclaimed, conflating issues and reiterating his claim that as president-elect his negotiating skill had lowered the cost of F-35 Joint Strike Fighter, the most expensive airplane weapons system ever.

"Took me probably an hour if I added up all the time. But I will be saving, when we put that out over two, the two thousand five hundred planes, billions of dollars. Nobody ever wrote a story about that," Trump said.

In fact, many news reports had examined the issues. "I was able to get $600 million approximately off those planes," Trump said on January 30, in remarks uncritically quoted in many news reports. Trump said that as president-elect he resolved long-stalled price negotiations to get costs down.

The claim was pure Trumpian fantasy.

Lockheed Martin would indeed get less money for the next batch of F-35s it delivered to the Air Force, Marines, and Navy. White House press secretary Sean Spicer said on February 3 that Trump's negotiating would save taxpayers $455 million or about $5 million per plane, significantly less than Trump's claim of about $6.7 million per plane.

But the cost reduction was not news. The price per plane had been falling for years. "The price tag of the F-35A, the version flown by the U.S.

Air Force and most allies, has fallen with each order. For example, F-35As in the seventh order cost 5 percent less than those in the sixth order, and so on," the Jordanian-owned news service Defence Monitor Worldwide reported right after Trump's January claims.

Lockheed had resisted cutting the price of Lot 10 by as much as the Pentagon wanted. Negotiations dragged on for fourteen months. Then, six days before the November election, the Pentagon invoked a take-it-or-leave-it clause in the F-35 contract mandating a lower price. Trade publications that track Pentagon contracting noted that Christopher Bogdan, the lieutenant general in charge of the F-35 program, had told reporters months earlier that he expected the cost per plane for Lot 10 to be 6 percent to 7 percent lower than Lot 9. Trump's initial claim about the Lot 10 aircraft worked out to 6.5 percent less per plane, meaning Trump contributed nothing to the lower price, he just claimed credit for what others had already done.

Lockheed, which counts on the federal government for about 71 percent of its revenue—and a third of that government money is for the F-35. That explains why Lockheed trod cautiously in a public statement responding to what Trump said. Even though it had informed shareholders in writing that Trump had nothing to do with the lowered price for Lot 10 planes, it took care to avoid disputing Trump. The weapons company said tepidly that it appreciated Trump recognizing "the positive progress we've made on the F-35 program."

To sell the public on a $54 billion boost in military spending, Trump proposed to cut spending elsewhere. His 2018 budget year plan includes cuts of more than a third in spending on diplomacy and aid to poor countries. And he wants to address the future of warfare in a most unusual way. The focus of global conflict is shifting from traditional battlefields to cyberspace, where theft by hacking and inflicting damage by planting computer viruses abound. Russia is a leader in both, including the help it gave Trump in the 2016 elections. But Trump's idea is to partner with the Russians.

Soon after Trump's unintentionally revealing comments to *Time*, he left on his first foreign trip, flying to Saudi Arabia where, as we have seen, what he did not know created new problems.

PART VI

EDUCATION

Promises and Performances

On the campaign trail Donald Trump repeatedly argued that he was the one true champion of African Americans, especially when he talked about education. He described African Americans as homogeneous—uniformly impoverished, poorly educated, living in communities of dilapidated housing, overrun by drugs and violent crime—ignoring the many black entrepreneurs, industrialists, physicians, scholars, and scientists. Again and again he would say to African Americans, as well as to Latinos, that the Democrats were their real enemy.

"What the hell do you have to lose?" by voting for him, Trump would ask. Trump declared that he would do more for black Americans than anyone ever had. He said that Hillary Clinton had done more harm to them than any other living politician, a bizarre claim he failed to support with any facts.

Only about 4 percent of African American voters said they planned to cast their ballots for Trump, although about 8 percent actually did. This broad rejection was not surprising given Trump's long and documented history of discriminating against blacks in renting apartments and in employment at his casinos. At campaign rallies, he repeatedly singled out African Americans, ordering police to eject people of color or urging the crowd to rough them up.

Just days before the election, Trump held a public rally in Kinston, North Carolina, where two thirds of the populace are African American. His audience was nearly all white. One black man who had arrived early to get a good spot stood near the podium. Trump assumed he was a protester. "Were you paid $1,500 to be a thug?" Trump shouted, ordering security to remove him. As it turned out, the man, C. J. Cary, is a former Marine who had come to show his support for Trump. He stood up front because he hoped to hand Trump a note suggesting he would get more votes if he showed more respect to four groups of people: blacks, women, the disabled, and college students.

In posturing as the true champion of African Americans, the Republican standard-bearer earlier that day in Charlotte, had compared himself to Abraham Lincoln. Trump evidently thought his audience was ignorant of the Civil War president's political affiliation, saying twice that "a lot of people don't know" Lincoln was a Republican, a point he continued making after the election.

The well-known fact that Trump offered about Lincoln as if it were a revelation came during a scripted address in a private meeting. "I'm asking today for the honor of your vote and the privilege to represent," he said.

In an uncharacteristically subdued voice Trump then proposed his "New Deal for Black America."

Anyone watching the official video reasonably would have thought his audience consisted of black North Carolinians. After being introduced by a black pastor, Leon Threatt of Christian Faith Assembly in Charlotte, Trump said he wanted to make an important announcement to "a small group of very, very powerful people in the African American community."

The video camera operator did not show the audience, unlike news cameras that typically pull back to show the audience at Trump rallies and other events. Had the camera panned the room, it would have shown that the seven hundred guests were not "very, very powerful people in the African American community." Trump's invited audience was nearly all white.

Trump said he had a three-prong plan to expand the African American middle class through education, jobs, and investment. It was typical Trump, slogans and claims without substantive policy proposals. Trump did make one clear and specific pledge. It concerned the future of America's 107 historically black colleges and universities (HBCUs). "My plan will also ensure funding for historic black colleges and universities," he promised.

In February, the White House invited leaders of the HBCUs to two days of meetings. Among those present was Betsy DeVos, the billionaire from western Michigan whom Trump had named education secretary even though she had no experience as a teacher, education professor, or administrator.

The sessions were billed as listening sessions so Trump and his appointees could hear the concerns of HBCU presidents. The meetings did
not proceed as promised. "There was very little listening to HBCU presidents," Walter M. Kimbrough, president of Dillard University in New Orleans, said afterward. "We were only given about two minutes each, and
that was cut to one minute," he said. Few of the college presidents got to
speak at all.

Had Kimbrough gotten a chance to be heard, he would have said that
a half century ago "a philosophy emerged suggesting education was no
longer a public good, but a private one. Since then we've seen federal and
state divestment in education, making the idea of education as the path to
the American dream more of a hallucination for the poor and disenfran-
chised. There is no doubt who is left to hallucinate. In the past decade, the
wealth gap between whites and blacks has gone from seven- to thirteen-
fold. The median net worth of a single-parent white family is twice that
of the two-parent black family. Black students graduate with 31 percent
more college debt than their white peers." To shrink the wealth gap, Kimbrough wanted to say, Trump should expand Pell Grants to poor students.
Pell Grants support 70 percent of students at historically black colleges,
compared to a bit more than a third of American college students overall.
And Pell Grants needed to be increased, many education leaders had argued elsewhere, because in 2017 their value measured as a share of typical
public college tuition was at its lowest level in four decades.

Kimbrough also wanted to propose a simple reform that would end a
structural bias against poor students. He wanted Pell Grants made available to part-time students because poor students generally must work
while attending college, making it difficult to do the study required with
a full course load.

The next day a score of other black college presidents were abruptly
ushered into the Oval Office by Omarosa Manigault. She was the repeat
guest on Trump's television shows who late in the campaign said that every
Trump critic would be forced to "bow down" to the new American president. The college presidents and Michael Lomax, president of the United
Negro College Fund, which has raised $3.6 billion to educate more than
400,000 African American young people since World War II, assembled
around Trump's desk.

With White House cameras rolling, Trump skillfully created the impression that he was very familiar with these educators, grabbing one and pulling him forward. To the casual viewer, Trump seemed to heartily embrace the idea of investing more federal tax dollars in improving young African American minds. Trump promised to "do more" for students at these colleges than any previous president. "We will make HBCUs a priority in the White House, an absolute priority," said Trump, looking into the camera. He pledged to "bring education and opportunity to all of our people."

With a flourish and awkward attempts to inject some laughter into the televised ceremony, Trump read from a statement announcing that he was signing an executive order establishing the President's Board of Advisors on Historically Black Colleges and Universities. Its twenty-five members would advise him "on all matters pertaining to strengthening the educational capacity of HBCUs" so that they would "remain fiscally secure institutions." This board was nothing new. It had existed for more than a third of a century. Its genesis was an order issued by President Jimmy Carter to strengthen the HBCUs and address historic discrimination in education funding. President Reagan created the board and every president who followed renewed it. Its annual budget was minuscule at less than $100,000. Any hope that this White House event showed that Trump would follow through on his campaign promises and expand federal financial support for HBCUs evaporated a few weeks later when the so-called skinny budget came out.

Called "skinny" because it lacked details, the skeleton plan included stripping about $10 billion from federal education spending in the 2018 budget year, a 13.5 percent reduction. Taking into account inflation and population growth, the budget cuts would be relatively larger. Proposing severe budget cuts when Trump had run promising to do more for education set off alarms at the American Council on Education, the largest association of colleges and universities. Terry W. Hartle, a council vice president, called it a "historic assault on college affordability" that "would undermine opportunity for millions of low-income and working-class students who see higher education as the gateway to a better life."

Trump would damage "nearly every program that helps students afford college," Hartle said. Student loans would cost more and they would be harder to get. The Federal Work-Study program was to be cut almost in half, with spending plummeting from $990 million to $500 million. The remaining funds would go mostly to undergraduate students.

Judith Scott-Clayton, a Brookings Institution education economist who believes the work-study program is ripe for reforms, said that even though she found the existing program wanting, "it's not possible to cut the program in half without sharply reducing access for those students that appear to benefit most: low-income students at public institutions." Halving the program would have a second negative consequence. Many poor students have no familial or practical experience working in a white-collar environment. Instead of operating cash registers or washing dishes to support themselves in college, the work-study program provided many poor students with an introduction to the white-collar work environment by doing chores in labs, gathering data alongside field researchers, or just handling administrative chores in offices like getting students identification cards and solving financial aid problems. Without such soft experiences, many students may earn a degree yet never fulfill their potential because they arrive at their first career position ill-prepared for a sudden transition from how they grew up to what is expected in workplaces for jobs requiring a college degree. While the budget was skinny, it was also revealing about where Trump wanted to redirect federal money. Short version: poor kids dreaming of college should forget their dreams of future prosperity because instead Trump wanted to increase military spending by more than a billion dollars a week and bolster the budgets for Homeland Security and rounding up undocumented immigrants even if they led exemplary lives. The planned cuts made it clear that the HBCUs and their students were not at all important to the new president.

Lomax was aghast at the flip-flop from Trump's unequivocal campaign and Oval Office promises of more government money and support for HBCUs and their students to severe federal budget cuts. The United Negro College Fund's motto, "A mind is a terrible thing to waste," had been updated a few years earlier by adding "but a good thing to invest in." Like the HBCU college presidents, he had every expectation that Trump meant what he said about investing in HBCUs and their students.

"President Trump pledged to do more for HBCUs than any other president has done before," Lomax said. "However, this budget is not reflective of that sentiment."

The Trump plan to savage education was not aimed directly at black students and the HBCUs, at least not blatantly. It was aimed at all students whose parents were not prosperous enough to pay for two years of community college or for the seven or more years required for college and professional and advanced degrees after high school. But the way the Trump administration designed the cuts, HBCUs and their students would suffer much more than the average college. This is how institutional racism works, seemingly evenhanded on the surface, the barriers hidden in the structure of funding mechanisms.

Right after the meeting at which the college presidents who came to speak were kept mostly quiet, Education Secretary DeVos issued a statement. It is significant because unlike off-the-cuff remarks that can be gaffes, this one was written, reviewed, and edited. Here are DeVos's written words, in which she seized on the opportunity to promote her Johnny one-note education policy:

> HBCUs started from the fact that there were too many students in America who did not have equal access to education. They saw that the system wasn't working, that there was an absence of opportunity, so they took it upon themselves to provide the solution. HBCUs are real pioneers when it comes to school choice. They are living proof that when more options are provided to students, they are afforded greater access and greater quality. Their success has shown that more options help students flourish.

DeVos's statement, to be polite, is nonsense. It is an example of the Trump kakistocracy in which the worst among us, especially the utterly unqualified and ignorant, hold high positions in the federal government.

While the first of these colleges was founded in 1864, as the Civil War raged, most HBCUs were formed during the Jim Crow era. By law and practice, even the smartest and most capable black students were barred by law or custom from almost every college, public and private, especially in the South. The existence of these schools reflects not choice but the racist politics of exclusion. African Americans had no choice but to create a separate, and poorly funded, parallel system of higher education because of the absurd belief that skin color determines character and intelligence.

Trump's casual cruelty was evident in the plan to eliminate a program for the poorest of poor students, known as Supplemental Educational Opportunity Grants. Each year more than a million and a half college students get an average of about $500 from the program. That is pocket change to Trump or DeVos, but to many students such small sums are the difference between getting an education and dropping out of school, between eating healthy meals and going hungry.

A few months later a presidential signing statement, attached to a spending bill, suggested that providing any federal funds for the historically black colleges and universities constituted official racial discrimination and thus was illegal.

This was part of a Trump meme that would grow over time, the assertion that the real victims of racial discrimination in America are whites, a message aimed at working-class whites in what for decades were factory and mill towns until the owners moved the jobs to Mexico or China or automated and made the jobs obsolete.

Cutting much needed help for poor students, especially poor black students, was not the end of the new policies that would ensure long-term harm to these strivers while helping the very people and institutions that candidate Trump accused of taking care of themselves in Washington at the expense of others. The Trump administration came out foursquare for bankers who loan money to students and their parents, taking Wall Street's side against any people who run into difficulty repaying these debts, a subject I will examine later.

Overall the budget messages were clear: campaign promises to build bridges to a better life, especially for African American young people, were not just the usual hot air from a politician who fails to deliver, but were in fact calculated lies that exploited dreams of a better future when the real plan was to create a nightmare for young strivers no matter how hard they studied in school. Trump's plan was not to make things better for them, but to make them much worse.

*   *   *

Taking an axe to education spending contradicted both Trump's America First policy and Make America Great Again slogan. A reduced commitment to education makes America less than great now and especially in the future. As noted, half of America's economic growth since World War II arose from taxpayer investments in scientific knowledge, which requires advanced education. Other countries, especially those in Asia with advancing economies, were pouring more money into education. China had begun experimenting with giving some freedom in the classroom for debate and even challenging professors to encourage entrepreneurs and scientists, rather than producing graduates reared on unquestioned fealty to their instructors and future bosses. Trump's cuts could make America second or third or worse, creating a future that would be less prosperous and leave America in the back of the class compared to other modern countries as an increasingly complex world requires much more rigorous intellectual development to prosper.

It got worse when the full 2018 budget came out weeks later. Over ten years, the cuts to education spending would come to $142 billion. Poor students of modest means would be hit hardest by the Trump budget.

DeVos defended these cuts. She had made a name for herself in asserting that public schools were not doing a good enough job, though many of her remarks suggested her deeper agenda was moving away from secular schools toward religious-based education. Her family has poured vast sums into electing politicians who support her vision of public schools, which she largely succeeded doing in Detroit.

After two decades, the Detroit charter schools she championed have not improved the miserable state of Motor City education and in some ways made it worse and less accountable, the *Detroit Free Press* found. Public schools in Detroit did far better than charter schools, the newspaper reported. Among all Michigan schools, 23 percent of Detroit public school students performed in the bottom quarter. But 38 percent of Detroit charter school students were in the bottom quarter. That was one of the milder problems the newspaper uncovered in a year-long investigation published in 2014 and updated in 2017.

The newspaper's editorial page, which advocates for school choice and charter schools as one way to reform education, ran a scathing editorial about DeVos's lack of qualifications to become education secretary. Stephen Henderson, the *Free Press* editorial page editor who has followed DeVos for years, described her as "willfully impervious" to facts. Two decades of DeVos family money pushing charter schools, the editorial said, have made the Detroit school system "a laughingstock in national education circles, and a pariah among reputable charter school operators."

All DeVos accomplished, Henderson wrote, was donating so much money to politicians that she managed "to bend the conversation to her ideological convictions despite the dearth of evidence supporting them." Worst of all, the paper found no indications that DeVos "is even interested" in issues of accountability, performance, and quality in education, unswayed that few Detroit charter schools are high performers. "DeVos and her family have not been daunted by these outcomes. It's as if the reams of data showing just incremental progress or abysmal failure don't matter. Their belief in charter schools is unshakable, their resistance to systematic reforms that would improve both public and charter schools unyielding," Henderson summed up.

That background grows in significance when evaluating what DeVos said about Trump's budget for education. She said it demonstrated "a series of tough choices we have had to make when assessing the best use of taxpayer money." Those choices were to cut education in favor of militarism and policing. Think of it as jettisoning brains for bullets.

Next on the Trump chopping block were subsidized federal loans, called Stafford Loans. These loans are free of interest so long as a student remains in college, in contrast to other student loans, on which interest accrues as soon as loan proceeds are disbursed.

In a direct contradiction to his promise to limit student loan repayments to fifteen years and no more than 12.5 percent of income, Trump sought to eliminate all repayment-based-on-income subsidies for students from large or poor families or those who go into low-paid fields after graduation.

Also to be ended was loan forgiveness for students who perform several years of public service by working for government, Native American tribal organizations, or charities and faithfully make their monthly payments for ten years. Trump even proposed ending Perkins Loans, in which colleges share in the cost, a sign of their commitment to students.

These Trump cuts could reasonably be interpreted as a war on the poor, especially the nonwhite poor, which critics said all along was what should be expected from a Trump presidency despite all his campaign claims to the contrary. Brains are not distributed according to the wealth of parents. Many rich kids grow up to be intellectual, moral, or performance duds. History is rich with examples of artists, inventors, politicians, scientists, and generals who grew up in poverty that they escaped through education, leaving an important mark on the world.

Cutting avenues to success for poor, working-class, and even middle-class young people is a Make America Worse policy. The most valuable assets possessed by America—or any modern country—are the brains of its young people. The world of today and tomorrow requires rigorous development of intellectual skills of all kinds. In the twenty-first-century economy, reading, writing, and arithmetic are not even a sufficient base. In the knowledge-driven society in which we now live, the arts, law, music, philosophy, and poetry take on new meaning to deepen one's understanding. Critical-thinking skills to perceive and analyze problems not yet imagined are the building blocks of a great nation. And given the many belief systems, desires, and interests of people not just in America but around the world, developing a sophisticated understanding of other cultures is also crucial to peace and progress.

There are more dimensions to this Trump assault on the brains of the young and poor. Trump the candidate ran against Wall Street and abuses by financial interests, and said he would also champion veterans. Instead, in a move rich with irony, Trump and DeVos took up the side of the bankers against the borrowers, as we shall see in the next chapter.

Bankers Before Brains

On the campaign trail, Donald Trump spoke passionately about a crisis in student loan debt. He sought to position himself as friendlier to young strivers than Barack Obama, who was forty-two years old when he paid off the last of his student loans in January 2004.

"Students should not be asked to pay more on debt than they can afford," Trump said less than a month before the election. "Debt should not be an albatross around their necks for the rest of their lives."

The burdens of student loan debt matter not just to those who take out loans or forgo higher education because they are unwilling to go into debt. These burdens, as we shall see, impose huge costs on society. They retard economic growth in ways as powerful as they are subtle. And they distort the demographics of generations to come with the potential for profound consequences about the future of life in America.

Trump proposed that students who faithfully pay on their loans every month for fifteen years be excused from the remaining balance. Obama had proposed twenty years, George W. Bush twenty-five years. However, Trump also wanted students to turn over up to 12.5 percent of their income, not the 10 percent Obama proposed.

The net effect of the Trump shorter term but higher payment would be a 6 percent discount compared to the Obama plan, not that people attending his rallies were likely to take out a calculator or pen and paper to run the numbers. But Trump's proposal also came with one serious flaw—the 12.5 percent maximum increased the chances of defaulting on the loans, which would wipe out the forgiveness benefit.

Trump also said he would make colleges and universities reduce tuition by getting rid of administrative "bloat." He never cited any legal authority for this. Nor did he offer any data indicating how much administrative expenses could be reduced or whether there was enough waste in higher education administration to enable meaningful tuition reductions.

He also threatened to take away the charitable deduction for donors to colleges unless colleges spend more from their endowments on student aid. Trump could never do that. Only Congress makes laws. And that idea had about as much chance of becoming law as Congress had of banning college football.

Within days after the election, Trump the incoming president began parting ways with Trump the candidate. The rhetoric that made Trump appear to be a champion of indebted students stopped. Trump made appointments that showed he would take the side of the for-profit schools that charged high fees for schooling of little value and the lenders who made those schools so lucrative by selling debt to students. Trump the champion of students, the modern knight who promised to slay the financial dragon of student debt, decided to feed the dragon more of the cash students hoped would be theirs because they stayed in school to get their degrees.

Casting aside the concerns of student borrowers, and the parents and grandparents who guaranteed their loans, the Trump administration brought in people right out of the commercial colleges, which depend on student loans for nearly all of their revenue. And these appointees came armed for battle against the borrowers.

By picking Betsy DeVos to be education secretary, Trump signaled that he was never serious about what he said during the campaign. At her confirmation hearing, DeVos was unable to articulate issues that any former education secretary could have expounded on with facts and insights aplenty. Two Republican senators could not bring themselves to vote for DeVos and so she was confirmed only because Vice President Mike Pence, as presiding officer in the Senate, cast the tie-breaking vote.

Two aides brought in by DeVos fit perfectly Trump's description of the Washington swamp dwellers he had promised to flush down the drain, not elevate to positions of power and influence. Both came from jobs where their salaries depended on their skill at vanquishing student loan borrowers.

DeVos named as one of her special assistants a lawyer, Robert S. Eitel, with a solid résumé in commercial education.

Eitel took a leave of absence from his job as vice president in charge of regulatory matters for Bridgepoint Education, Inc., a California company operating for-profit colleges with 45,000 students. Student loans provided Bridgeport with more than 80 percent of its revenue and, the company disclosed in a footnote to a regulatory filing, perhaps more than 90 percent.

The company warned shareholders that it faced significant difficulties because of federal regulations adopted by the Obama administration. These regulations were designed to protect students and taxpayers from unscrupulous and worthless schools. The regulations required such schools to show that a substantial number of their students found work in the fields in which they paid to learn. Getting rid of that rule and another one limiting student loans to less than 90 percent of school revenues were top priorities for Bridgepoint and its for-profit peers.

Bridgepoint was not thriving as a business. From 2013 through 2016 its annual revenue steadily shrank with a net loss over those years of $44 million.

Potentially much more serious problems than losing money, and filling nine pages near the end of its annual disclosure report to shareholders, were some footnotes on "commitments and contingencies." These footnotes told of audits and subpoenas in actions brought by the Justice Department, the Education Department's inspector general, the attorneys general of California, Massachusetts, New York, and North Carolina, as well as several lawsuits. The litigation had been brought by investors claiming Bridgepoint executives were lining their own pockets at the expense of shareholders and other alleged dishonest behavior.

Despite the financial losses and unsettling allegations, Bridgepoint stock shot up after Election Day, from $6.35 just before voting to $15.19 in June 2017, a phenomenal 139 percent gain. This remarkable growth came despite only a sliver of increased revenue in the first half of 2017. The stock price rise suggested that speculators were betting not on a boom in profitable business, but on the Trump administration improving the business climate for the company.

DeVos assigned Eitel, during his leave of absence from Bridgepoint, to guide the rollback of federal regulations. This posed obvious conflict-of-interest issues. The top lawyer for an anticorruption nonprofit organization, Scott Amey of the Project on Government Oversight, said Eitel's position "raises considerable red flags, especially due to the fact that this company was under investigation."

Senator Elizabeth Warren, the Massachusetts Democrat who made a name for herself exposing abusive financial practices and designing the Consumer Financial Protection Bureau, asked DeVos about this. In a letter, she noted that Consumer Financial Protection Bureau had reached a $23.5 million settlement with Bridgepoint over its practices in advising students about loan repayment.

Bridgepoint had agreed to a consent order stating that Bridgepoint sales agents, called financial advisers, "made oral statements to Students about the potential costs of the loans, including that Students normally paid off Institutional Loans . . . with $25 monthly payments." Monthly payments would, of course, have had to be much larger than $25 just to cover interest.

Numerous studies have shown that most Americans woefully underestimate interest costs on loans. Many cannot calculate simple interest and even fewer understand compound interest. The for-profit colleges aimed their marketing at poor and ill-educated young people, many of whom would not be proficient at math.

Lending to students is "a largely unregulated financial market and opaque industry [that] cries out for transparency and consumer-focused regulation," Bruce H. Adams, the Connecticut Department of Banking general counsel, wrote in urging federal and state banking regulators to cooperate in ensuring that "robust enforcement authority" is exercised on behalf of students.

"Our vulnerable student borrowers . . . will do anything to chase the American Dream," Adams wrote, making them easy prey for predatory student loan firms.

Senator Warren's letter to DeVos also questioned the legality of employing Eitel and a second man, Taylor Hansen, as her special assistants. Warren, a former Harvard Law School professor, raised the specter of criminal violations of federal integrity laws. Congress prohibits government officials from any involvement on issues in which they have a financial interest. Warren noted that rather than sever his ties to Bridgepoint, Eitel was only on unpaid leave.

Eitel immediately resigned from Bridgepoint. For weeks he had worked on undoing a host of Education Department regulations under an executive order Trump issued in March. As regulatory reform officer he issued a fifty-three-page report in late May outlining a plan for sweeping reforms. The task force operated in what a variety of education interest groups, education journalists, and congressional staffers all described as extreme secrecy.

The other special assistant DeVos hired, Taylor Hansen, had been on the payroll of the largest association of for-profit schools, Career Education Colleges and Universities. As its lobbyist, Hansen sought to roll back rules, especially a "gainful employment" rule that vexed for-profit schools. This Obama regulation was intended to weed out schools that were outright scams or trained students for careers in areas where there were no jobs. Getting rid of it was a top priority for the lobbying arm of the commercial schools.

News reports documenting in vivid detail the mistreatment of student loan borrowers by the lenders and their collection agents had been widely reported in print and broadcast for several years before the 2016 presidential campaign. These articles included images of canceled checks and other documentation showing that student borrowers had made their monthly payments on time, or obtained forbearances, and in some cases entirely paid off the debts. Yet they were being hounded because the lenders insisted that money was still owed.

To rein in these abuses, the Obama administration instituted a formal rulemaking. In most regulatory proceedings only the affected industry and executives from individual companies, along with state-level regulators, file comments. But in this case more than ten thousand Americans wrote to express their anger and frustration. These comments overwhelmingly favored regulating the lenders, especially giving relief to borrowers when the lenders either refused to acknowledge payments that had been made or to abide by the terms of loan modification agreements.

Obtaining forbearance from bankers had been a Trump specialty for a quarter century. No one knew better than he that banks will rework the terms of the loan to help borrowers burdened with more debt than they can handle or who are the unfortunate victims of events beyond their control like the Great Recession that cost nearly nine million Americans their jobs.

At campaign rallies, Trump said a big problem he would address as president was that after taking out loans and earning their degrees many students discovered "there are no good jobs." Six weeks after becoming president, though, the Trump administration delayed implementing the Obama era rule requiring for-profit schools to show that a significant number of their students found "gainful employment."

The Education Department granted the for-profit colleges and loan servicers this favor the day that Senator Warren's letter arrived. The favor was especially valuable to the biggest student loan servicer, which in its financial statements disclosed that it stood to gain perhaps $15 million per year if the Obama era rule was reversed. That servicer just happened to have been run until the start of 2017 by Bill Hansen, father of DeVos special assistant Taylor Hansen.

DeVos, two months into the Trump administration, issued a letter saying, in effect, that the federal Education Department would not protect student loan borrowers when lenders refused to honor their signed agreements modifying loan payments. The Education Department simply "will not require compliance with the interpretations" of the Obama administration that such agreements be honored, the letter said.

Under laws passed by Congress, regulations are not casual words, like tweets, that can be ignored. Regulations are indeed interpretations of how laws will be enforced, and they carry the force of law if they have been properly, in legal parlance, *promulgated*. The Obama era rule had been promulgated; the Trump era policy had not.

Senator Warren, the former Harvard law professor, in a stinging letter told DeVos that she had no legal authority to ignore any regulation. If the Trump administration wanted to change the regulation, it had to follow the Administrative Procedure Act procedures. That law required formal notice, time for public comment, and an opportunity for all interested parties to be heard. These requirements are rooted in the First Amendment's guarantee of the right to petition the government for a redress of grievances.

DeVos's letter also drew a sharp rebuke from 130 members of Congress, all Democrats. They pointed out that her letter benefits lenders who had abused veterans, whom Trump said he would always look out for and help. It also noted that at her confirmation hearing, DeVos said the Education Department "should to do everything possible to ensure that our students are getting excellent servicing of their student loans." They said her letter contradicted her testimony and "signals an unwillingness to support and safeguard the best interests of borrowers."

"Your decision to rescind these memos—including the guidance making servicers' past performance and record of compliance with the law the most important non-cost factor in the evaluation—will put millions of borrowers and taxpayers at risk. Without accounting for past performance, federal contracts will be open to bidders that have previously violated state or federal consumer protection laws, mistreated members of our military, and consistently ignored the needs of their borrowers," the senators and representatives wrote.

DeVos never acknowledged the letter, a practice widespread in the Trump administration.

Maura Healey, the Massachusetts attorney general, interpreted the nonresponsiveness of DeVos as both high-handed and a sign that the Trump administration has little to no regard for the law. Healey filed a lawsuit to block what she called the "unlawful rescission" of the rule protecting diligent borrowers from financial abuse. Healy persuaded the attorneys general from seventeen other states and the District of Columbia to join her.

Federal law "does not permit the [Education] Department to delay" implementing a properly adopted "regulation in order to work on a replacement," the attorneys general argued. They said the rationale DeVos put forth for delaying the rule was "mere pretext," an excuse to evade following the existing rule until the department went through the legally mandated steps to adopt a new regulation.

They also argued that DeVos was delivering a hugely lucrative favor to loan servicers and the related commercial schools that charged a lot and delivered little. The attorneys general, all Democrats, said the "borrower rule" was "designed to hold abusive post-secondary institutions accountable for their misconduct and to relieve their students from federal loan indebtedness incurred as a result of that misconduct."

Their lawsuit noted that for-profit schools are very expensive. For each dollar community colleges charged, the lawsuit said, for-profit schools typically charged $4.50.

"For-profit schools have directed their marketing toward low-income and minority students, particularly low-income women of color," the attorneys general said. They noted that just a tenth of college students attend commercial schools, but they take out a quarter of all student loans.

The DeVos letter was suspect for another reason. DeVos was an investor in companies that seek to profit from education. Among them was LMF WF Portfolio. It finances a firm that collects student loans. The bigger the debts owed, a figure that would increase significantly if the Obama era regulation was ignored, the greater the value of her investment. DeVos had more than $1 million invested with that firm, although that was only a small part of her overall portfolio.

DeVos had to divest, but people close to her did not. And she had to divest only her financial holding, not any allegiance to people like herself who had enjoyed profits from practices that exploited poor people trying to better their lives.

DeVos's haughty dismissal of a properly adopted regulation, and the complete turnabout from what candidate Trump promised to what President Trump did would have surprised no one who had read Trump's campaign book.

In *Great Again: How to Fix Our Crippled America*, Trump wrote that "we can't forgive these [student] loans." It was a clear signal that he had no interest in allowing overburdened students to repudiate their debts as he had done when he got his bankers to permit him an allowance of $450,000 a month of personal spending money in 1990 when he accumulated massive debts.

Trump's book did say, "We should take steps to help students." The way to do that, the book said, was to make sure the federal government did not profit from these loans. As for abuses by loan servicers and mendacious sales pitches to get students to take out loans, there was not a word in the book.

By favoring bankers over borrowers, the Trump administration is punishing not only current students but also the working adults who have been struggling to settle their student loan debts and build their lives after getting their education. Behind them is a generation of workers-to-be who may never be able to sit in a college classroom if funding is cut to every program that might allow them to attend. The long-term cost to the American economy could be devastating if many thousands of our brightest minds are shunted into low-wage, low-skilled jobs.

PART VII

LAW AND ORDER, VETERANS, RACE AND GUNS, IMMIGRATION

Above the Law

In late August of 2017, Donald Trump flew to Phoenix to hold a rally for the 2020 election. To those who heard his entire speech and understood the context, his remarks raised troubling, even frightening new concerns about the future of America as a democracy under law.

Phoenix signaled an important change in Trumpian rhetoric that revealed just how far his contempt for the rule of law could go. He replaced his many wink-wink and dog-whistle comments—subtext intended to be understood by his fellow racists, but not most people—with a rhetorical bullhorn. He aimed the message at two audiences. One consisted of his die-hard supporters, some of whom told television journalists that any effort to remove Trump via impeachment would be met with violence, perhaps even a civil war.

The other audience consisted of Republicans in Congress who might be thinking that Trump was a danger to the nation or the Republican Party—and needed to go. Journalists and anyone who might challenge Trump also came in for a not at all subtle threat that he could pursue them using the powers of the presidency, if only to harass them.

Given the rapidly advancing Russia investigation by special prosecutor Robert Mueller, Trump's need to signal Capitol Hill Republicans that they had better stay quiet or face the wrath of Trump voters in 2018 was pressing. That Trump's popular support was down to about a third of all voters mattered far less than the vast majority of Republicans who still stood firmly with him. They represented plenty of votes to sway Republican primary elections to those who vowed fealty to Trump and away from anyone who challenged his fitness to hold office.

While not using these words in Phoenix, Trump articulated clearly that his administration stood for two standards of justice, separate and unequal. One standard was for those in positions of power who shared his views and took actions he liked, even if they were unlawful. The other standard was for everyone else. Those who were with him would be protected, if necessary with pardons or clemency. They would not be held accountable for lawless behavior, no matter how egregious, provided it was in Trump's personal or political interests to shield them. His support for former sheriff Joe Arpaio, whose pardon Trump had hinted at for days, exemplified Trump's protection of those he liked or whose allegiance he needed to shield himself from the Mueller probe.

The other standard of justice was for those who opposed Trump and found themselves in trouble in any way. That group was sent a simple message: expect no quarter from the Trump administration, which intended to use every tool at its disposal to vanquish those he perceived as unworthy or, worse, as enemies.

In Phoenix, Trump quickly riled up the crowd on behalf of Arpaio by attacking the legitimacy of the law enforcement people who had brought him to justice through years of diligent work, culminating in a three-week trial for criminal contempt of court for brazenly violating a federal judge's order again and again. Criminal convictions for contempt of court are rare both because such conduct is extraordinary and because there are so many ways to create the appearance of lawful compliance without actually doing so. Trump, though, made it seem as if Arpaio was railroaded.

"So, was Sheriff Joe convicted for doing his job?" Trump asked. The crowd responded with shouts of "yes!"

The responses grew louder when Trump went on to declare his intent to pardon Arpaio. Playing coy with the audience, Trump said, "I won't do it tonight because I don't want to cause any controversy." He waited for the applause to die down before adding, "I'll make a prediction: I think he's going to be just fine."

By pardoning Arpaio, Trump signaled those who might turn against him to avoid long prison terms for their own crimes that so long as they are with Trump, so long as he trusts in their loyalty to him, he wants them to think they are safe.

The president then launched into an angry and unscripted denunciation of journalists. Less than a month after taking office, he had declared that journalists are "the enemy of the people. SICK!" As a candidate, he said that no one should be allowed to publish stories about him that he did not agree with, a position at complete odds with the First Amendment to the Constitution, with its prohibition against government blocking the press.

"It's time to expose the crooked media deceptions. They're very dishonest people," Trump continued. "The only people giving a platform to these hate groups is the media itself and the fake news."

Following up his wink-wink promise to pardon Arpaio in the future with an attack on journalists made perfect sense from Trump's perspective, though it was not at all obvious to casual observers. What would discredit an Arpaio pardon would be widespread knowledge of what Arpaio had done, which would happen only if national journalists reported the facts about his decades of lawless behavior.

Arpaio was criminally convicted for not doing his job. Instead of enforcing the law under the Constitution's rules, Arpaio ran roughshod over the rights of people based on their appearance or accent. But it was thumbing his nose at a federal judge who had ruled that he must stop his illegal roundups, his public boasting that he would never obey, that made him a convicted criminal. And that was not what Trump wanted his audience, or anyone else, to know.

Trump then tried to call into question the legitimacy of the trial in which Arpaio was convicted of criminal contempt of court. "He should have had a jury," Trump said.

It was Arpaio's choice to be tried by Judge Susan R. Bolton rather than a jury, but to those not familiar with how the criminal justice system works, Trump left the impression that Arpaio had been railroaded.

Arpaio tried to purge Phoenix of Latinos, not just people who entered the United States without permission. "They hate me, the Hispanic community, because they're afraid they're going to be arrested. And they're all leaving town, so I think we're doing something good, if they're leaving," Arpaio said in a 2009 television appearance.

In 2008, he referred to one of his jails as "my concentration camp." Just as Trump denies saying things despite videos recording his words, Arpaio later denied at a press conference that he said that despite videotape of his remarks. In a Trumpian move, Arpaio turned the tables on the reporter who brought this up, fabricating a story that "concentration camp" was part of an accusation others concocted to harm him.

In a 2001 interview with the network news program *60 Minutes*, Arpaio proudly confirmed that his office spent $1.15 per day on food for each jail dog, but only 90 or 95 cents for inmate food. He said he was protecting taxpayers.

That was far from the worst of it. From 1995 through 2015, sheriff's records examined by the *Phoenix New Times* showed that 157 prisoners died in custody. That was a death rate far out of line with other large jails. A fourth of the dead were reported as suicides. The sheriff's office listed 34 people as simply found dead in jail, 37 dying in the county hospital with no explanation why, and 39 as suicides by hanging.

Not on the official list of deaths was Deborah Braillard, a diabetic who pleaded for insulin. Jailers waived off her requests, saying she was just a heroin addict kicking a habit. When Braillard grew visibly sick, fellow inmates pleaded on her behalf to no avail as over the hours her condition deteriorated from vomiting to convulsions to coma to death.

Braillard's death from denial of medical care was no isolated case. Arpaio's jail staff often denied medical treatment or delayed it for hours. Women in childbirth were shackled to beds, even those being held before trial on suspicion for nonviolent crimes. At least one woman's child was stillborn because deputies refused medical care. Women prisoners, more than a thousand of whom over the years were pregnant, got their water from a well contaminated with mouse feces, which can carry the *Toxoplasma gondii* parasite and thus put their fetuses at risk of blindness and lifelong ill health.

Sometimes Arpaio's department fabricated reasons to investigate and, in some cases, obtain criminal charges against those who questioned his conduct. One Arpaio critic, Israel Correa, said he was arrested when he could not produce his driver's license fast enough to please a deputy who had stopped him. His said his declarations that he was born in Arizona were derisively dismissed as he was handcuffed and hauled off to jail. When he got his wallet back he said $2,000 was missing. It was not the only complaint by Hispanics that Arpaio's deputies robbed them.

In a chilling indication of conduct that Trump regards as legitimate, Arpaio's deputies arrested or obtained criminal charges against Mary Rose Wilcox, a former county supervisor; Gary Donahoe, a superior court judge; and Dan Saban, a candidate for Arpaio's job. There were also middle-of-

the-night raids to roust from their homes Mike Lacey and Jim Larkin. Together, they owned the *Phoenix New Times,* the weekly newspaper that had
fearlessly documented Arpaio's misconduct for years. Taxpayers eventually
paid $3.75 million to settle the wrongful arrest case brought by Lacey and
Larkin. Don Stapley, a former county supervisor, received $3 million in an
unrelated case over false charges.

Two weeks after Arpaio was found guilty, Trump started focusing the
thoughts of those who would attend his Phoenix rally the next week. It
began with an off-air interview with a television pundit working for Fox
News, the reliably Trump-supporting cable channel.

"Is there anyone in local law enforcement who has done more to crack
down on illegal immigration than Sheriff Joe?" Trump asked Fox's Gregg
Jarrett. "He has protected people from crimes and saved lives. He doesn't
deserve to be treated this way." Jarrett said Trump also told him, "I am
seriously considering a pardon for Sheriff Arpaio. He has done a lot in the
fight against illegal immigration. He's a great American patriot and I hate
to see what has happened to him."

Not a skeptical word from Jarrett, a lawyer, who on Fox's Sean Hannity
show told only part of the story. Jarrett called the case a "political prosecution that began in the Obama administration," speaking more like Arpaio's
lawyer than a news analyst.

The case began during the George W. Bush administration and the
decision to prosecute for criminal contempt came during the Obama era.
It was during the Trump administration that Arpaio was tried for criminal
contempt of court and convicted.

That Trump is thinking about using pardons to compromise the
Mueller investigation was beyond doubt after the Phoenix rally. While the
pardon power appears to have no limits, other than using it to prevent impeachment, Trump's willingness to use it is fraught with peril for himself
and the Republic. Using pardons strategically could seriously hamper the
Russia and other investigations.

Pardons are for "offenses against the United States." By accepting a pardon, a person admits guilt for committing the crime. Anyone is free to accept or reject a pardon, as a principled person might who believes that he
or she was innocent and had been wrongly convicted. There are plenty of
examples of people who refused to say they committed a murder, rape, or

other crime just to get out of prison, even if it meant staying behind bars until they died.

Anyone who accepts a Trump pardon, including Arpaio, is admitting he committed offenses against the federal government. But there is a way around this. The Constitution also gives the president the power to grant reprieves, such as letting a prisoner get out of jail early, without settling the issue of guilt or innocence. Such clemency is not optional. If the president orders someone freed from prison or otherwise relieved of criminal punishment, that person cannot say no.

Pardons can be issued preemptively, before any criminal charges are brought, as President Gerald Ford did when he relieved Richard Nixon and the country of the prospect of Nixon being tried for a host of felonies, including conspiracy and income tax evasion (for which Nixon's lawyer did go to prison).

That explains why strategically issuing pardons and reprieves would likely occur late, not early, in the Mueller probe and those by House and Senate committees. The problem issuing pardons poses for Trump is that anyone who accepts a pardon loses his or her Fifth Amendment right against self-incrimination. If you have been pardoned, you cannot be tried and therefore must testify in criminal proceedings and before Congress. Lying in such proceedings, including falsely claiming you cannot recall something, subjects you to prosecution for that criminal conduct.

Nothing in the Constitution would prevent Trump from issuing serial pardons, either. Thus, he could pardon someone who had evidence that Trump would not want used against him, and if the person was indicted for refusing to testify, he could, as with Arpaio, pardon them again even before they were found guilty of contempt of court.

Presidential pardons apply only to "offenses against the United States." This means that state prosecutors are free to bring charges for crimes within their jurisdiction, which helps explain why Mueller's team is working with Eric Schneiderman, the New York State attorney general. Should Trump pardon, for example, his sons or his son-in-law, or Paul Manafort, his former campaign manager, or others, Schneiderman would be free to bring state level charges. To appreciate the importance of the shift Trump made during his Phoenix rally for the 2020 campaign from wink-wink to open dismissal of the rule of law, we need to go back and review what Trump said a month earlier to police on Long Island, remarks he harked back to in Phoenix. He made a speech full of gore, urging official lawlessness, with anecdotes that have no basis in fact and may well have been delusional.

Trump focused his Long Island talk on La Mara Salvatrucha, a Latino gang sometimes called MS-13.

"We're going to restore safety to our streets and peace to our communities, and we're going to destroy the vile criminal cartel MS-13 and many other gangs," he said. Trump linked the gang to all illegal immigrants from south of the border even though many MS-13 gang members are American citizens or lawful residents. In doing so he blurred distinctions, suggesting—even if unintentionally—that all Latinos in America are at least suspect.

"MS-13 is particularly violent," Trump continued. "They don't like shooting people because it's too quick, it's too fast. I was reading—one of these animals was caught—in explaining, they like to knife them and cut them, and let them die slowly because that way it's more painful, and they enjoy watching that much more. These are animals."

Seven times Trump called the gang members animals. Vicious as any criminal may be, one of our great historical advances has been treating all people as human beings and applying the rule of law even to those who commit despicable acts. Under the Constitution that Trump swore to faithfully uphold, every individual human being is innocent, even after being arrested and charged, until proved guilty beyond a reasonable doubt. Animals, on the other hand, have no such rights. A vicious dog can be shot on the spot.

Trump's bloody description of murder by torture for pleasure was not one of his frequent fabricated or delusional comments. There was indeed an MS-13 case that fit his description. But it was a crime of passion. A teenage love triangle in Virginia ended with a furious stabbing, followed by arrests. It was, in other words, not the kind of crime that should frighten people not involved with the gang. And it was not the kind of crime that any degree of law enforcement can prevent.

The rest of the speech strayed farther from the truth. "We have your backs—believe me—we have your backs 100 percent. Not like the old days.

Not like the old days." This was another of his many remarks suggesting that Democrats in general and especially Barack Obama were antipolice and supported criminals, a charge that surveys show has gained some currency with the public despite the lack of any factual basis.

MS-13 operated, Trump continued, "because of weak political leadership, weak leadership, weak policing, and in many cases because the police weren't allowed to do their job. I've met police that are great police that aren't allowed to do their job because they have a pathetic mayor or a mayor [who] doesn't know what's going on. . . . But hopefully—certainly in the country, those days are over. You may have a little bit longer to wait. But from now on, we're going to enforce our laws, protect our borders, and support our police like our police have never been supported before. We're going to support you like you've never been supported before."

Again, there is no evidence that any mayor has held police back from investigating crimes by MS-13 or that police were "weak" in performing their duties. But Trump has a long and well-documented history of making stuff up and, when called on it, asserting that someone told him or he saw it on the Internet or he never said it.

Trump went on to promise military-grade weapons for police. Resuming his gory theme, he said MS-13 members "slash them with machetes, and they stab them with knives. They have transformed peaceful parks and beautiful, quiet neighborhoods into bloodstained killing fields. They're animals." The references to machetes had an interesting antecedent.

In Phoenix, a middle-aged black man sat right behind Trump so the cameras captured him, as they did at many Trump events. "TRUMP & Republicans Are Not Racist" was stenciled on his T-shirt.

He goes by the name Michael the Black Man, but when he was known as Maurice Woodside, he was part of the Temple of Love, a Miami cult whose leader had drifters grabbed at random and killed, their ears taken as trophies. Perceived enemies of the cult were tortured to death. Sometimes they were slowly beheaded with dull machetes. The cult leader and most of his top aides were convicted of a host of crimes, but the jury acquitted Woodside after he took the stand, sang a childish song about being a sheep, and offered nonsense statements. One of the prosecutors called it acquittal by mercy. Interviewed after the Phoenix rally by Jon Hotchkiss of factbox.tv, Woodside delivered one of his many strange monologues, saying among other bizarre statements that Hillary Clinton keeps slaves.

That Trump denounces MS-13 and calls its members animals yet repeatedly has Woodside seated squarely behind him at rallies, shows how Trump manipulates the public into thinking he enjoys broad support among African Americans and that he has a firm line on dealing with those who have engaged in violence.

"I spoke to parents, incredible parents," Trump told the Long Island police. "I got to know so many parents of children that were so horribly killed—burned to death, beaten to death, just the worst kind of death you can ever—stuffed in barrels." There is not a single reported case in Long Island or the rest of the United States of children being burned to death or beaten to death and stuffed into barrels by gang members, nor of Trump ever having spoken to parents of victims of such crimes. This paralleled his claims that many of the people who died when the Twin Towers collapsed in 2001 were his friends. Trump did not attend a single funeral, as would be expected if Trump considered anyone who died that day a friend.

Long Island was then described by Trump, who grew up in Queens at the urban western portion of the island, as a war zone, a description that no one among the nearly eight million people who live on Long Island would recognize.

"One by one, we're liberating our American towns," the president said. "Can you believe that I'm saying that? I'm talking about liberating our towns. This is like I'd see in a movie: They're liberating the town, like in the old Wild West, right? We're liberating our towns. I never thought I'd be standing up here talking about liberating the towns on Long Island where I grew up, but that's what you're doing."

No one laughed at the ridiculousness of what he said. None of the uniformed officers standing behind Trump even rolled their eyes or looked at their shoes. Many news accounts gave it passing mention or none, so accustomed had politics reporters become to Trump's fashioning stories out of whole cloth.

In case anyone missed the message that because of these crimes—real or imaginary—police should ignore the Constitution, Trump offered up his preferred way of handling gang members after an arrest. "When you see these thugs being thrown into the back of a paddy wagon—you just see them thrown in, rough—I said, please don't be too nice. Like when you guys put somebody in the car and you're protecting their head, you know, the way you put their hand over? Like, don't hit their head and they've just killed somebody—don't hit their head. I said, you can take the hand away, okay?"

The "don't be too nice" remark drew hearty laughter from the assembled police officers. But combined with the last remark it was too much for the police brass in Suffolk County, where Trump spoke. "As a department, we do not and will not tolerate roughing up of prisoners," the Suffolk County police headquarters soon tweeted. They may have reacted in part because the department had had its independence taken away, forcing it to operate under the aegis of the U.S. Justice Department, because of a history of discriminating against Latinos, including failure to investigate hate crimes.

From New York to New Orleans to Los Angeles, police chiefs denounced Trump's remarks on mistreating prisoners, some saying that even if intended in jest, they were utterly inappropriate. Many expressed disgust at the applause from uniformed officers standing behind the president. The International Association of Chiefs of Police criticized Trump without naming him. It said treating everyone, including criminal suspects, with "dignity and respect" is "the bedrock principle behind the concepts of procedural justice and police legitimacy."

A stronger message came from the Police Foundation, which encourages research to develop more effective law enforcement strategies to deal with crime. Its president invoked a powerful word to suggest that Trump was profoundly immoral and malevolent. "We cannot support any commentary—in sincerity or jest—that undermines the trust that our communities place in us to protect and serve," said Jim Bueermann, a retired California police chief. "That is what separates us from evil as we follow the rule of law."

Chuck Rosenberg, a career prosecutor who was acting head of the Drug Enforcement Administration, sent an email to its more than ten thousand employees telling them, "The President, in remarks delivered yesterday in New York, condoned police misconduct regarding the treatment of individuals placed under arrest by law enforcement. . . . I write because we have an obligation to speak out when something is wrong. . . . We must earn and keep the public trust and continue to hold ourselves to the very highest standards. Ours is an honorable profession and, so, we will always act honorably."

Two months later Rosenberg resigned, telling associates that he feared Trump lacked respect for the rule of law.

Not abusing prisoners also helps solve crimes, although Trump has never shown any understanding of how police do their jobs. It is citizens who help police solve crimes by coming forward with information and physical evidence that detectives then assemble, connecting dots to present a case to prosecutors. Without community trust and cooperation, criminals can and do get away with their deeds. Further, police who rough up suspects risk suspension, firing, and even indictment, while the taxpayers can be hit with lawsuits requiring costly litigation or settlements.

The logical implication of Trump's remarks is that he would repeal the laws, procedural rules, and moral standards that protect the rights of everyone, including suspects. That is how it is done in Russia, whose autocratic leader Trump praises at every opportunity as a great leader. He has similarly praised the autocratic rulers of the Philippines, Saudi Arabia, and Turkey, three other nations whose leaders keep their people in line.

Trump's clear statements characterizing members of MS-13 and other criminal gangs as bloodthirsty savages unworthy of respect for their Constitutional rights fit perfectly with the Arizona address that left no doubt Trump hopes to create an America with two standards of justice, one for his supporters and one for everyone else. His first federal budget proposal supported this interpretation.

Trump wants the federal government to become a much more militaristic and paramilitary policing organization while making drastic cuts in the civilian workforce, a story no mainstream news organization covered until I broke the news at DCReport.org. The budget memo referred to increasing spending only on militarism and enforcing immigration laws as part of "broader efforts to streamline government by ensuring that the federal government spends precious taxpayer dollars only on worthwhile policies, and in the most efficient, effective manner." Civilian agencies

were instructed not even to ask for more money. Instead, they were ordered to identify programs for reduction or elimination so money could
be shifted to the military and policing.

Trump never told those at the rally that he had tried to stop the Arpaio prosecution. He telephoned Attorney General Jeff Sessions to intercede, just as he had asked James Comey to drop the FBI investigation of
retired General Michael Flynn, who was Trump's first national security
adviser. Sessions, like Comey, declined. Sessions even told Trump that his
request would be improper, three people with knowledge of the call told
The Washington Post.

While Sessions has never been a friend to minorities or criminal suspects, he knew that the Justice Department is supposed to be independent
of the president for many reasons. Furthermore, stopping a criminal prosecution, calling off an FBI investigation, or initiating one for political or
personal reasons could be an impeachable offense and, after removal from
office, prosecutable as a felony.

Under long-standing protocols, White House staff generally cannot even talk directly to Justice Department lawyers about potential or
pending cases, except in some matters of national security. In 2007, when
George W. Bush was president, the Justice Department issued precise
rules limiting contact on matters civil and criminal as well as pardons.
Most inquiries must go through high-level Justice Department officials
and the White House counsel. The guidelines state that the purpose is to
ensure the "president's ability to perform his constitutional obligation to
'take care that the laws be faithfully executed' while ensuring that there is
public confidence that the laws of the United States are administered and
enforced in an impartial manner." The guidelines also require those seeking pardons to have served much of their sentence and to express remorse.
Arpaio had yet to be sentenced. He might have gotten off with probation.
Given Arpaio's age—he was eighty-five—and the fact that he was out of
office, it was unlikely he would have gotten the maximum of six months
behind bars. But Trump didn't wait to see what punishment would be imposed, because relief for Sheriff Joe was not the point of the pardon; sending signals was.

The Constitution does not require that presidents follow or even give
a nod to the Justice Department guidelines. But presidents who have bent

or ignored the guidelines have touched off firestorms of criticism, including from Jeff Sessions. As a Republican senator from Alabama with a long pedigree of hard-line law-and-order positions, Sessions expressed outrage in 2014 not over a pardon, but a new policy outlining who could ask for clemency to reduce a prison term.

President Obama had decided that nonviolent drug offenders could apply for clemency because he thought many such sentences were excessive, especially sentences for crack cocaine. Congress had enacted long mandatory sentences for amounts of the illegal drug that in powdered form would have seen offenders released in a jiffy. Crack was much more widely ingested by black Americans; whites preferred powder.

"An alarming abuse of the pardon power," Sessions declared. "If this latest unilateral action becomes the norm, then what kind of Pandora's box has the president opened? Can a president pardon all people convicted of financial fraud, or identity theft, or unlawful re-entry into the country, or any category of crime when Congress does not act as the executive wishes?"

Sessions also said that "to unilaterally determine that a sentence was unjustified simply because the president disagrees with the underlying criminal justice policy is a thumb in the eye of the law enforcement officers, prosecutors, defense attorneys, judges, court and prison personnel who put time and resources into these cases."

Given the standard Sessions set for changing the rules on merely asking for mercy, the Arpaio pardon should have ignited the attorney general's fury. He said nothing.

Wounding the Veterans

Visit the White House webpage titled "Making Our Military Strong Again" and you will read that "the Trump Administration will rebuild our military and do everything it can to make sure our veterans get the care they deserve."

Then come these firm promises:

Let us never forget that our military is comprised of heroic people. We must also ensure that we have the best medical care, education and support for our military service members and their families— both when they serve, and when they return to civilian life.

We will get our veterans the care they need wherever and whenever they need it. There should be no more long drives. No more wait lists or scheduling backlogs. No more excessive red tape. Just the care and support our veterans have earned through sacrifice and service to our country. The Trump Administration will transform the Department of Veterans Affairs to meet the needs of 21st century service members and of our female veterans. Our reforms will begin with firing the corrupt and incompetent VA executives who let our veterans down, modernizing the bureaucracy, and empowering the doctors and nurses to ensure our veterans receive the best care available in a timely manner.

Under the Trump Administration, America will meet its commitments to our veterans.

That breathtaking commitment delighted millions of veterans and their relatives who voted for Trump. The webpage is consistent with the many specific and repeated promises the candidate made to veterans, especially about long wait times to get medical care at the 150 Veterans Administration hospitals and more than eight hundred VA clinics. The Department of Veterans Affairs, the fifth largest federal agency, is authorized by Congress to spend $180 billion during the 2017 budget year, a sum almost equal to the budget of Turkey, a country with 80 million people. But even that sum was not nearly enough to promptly and fully serve the nation's more than 23 million military veterans.

More than 2.3 million veterans were receiving disability benefits in 2000. Then came 9/11. Less than a month later, troops invaded Afghanistan, followed in 2003 by the invasion of Iraq. By 2015 almost 4.2 million veterans received disability benefits, in large part because modern medicine saved many causalities from wounds that would have been fatal in wars past. In World War II for every airman, sailor, and soldier killed in combat, 2.3 wounded survived. This ratio grew to nearly nine survivors for each combat death in Afghanistan and Iraq.

Anyone who paid attention after those undeclared wars as well as the 1991 Gulf War knew that Congress was not giving the VA enough money to fulfill the promises Congress and various presidents had made. Trump's message was like a wonderful song to those frustrated by the slowness in getting health care, fighting for disability benefits, and getting lost in the VA bureaucracy.

These problems persisted even though the VA's total budget, adjusted for inflation, nearly tripled between the 2000 and 2017 budgets. Congress not only failed to fully adjust spending to keep pace with the higher survival ratios from combat wounds, it also did not consider the soaring costs of technology-based medical care and the longer lives disabled veterans were likely to have provided they got proper medical care and monthly disability checks sufficient to make their lives passably pleasant. Among these were the costs of mental and emotional trauma, known as posttraumatic stress disorder, PTSD, a condition heightened by the nature of twenty-first-century conflicts with women and children suicide bombers, sudden attacks on American troops by ostensibly friendly local forces, and the lack of clear front lines and combat zones.

Candidate Trump repeatedly promised voters he would make sure veterans got all the help they had earned and without long delays to be seen by doctors even if that meant paying for private physicians instead of VA staff.

Trump had no military experience, though he sometimes told audiences about attending a New York military academy. His father sent him there the summer he turned thirteen because he was constantly getting into trouble. Fred Trump believed his son needed discipline, his son later said. When the Vietnam War loomed, some men of wealthy families who could have pulled strings to escape service volunteered, notably future Democratic Party presidential candidates Al Gore and John Kerry. Trump got deferments as a college student. When those ran out he got a medical deferment. His doctor said Trump was unfit for service because of a bone spur in one foot. During the presidential campaign, Trump said he could not recall which foot.

But Trump did not just avoid military service, he repeatedly denigrated those who went to war. During one of his many guest spots on the radio show of Howard Stern, the "shock jock" who specializes in crude commentary on women's bodies, Trump compared not contracting a venereal disease from his sexual conquests to serving in combat. "If you have any guilt about not having gone to Vietnam, we have our own Vietnam. It's called the dating game. Dating is like being in Vietnam. You're the equivalent of a soldier going over to Vietnam."

Four years later, in 1997, Stern again asked him about sexually transmitted diseases. This time Trump compared himself even more favorably to soldiers in combat. "It's amazing, I can't even believe it. I've been so lucky in terms of that whole world, it is a dangerous world out there. It's like Vietnam, sort of. It is my personal Vietnam. I feel like a great and very brave solider."

In the early 1980s Trump agreed to be co-chair of the New York Vietnam Veterans Memorial Commission, but after the press announcement he attended only two meetings, one of them when he was accompanied by a reporter writing a magazine profile of him. Asked about this by writer Lois Romano in 1984, Trump said he would resign from the board. "They're very small thinkers," he said of the other trustees. "They're stockbrokers that were in Vietnam and they don't have 'it.'"

An early sign that Trump's lack of military experience, combined with his lack of interest in reading anything not about him, would limit his knowledge of veterans' issues emerged when he made a campaign stop at the Retired American Warriors Political Action Committee in Herndon, Virginia. A congenial moderator asked about services for veterans, especially those who suffer with post-traumatic stress.

"When you talk about the mental health problems when people come back from war and combat, and they see things that maybe a lot of the folks in this room have seen many times over, and you're strong and you can handle it, but a lot of people can't handle it," Trump said. The implication of his remark—that those suffering from post-traumatic stress are weak—prompted many veterans' group leaders and individuals to call Trump insensitive, ill-informed, or ignorant. But they did not abandon him.

What kept many veterans' groups behind Trump were the promises he made moments after the ill-considered comment on the psychological effects of modern war, promises he repeated in the months that followed. Near the top of his White House to-do list, Trump said, would be mental health services for vets. "When you hear the 22 suicides a day that should never be. That should never be," Trump said. "So, we're going to be addressing that very strongly and the whole mental health issue is going to be a very important issue when I take over and the V.A. is going to be fixed in so many ways but that's going to be one of the ways we're going to help. And that's in many respects going to be the number one thing we have to do."

Two months earlier he had pledged to another veterans' organization that he would personally solve problems veterans had with the VA.

"I will create a private White House hotline," Trump announced. Then he shifted verbal gears to lighten the moment, saying, "This could keep me very busy at night, folks. This will take the place of Twitter." That drew mild laughter.

Resuming his pitch, Trump promised that the White House hotline would be "answered by a real person 24 hours a day to make sure that no valid complaint about the VA ever falls through the cracks. I will instruct my staff that if a valid complaint is not acted upon" it then must be "brought directly to me—and I want to have it—will bring it directly to me, and I will pick up the phone personally and get it completed and get it taken care of."

The promise of immediate and personal action turned out to be just another Trump con. More than six months after taking office, no hotline had been set up inside the White House or at any other government facility. The White House said it did not know when a hotline might be activated. The VA public affairs office said nothing. Worse, Trump's budget proposed not more money to care for veterans, but cuts.

Trump's administration did act on some VA promises. In June Trump signed into law the Veterans Affairs Accountability and Whistleblower Protection Act, one of his very few legislative accomplishments. The law made it much easier for the man whose signature television line was "You're fired" to discharge VA employees. The new law drew a mixed response, hailed because it made removal of corrupt as well as poor performers easy, but denounced by those who feared it would be used to slash VA staff in future Trump budget cuts. Some feared it was just the first step in removing the civil service rules that for more than a century had encouraged dedicated professionals to work for our government by insulating them from patronage politics.

While Trump promised that veterans would get all the care they had earned with their military service, his first budget showed otherwise. He proposed spending on mental health care and assistance for homeless veterans at the same level as Obama's last budget, which means a slight cut due to inflation.

The biggest cut Trump proposed was ending a benefit for disabled veterans once they reach the minimum age for Social Security benefits. These veterans would see their income plunge from almost $35,000 annually to less than $13,000 if the Trump plan becomes law.

Many veterans rated less than 100 percent disabled cannot get anyone to hire them because their injuries from combat or accidents severely limit their capacity to work. Under our government's Individual Unemployability program, veterans at least 60 percent disabled can get the same disability benefits as those rated 100 percent disabled. Being unable to work also means they cannot qualify for pensions or save from their earnings for retirement. The Trump budget calls for ending veterans' unemployability benefits as soon as a veteran becomes eligible for Social Security, asserting that receiving both amounts to a double dip at the expense of taxpayers. The change would save $3.2 billion in the 2018 budget year and much more in future years. But annual income could fall by as much as $22,200 per veteran with an average cut of more than $14,000, not exactly the song candidate Trump sang in his numerous appearances before veterans groups.

Congressman Mark Takano, a California Democrat, raised the issue of how much fear the budget cuts had put into the hearts of disabled veterans when Trump's secretary for Veterans Affairs, David Shulkin, appeared before the House Veterans' Affairs committee. "If you end the payments to veterans like this, don't you risk plunging them into poverty?" Takano asked at a May hearing.

In seeking to reduce federal spending, Shulkin said the Trump administration was "looking at where we can make the program more responsible." It was a not well considered response given that, as Takano noted, the 225,000 veterans who would have their benefits cut in the first year could not work, could not save for retirement, and had put their lives in the hands of our government. Takano also got Shulkin to acknowledge that seven thousand of these veterans were age eighty or older.

Shulkin's response aroused the ire of veterans' organizations. Joe Chenelly, executive director of AMVETS, said the prospect of these cuts terrified many vets and would spread misery if enacted because many would become homeless and some would surely commit suicide. "These scared veterans need real assurance now that this proposal is a non-starter. We cannot subject these veterans to a long, stressful summer." The Trump administration later backed off this plan, but not its proposed cuts to veterans.

The Trump budget also called for reducing housing vouchers for veterans. The number of homeless veterans had been shrinking since 2010, a trend likely to be reversed if fewer subsidies would be available for housing veterans who are unemployed or can find work only episodically, as Trump's budget proposed. And the budget called for eliminating the $3.5 million for an interagency council that coordinates efforts by nineteen federal agencies to reduce duplication of government services while working to reduce homelessness among veterans.

Then there was the issue of jobs for veterans. As we've seen, Trump the candidate promised to be laser-focused on job creation.

Upon taking office, Trump issued an executive order freezing the federal workforce. That hurts veterans. Federal civil service laws give veterans significant preferences in getting hired. As people retire or move on to other work, the federal government hires replacements, close to 100,000 people per year. More than 70,000 of them are veterans, including nearly 32,000 partially disabled vets. Studies done for Congress have shown that past hiring freezes, like the one President Ronald Reagan ordered in 1981, do not save money but add to the burdens on citizens and businesses as they deal with overwhelmed federal staffers and wait for both approvals and services. The federal workforce was not bloated, either. The executive branch employed a bit more than two million people when Trump took office, about the same as during the Carter, Reagan, and George H. W. Bush administrations, when the population was much smaller.

Closing off federal employment for disabled veterans would only increase requests for the unemployability benefit that Trump proposed eliminating. In addition, the hiring freeze would have a second detrimental impact on veterans. The freeze would prevent the VA from hiring 300 more people to process veterans' claims and provide health care and other services. Between 2012 and 2015, the Obama administration had hired more claims examiners as it cut the backlog of veterans' requests for services from 536,400 to about 71,000. Reducing that to zero as Trump promised and then improving other services, however, was scuttled by the Trump budget plan.

No opportunity to reduce veterans' benefits was too small to escape the Trump budget team. The administration proposed to nickel-and-dime disabled veterans—literally.

In the 1990s, Congress ordered the VA to round down to the nearest dollar when calculating benefit checks to veterans. That saved about $6 annually per veteran. That policy ended in 2013 under Obama. Trump's budget called for restoring downward rounding. The annual savings would total about $20 million in 2018. Out of each dollar the VA spends, rounding down would save about a hundredth of a penny.

While Trump was focusing on pennies, a violent political storm was brewing over much bigger issues of race, a storm he would do nothing to calm.

The Road to Charlottesville

"**I** am the least racist person that you've ever encountered," Donald Trump said in 2015, not long after he launched his campaign by calling Mexicans rapists and murders.

One of the great victories of the civil rights movement is that, in America, it has become unacceptable to espouse racist views publicly, though many people harbor them, sharing their biases only with those they trust. Many whites do not care to sit next to Latinos in a restaurant, fly with an Asian pilot, or report to a black woman boss.

Not many people go so far as to support the Ku Klux Klan, as Trump's father, Fred, was doing in 1927 when New York City police arrested him during a violent demonstration. But thanks to the ease of Internet communications, and laws in most states permitting people to walk around carrying assault rifles and other weapons of war, the current crop of neo-Nazis, skinheads, and various hard-core hatemongers can easily recruit their niche audiences while putting fear into the hearts of other Americans.

The FBI and other law enforcement agencies have files on thousands of people associated with such groups During the George W. Bush administration, Homeland Security and other federal officials warned that far-right hate groups posed a serious threat. The FBI and Homeland Security have a database of extremist attacks, which shows that from the day after 9/11 through the end of 2016, far-right extremists killed 106 people in America in 62 attacks, while violent self-professed Muslims killed 119 people in 23 separate attacks. The Southern Poverty Law Center tracks more than 900 such groups it regards as proselytizers of hate.

A vastly larger group of white Americans is uncomfortable with the changes wrought by the civil rights movement and the subsequent liberating movements of women, gays, and other people they imagine are not like themselves. This truth reveals itself in the vile emails frequently made public in lawsuits over alleged discrimination and in subtle societal assumptions, such as when news reports specify the race of suspects who are other than Caucasian. All this falls under the broad rubric of white privilege, a social disease that is highly persistent and rarely discussed. Many white people are blinded by the presumed normality of their skin and the harm their inability to see others as equals causes everyone, including themselves, as revealed by the defensive statement, "I'm not a racist."

Millions of Americans watched live as the violence unfolded in Charlottesville as young men marched shouting Nazi slogans while anti-facists (or antifa)* counterdemonstrators stood their ground. They saw cell phone videos of the terrorist attack by a man driving a Dodge Charger that killed Heather Heyer, one of hundreds of mostly white counterprotesters who came to oppose the racists. Some may even have found amusing the images of a legion of young white men in khakis and polo shirts bearing backyard tiki torches burning scented mosquito repellent oil as they shouted Hitlerian slogans including "blood and soil" and "Jews will not replace us."

The liberal columnist Eric Alterman accurately ridiculed them in *The Nation* as "Third Reich fantasy re-enactors." Trump has a fondness for some of the racist marchers, the ones he repeatedly said were "fine people."

What Americans did not see on live television, however, were two equally ominous scenes. One was of a white man, a Ku Klux Klan leader from Baltimore, firing a shot at some of the people who came to oppose hatemongering. No one was hit by his bullet and he was later arrested.

The other images were of a band of thirty-two men who had come down from New York State ready for war. They wore camouflage fatigues and military-grade combat boots. Slung over their shoulders were loaded military assault rifles with ninety backup rounds of ammunition. They strapped semiautomatic handguns to their hips. Their chests were protected with Level 3 body armor designed to stop the most widely used military assault rifle bullets and thrusts from bayonets. To protect their

---

* *Antifa* is shorthand for *antifacists* and used by the neo-Nazis to describe the counterdemonstrators in Charlottesville.

heads, they wore bullet-resistant Kevlar helmets with battlefield shooting glasses shielding their eyes. They carried water, two-way radios, and first-aid kits.

"You saw the militia walking down the street, you would have thought they were an army," Virginia governor Terry McAuliffe said, adding the militias "had better equipment than our State Police had."

On the first night in Charlottesville, hundreds of mostly young men, some wearing swastikas, marched past Congregation Beth Israel. Torches lit the way as they shouted the Nazi salute "Sieg Heil," the Nazi slogan "blood and soil," and other anti-Semitic chants, loudly pointing out the synagogue.

The next day, during services, three men showed up in full combat gear. They paced back and forth on the sidewalk across the street. "Had they tried to enter, I don't know what I could have done to stop them, but I couldn't take my eyes off them, either," the rabbi told congregation members later. Rabbi Zimmerman had hired a security guard and stationed him out front. "Perhaps the presence of our armed guard deterred them. Perhaps their presence was just a coincidence, and I'm paranoid. I don't know."

In Virginia, it is perfectly legal to go about alone or in a pack dressed and equipped for warfare. Every American state allows some form of "open carry" for rifles and shotguns, a major shift from the gun control laws of the twentieth century, which in some states required rifles to be carried in the locked trunks of cars or that bullets be kept in a separate compartment from firearms.

Among the states that ban open carry of handguns, the laws are shot through with almost as many holes as firing range targets. In Washington State, a court ruling forced changes to a Kitsap County ordinance; in county parks, people are free to carry firearms among the picnickers and sunbathers, but they may not use a BB gun or a slingshot. Only the nation's capital has a strict law against open carry. While that is a local ordinance, it is another example, perhaps, of Trump's argument that the powerful in Washington take care of themselves first.

Open carry laws and the ability to buy weapons of war over the counter were enacted before Trump took office. These policies come not from any popular will. Surveys show overwhelming support for strict gun controls, especially on handguns and weapons of mass killing, and banning the seriously mentally ill from access to guns, an issue we will return to.

These laws are weakened because of the sustained and concentrated pressure brought by the National Rifle Association and the campaign donors aligned with it. While founded as an association of sportsmen, the NRA has become the slavish handmaiden of gun manufacturers.

Its success has created a nation that in 2009 counted 315 million guns in private hands, more than one per person. That estimate by congressional researchers came out one month before the 2012 massacre of twenty first graders and six adults at Sandy Hook Elementary School in Newtown, Connecticut. Since then many states have weakened their gun laws.

Throughout his campaign, Trump embraced guns and spoke against gun controls, often in the context of urging violence.

In February 2016, Trump the candidate told a crowd in Cedar Rapids, Iowa, that when encountering Trump protesters, they "should knock the crap out of them—seriously. Just knock the hell—I promise you, I will pay for the legal fees. I promise, I promise."

At a Las Vegas rally that same month, as a protester was being escorted from a rally, Trump lamented that "we're not allowed to punch back anymore," saying, "I'd like to punch him in the face, I'll tell you that." The billionaire said he missed the "good old days," adding, "You know what they used to do to a guy like that in a place like this. They'd be carried out on a stretcher, folks."

Trump even planted the idea of killing people who oppose him during a December 2015 rally in Grand Rapids, Michigan. Standing before a huge American flag, Trump referred to protesters, saying, "By the way, I hate some of these people, but I'd never kill 'em. I hate 'em. . . . these people, I'll be honest—I'll be honest, I would never kill them [laughter] I would never do that, ah, well . . ."

As president, he used his power to ensure that about 75,000 people so mentally ill that they are not allowed control over their finances could easily buy guns. With no cameras, none of the fanfare of other actions, he signed into law a joint congressional resolution ending the background checks Congress required, at Obama's urging, after the Sandy Hook massacre. Senator Chris Murphy, a Connecticut Democrat, argued against the resolution. "Someone who can't literally deposit their own paycheck probably can't, or likely can't responsibly, own and protect a gun," he said.

"The polls say I have the most loyal people," Trump told an Iowa audience in January of 2016. "I could stand in the middle of Fifth Avenue and shoot somebody and I wouldn't lose any voters, OK? It's, like, incredible." The next day Trump responded to criticism, telling another Iowa campaign rally he didn't have time to be nice while campaigning, but that as president, "the demeanor would be a little bit different but, don't worry, it would be the same attitude."

In June, after Omar Mateen slaughtered forty-nine people in a lone-wolf terrorist attack on a Florida nightclub, candidate Trump told a rally it would have been "beautiful" if the partiers had been armed.

"If we had people, where the bullets were going in the opposite direction, right smack between the eyes of this maniac," Trump said, his hand simulating a gun held between his eyes. "And this son of a bitch comes out and starts shooting and one of the people in that room happened to have [a gun] and goes boom. You know what, that would have been a beautiful, beautiful sight, folks."

His Woodlawn, Texas, audience went wild at the idea of a shootout between drunken nightclub patrons and a terrorist. But the remarks drew rebukes from many sides, including the National Rifle Association, which noted that guns have no place in bars. As he often does, Trump sort of, but not really, tried to walk back his remarks.

Then, two months before the election, he also said Hillary Clinton could literally get away with murder. Clinton is "being so protected. She could walk into this arena right now and shoot somebody with 20,000 people watching, right smack in the middle of the heart, and she wouldn't be prosecuted." Then, mimicking a gun with his hand, he said, "Right smack in the middle of the heart and she wouldn't be prosecuted, OK?"

These incidents illustrate Trump's casual use of violent imagery and how many words come out of his mouth without any filter, a situation that did not change after he became president. But they also go to a deeper problem in America, one that costs many lives and seems highly likely to cost many more as Trump spreads his violent rhetoric with the presidential seal as a prop.

Trump is not the cause of the forces making gun violence and perhaps urban warfare more likely, but he is not calming things, either. The NRA and other absolutists say any restrictions on guns violate the Constitution. But no constitutional right is without limits. The Second Amendment makes no mention of guns, only that "A well regulated Militia, being necessary to the security of a free State, the right of the people to keep and bear Arms, shall not be infringed." Following the logic of Second Amendment absolutists, each of us should be able to carry a howitzer or even a personal nuclear weapon. After all, they meet the definition of *arms*.

The issues of gun violence are just as real as examples of Second Amendment overreach are absurd.

Conflicts exist between the various guarantees in the Bill of Rights. For example, does a self-styled militia, like the New York State contingent in Charlottesville, interfere with the First Amendment freedom-of-religion rights of those attending Beth Israel for prayer? Would it matter if the armed men on patrol are shouting anti-Semitic slogans, like the marchers with the torches, but not brandishing their weapons? Does it matter that the militia is not recognized by any government? If it was recognized by a government, would the incidents at the synagogue interfere with the worshippers' First Amendment rights of religion and assembly? Does it matter that states, which under a Constitutional law concept known as *incorporation* are subject to the full Constitution, have elevated the opportunity for people with weapons to intimidate those exercising their First Amendment right to assemble peaceably or worship?

If and when a confrontation like Charlottesville turns into a bloody shootout, will it prompt any demand to amend gun laws? Will it provoke a serious debate about how the Framers of the Constitution, who lived in an era of single-shot long rifles owned by a mostly rural population, could not have contemplated city streets where packs of men flaunt military-style AR-15 rifles designed only for rapid killing?

Trump surely will never support limiting the types of guns sold or their open display. We know this because he said so three months after assuming office, when he became the first president since Ronald Reagan to address the NRA leadership. "As your president, I will never, ever infringe on the right of the people to keep and bear arms," Trump promised. "Never, ever. Freedom is not a gift from government; freedom is a gift from God."

The deaths at Sandy Hook and in Orlando and Charlottesville weigh unequally on the consciences of American policymakers. They apparently trouble Trump little or not at all. He did not attend Heyer's funeral, which could have made a powerful statement against those who promote hate and strengthen a national sense of conscience about hate crimes.

Just hours after Heyer was killed, Trump spoke from his New Jersey golf course clubhouse. His original intent for "this small press conference" was to sign a veterans health care bill, but after a few moments Trump switched to denouncing the "egregious display of hatred, bigotry and violence" in Charlottesville.

Had he stopped there, his words would have been viewed as the kind of healing comment Americans have come to expect of presidents after such awful events. But Trump went off script, adding an impromptu line that negated those words while giving aid and comfort to the racists he had just seemed to be condemning.

"We condemn in the strongest possible terms this egregious display of hatred, bigotry and violence—on many sides," he said, pausing for a moment and then using his hand for emphasis as he repeated "on many sides."

Trump made no mention of neo-Nazis, skinheads, and racists. This failure to identify, much less blame, was in sharp contrast to his long history of instantly blaming Muslims after various terrorist attacks in Europe, Kansas, California, and Florida.

The Nazis and racists quickly declared the president's words to be exactly what they had hoped to hear. They kept up that position as Trump flip flopped through clarifying comments over the next few days.

He read one statement in which he looked like a hostage making a video when the captive reads words but his body language, tone, and attitude show that his actions are being forced. The next time he spoke he went on the attack against journalists, defending his remarks and insisting he had done the right thing in his first remarks, which would include his turning his back on the reporters he had summoned to a press conference, walking off when they asked questions to clarify his original position.

To the hatemongers this first statement and what followed were taken as more wink-wink reassurances from Trump that with him in the White House their movement was in official favor. They told their members that

Trump had to throw some rhetorical bones to the race-mixing crowd, but that his remarks made it clear that their movement was ascendant because they had an ally in the Oval Office. And they warned that the day was drawing closer when blacks, Asians, Jews, Mexicans, homosexuals, and many young women should fear being rounded up, or worse.

Moments after Trump first spoke, the Daily Stormer, an American Nazi website that promotes making America a whites-only Christian nation, thanked Trump for blaming "many sides" for the violence rather than its readers:

> Trump comments were good. He didn't attack us. He just said the nation should come together. Nothing specific against us. He said that we need to study why people are so angry, and implied that there was hate . . . on both sides! He implied the antifa are haters. There was virtually no counter-signaling of us at all. He said he loves us all. Also, refused to answer a question about White Nationalists supporting him.
>
> No condemnation at all. When asked to condemn, he just walked out of the room. Really, really good. God bless him.

The next day the Daily Stormer "Summer of Hate edition" described the murder victim as a "fat, childless, 32-year-old slut." Heather Heyer should have been killed, the article argued: "Most people are glad she is dead, as she is the definition of uselessness. A 32-year-old woman without children is a burden on society and has no value."

Trump's treating anyone who marched with the Nazis and their ilk as moral equals of those who oppose hatred was more than many leading Republicans could bear. Senators John McCain, Lindsey Graham, and Mitch McConnell spoke out. They recognized the lasting damage these remarks could do to the Republican Party, which has worked ever since Nixon to persuade people that GOP policies that hurt nonwhite Americans aren't racist but instead are grounded in Constitutional principles and pro-growth economics.

From Kennebunkport, former presidents George H. W. Bush and George W. Bush released a clear statement that gave no quarter to the racists, highlighting the difference between Trump and them:

America must always reject racial bigotry, anti-Semitism, and hatred in all forms. As we pray for Charlottesville, we are reminded of the fundamental truths recorded by that city's most prominent citizen in the Declaration of Independence: we are all created equal and endowed by our Creator with unalienable rights. We know these truths to be everlasting because we have seen the decency and greatness of our country.

The Democrats were less restrained. Representative Ruben Gallego, an Arizona Democrat, said "the president is not actually condemning this white nationalism, this terrorism." Trump's rhetoric encouraged the hatemongers, Gallego said, a view supported by what their websites were telling followers that day. "He should treat the alt-right movement and the neo-Nazi movement the way he treats any occasion where there is a Muslim terrorist attack."

In Germany, Chancellor Angela Merkel denounced the neo-Nazis and racists in Charlottesville with a moral clarity and force lacking in Trump. Merkel spokesman Steffen Seibert called the white supremacists "evil" and "disgusting," and said those who took part in "the right-wing extremist march were absolutely repulsive—naked racism, anti-Semitism and hate in their most evil form were on display."

Trump's dog-whistle support for racists and neo-Nazis has a long history.

When Trump was divorcing his first wife, Ivana, he planted news stories some ran as covers of Rupert Murdoch's *New York Post* tabloid—that publicly humiliated the mother of his children. Ivanka, Don Jr., and Eric became estranged from their father, as they wrote and talked about for years, until as adults they went on Daddy's payroll and became his loyal aides.

Ivana's friends circulated a story she told them about a Trump Organization employee, John Walter. Each time he came into Trump's office Walter would click his heels and say, "Heil Hitler!"

Ivana also put into the public record in 1990 that Trump read now and then from a book of Hitler's speeches, which he kept in a cabinet next to their bed. Anyone seeking power and wanting to know how to manipulate people, especially in crowds, would do well to study Hitler's public addresses.

Marie Brenner asked Trump about the book of Hitler speeches while writing a 1990 *Vanity Fair* profile of Trump. Trump said the book was *Mein Kampf*, a gift from businessman Martin Davis, who Trump said was a Jew. Davis confirmed the story, but with two significant changes. Davis was not Jewish and the book was *My New Order*, Hitler's collected speeches, just as Ivana had told the story.

When Brenner went back to Trump he told her, "*If* I had these speeches, and I am not saying that I do, I would never read them."

The Nazi leader said in 1939 that he was aware that "I have no equal in the art of swaying the masses." Hitler also said, "Everything I have accomplished I owe to persuasion" and that the key to his success was constant repetition, a principle understood by anyone who has seen television commercials repeated so often they can quote them from memory.

That Trump lumps together many groups and labels them "enemy" fits with a 1925 Munich speech in which Hitler discussed the inability of the masses to focus when presented with multiple enemies. "It is part of the genius of a great leader to make adversaries of different fields appear is always belonging to one category."

Trump bundles together Mexicans, Muslims, journalists, climate change scientists, "elites," and the counterdemonstrators in Charlottesville as the enemy of what in his inaugural address he called "a historic movement the likes of which the world has never seen before."

During his campaign, Trump retweeted racist tweets, including from believers in "white genocide." That white Americans are the target of genocide is a delusional notion that American Nazis promote as an article of racist faith. Daily Stormer publisher Andrew Anglin in August 2017 sent a message to racists and American Nazis about how Trump is with them on white genocide:

Our Glorious Leader and ULTIMATE SAVIOR has gone full-wink-wink-wink to his most aggressive supporters after having been attacked for retweeting a White Genocide account a few days ago, Trump went on to retweet two more White Genocide accounts, back to back. . . . Whereas the odd White genocide tweet could be a random occurrence, it isn't statistically possible that two of them back to back could be a random occurrence. . . . Today in America the air is cold and it tastes like victory.

Rocky Suhayda, chairman of the American Nazi Party, endorsed Trump a few months before the election. Suhayda called blacks *savages*, saying, "If Trump does win, okay, it's going to be a real opportunity for people like white nationalists, acting intelligently to build upon that" if they just shift their rhetoric from negative to positive. "It has to be pro-white . . . we have to keep our eyes on the prize." Trump declined to reject the endorsements of various racists and Nazis. He even claimed he was unaware of David Duke, the former KKK leader and Senate candidate from Louisiana. Trump said on CNN four times within a matter of seconds that he didn't know who David Duke was:

Well, just so you understand, I don't know anything about David Duke, okay? I don't know anything about what you're even talking about with white supremacy or white supremacists. So, I don't know. I don't know, did he endorse me or what's going on, because, you know, I know nothing about David Duke. I know nothing about white supremacists. And so you're asking me a question that I'm supposed to be talking about, people that I know nothing about. I don't know any—honestly, I don't know David Duke. I don't believe I have ever met him. I'm pretty sure I didn't meet him. And I just don't know anything about him.

And yet Trump, who claimed during the campaign that he possesses "the world's greatest memory," had told the New York *Daily News* in 2000 that he was quitting the fringe Reform Party because it "would require associating with David Duke."

Trump's sympathy for the Charlottesville racists was more than Kenneth C. Frazier, CEO of the drug company Merck, could take. He resigned from Trump's American Manufacturing Council, a ceremonial group, to protest Trump's Charlottesville statements. The Nazi news site then called Frazier a "black bastard" and "dumb black guy" unqualified for his job.

Trump tweeted, "Now that Ken Frazier of Merck Pharma has resigned from President's Manufacturing Council, he will have more time to LOWER RIPOFF DRUG PRICES!"

Disney CEO Bob Iger and Tesla founder Elon Musk and others also quit the council. All of them are white. None was subjected to a Trumpian attack tweet.

Immigration

Protecting American jobs by preventing foreigners from taking them was a major theme throughout the Trump campaign. Soon after Trump won the Republican nomination, questions began to emerge about whether Melania Trump was among those people who had worked illegally in the United States. If she had, and her husband's proposed policies had been in effect, she would have been a high-priority target for arrest and deportation to Slovenia.

How Trump handled this potential crisis proved how clever he is at distorting an argument to avoid an issue. And it would show how what Trump told voters on immigration and jobs was mostly talk, not the promised action to make sure foreigners did not, legally or illegally, take American jobs.

Questions about whether Melania Knauss (sometimes spelled Knavs) worked illegally arose after Trump's favorite tabloid, the *New York Post*, ran nude photos of her on its cover and inside for two days, using stars to cover strategic spots. The photos included lesbian poses. That Trump or someone acting with his approval supplied the photos became clear when the freshly nominated Republican candidate's campaign was asked about them.

Instead of denouncing the newspaper, a spokesman called the photos art, though the setting—a mattress with a sheet, the bed pressed against a bare wall and harsh lighting—was not up to the standards of either *Playboy* or the late art photographer Robert Mapplethorpe.

As for his wife's immigrant status, Trump spoke up in August 2016 using his universal "they" to cover anyone in journalism.

"They said, 'Melania Trump may have come into our country illegally' and 'how would that be for Donald Trump?' Here's the only problem, she came in totally legally," he said, indicating they had spoken privately about whether to respond. "I said to her: 'No no, let it simmer for a little while. Let them go wild, let it simmer, and then let's have a little news conference.'"

Speaking in North Carolina, Trump said his wife entered the United States legally. "Let me tell you one thing. She has got it so documented, so she's going to have a little news conference over the next couple of weeks. That's good. I love it. I love it."

There was never such a news conference. No documents were provided, either.

That allowed Trump to get away with diverting the issue to one not raised. The issue was whether Melania had worked in the United States illegally. But just as with his tax returns, Trump promised but failed to deliver.

Months later, diligent reporters from the Associated Press uncovered business records from Metropolitan International Management, which had Melania's contract. It had later folded. The records showed that Melania Knauss had indeed worked illegally in the United States in 1995. She took at least ten modeling jobs that in all paid more than $20,000. She was an independent contractor, but the modeling agency gave her a pager, putting her at management's beck and call, and loaned her money, the business records showed.

Knauss turned twenty-five that year, making her old to be a fashion or swimsuit model. That may explain why she got so little work at modest pay and did nude photos with another woman.

Fashion shows and magazines prefer teenage girls. Until New York State passed a law in 2014 making models seventeen and younger subject to rules governing child actors the majority of fashion models were legally children, many only fourteen years old, according to the Council of Fashion Designers of America, which urged the legislation.

As a candidate, Trump promised to round up every one of the estimated 11 million people living in the United States without the government's permission, people some call undocumenteds and others call illegals. He was especially vocal about deporting those with jobs. Any noncitizen without a Green Card, shorthand for federal government permission to work, steals a job from an Americans and should be deported, Trump said over and over.

But while Trump railed against illegal work, his actions as a business owner were quite different, demonstrating a basic Trumpian philosophy—there are two standards. One is for the Trumps and anyone they like. It is soft and easy. The other is harsh. It's for everyone not aligned with the Trumps, especially those the president dislikes, most especially Mexicans and Muslims.

On the campaign trail, Donald Trump often railed against work visa programs allowing foreigners to enter the country and work for periods from ninety days up to ten years.

Candidate Trump said in a written statement that he was "totally committed to eliminating rampant, widespread H-1B abuse and ending outrageous practices such as those that occurred at Disney in Florida when Americans were forced to train their foreign replacements. I will end forever the use of the H-1B as a cheap labor program, and institute an absolute requirement to hire American workers first for every visa and immigration program. No exceptions."

H-1B is one of several programs that allowed American companies to use foreign workers. All of them had rules that made the workers temporary guests. To critics, especially software code writers, it was a program to push down wages.

Half of the foreign workers were hired by computer industry companies, many in Silicon Valley. And half of those workers earned $88,000 or less. Whether these guest workers were paid less than Americans, and thus depressed the wages of Americans, is hotly debated in Silicon Valley. The issue is further complicated by the fact that software coding could be done in a remote location, say India, where a large share of the work-visa hires come from. End the visa program and instead of hiring more American programmers, Silicon Valley might just outsource much of the work from Cupertino and Redwood City to Bangalore and Hyderabad.

The justification for high-tech guest workers is that there are not enough Americans with the skills to do the work. If that is so, then slowly, steadily shrinking the number of visas should result in rising wages, which would attract more Americans and prompt them to invest in skills worthy of higher pay. Continuing the program at roughly the same level only perpetuates any shortage of native workers and puts downward pressure on American wages.

In April 2017 Trump told an audience in Kenosha, Wisconsin, that he was about to take bold action on foreign guest workers. He promised to end the "theft of American prosperity." Foreign worker visas "should never, ever be used to replace American workers," he said.

But the executive order he signed was not bold, as Trump said, but tepid. It simply directed four cabinet agencies to "suggest reforms" with no deadline for submitting their ideas.

There are also work visas for low-skilled workers like the staff at Mar-a-Lago, which had for years relied on the very workers Trump wanted kept out—foreigners. Trump said during one of the Republican primary debates that Mar-a-Lago, like other local seasonal resort properties, had no choice but to import workers. "People don't want a short-term job," he said. "So, we will bring people in, and we will send the people out. All done legally."

Senator Marco Rubio of Florida broke in. "That's not accurate," he said, because at least three hundred Americans who sought work at Mar-a-Lago were not hired. That, Rubio said, helped Trump push down wages, the very issue Trump complained was caused by too many foreign workers in America.

"When you bring someone in on one of these visas they can't go work for anybody else," Rubio noted. "They either work for you or they have to go back home. You basically have them captive, so you don't have to worry about competing for higher wages with another hotel down the street. And, that's why you bring workers from abroad."

Trump kept interrupting Rubio, making it difficult for those watching to understand the debate unless they read the transcript later.

The public record showed that hundreds of local residents did want jobs but were not hired.

In July 2017 the Trump administration decided to let in more foreign workers, not exactly what Trump promised on inauguration day when he said every decision would be made to promote American jobs and buy American.

American "businesses in danger of suffering irreparable harm due to a lack of available temporary nonagricultural workers" would be able to hire an additional 15,000 foreigners in temporary low-skill, low-paid jobs.

That would increase supply by more than 40 percent for the second half of the year.

This was a prime example of Trump not walking his campaign talk in office, but also of driving down wages, just as Rubio had said was Trump's goal.

In Palm Beach, for example, hundreds of people were willing to work at the wages offered by Mar-a-Lago, roughly $10 to $13 an hour, for the 2016–17 season.

Locally four people wanted work for every low-skill resort job offered. That means there was no shortage of local labor for the seasonal positions. With so many workers available, hiring locals might not even put upward pressure on wages. When there is so much more demand for work than employers could supply, employers can offer less pay and still recruit people.

But workers who come from overseas on visas are subject to more control. Their employer can arrange pay that depends on their staying until the last day of the season and hold back part of their pay through "bemusing" arrangements. That means anyone who gets out of line, anyone who gets fired, gets shorted on his or her pay and sent home early.

President Trump declared July 24 the start of Made in America Week. Trump said he would be "recognizing the vital contributions of American workers and job creators to our Nation's prosperity."

The same week a tiny classified ad ran twice in the back pages of *The Palm Beach Post*. It offered work for "3 mos recent & verifiable exp in fine dining/country club." The jobs paid wages only—"No tips."

The ads did not identify the employer, but the fax was a Mar a Lago number.

A week earlier, Mar-a-Lago had applied to the Labor Department—run by a Trump appointee—for visas to import thirty-five people to wait on tables, twenty cooks, and fifteen chambermaids. All it needed to do was show that it offered work and not enough people showed up to take the jobs. That was easily accomplished. Run a tiny ad with few details. Tell locals to apply via fax, a technology few people seeking such low-paid seasonal work were likely to own. People could mail a letter but letters can get lost or take time being delivered.

Those two ads, and the predictably weak response, met the legal requirement necessary to import foreign workers under the H-2B visa program from October 2017 until June 2018.

There was, perhaps, one positive in these foreign workers being hired at Mar-a-Lago to wait on Trump's paying guests. Unlike Melania Knauss Trump, they wouldn't be violating American law.

Trump often states as fact that illegal immigrants are a drag on the economy. He complains of "Americans losing their jobs to foreign workers."

To stop that he supported the RAISE Act, for Reforming American Immigration for Strong Employment. It would fundamentally change the rules on legal immigration, something Congress did in 1924 and again in 1965. Ostensibly the bill's purpose is to "establish a skills-based immigration points system, to focus family-sponsored immigration on spouses and minor children, to eliminate the Diversity Visa Program, to set a limit on the number of refugees admitted annually to the United States."

That would mean that more people with job skills could enter the country, which in general will tend to depress wages for people with similar skills, but which may also help grow the economy. The focus on spouses and minor children means that grandparents, grandchildren, and cousins are out and the age of minors would be lowered from twenty-one to eighteen.

The bill was analyzed at the Wharton School at the University of Pennsylvania, the school Trump claims he attended when he went only to its undergraduate program in real-estate economics.

The analysis found that the bill would make wages grow briefly in the short term but that as the years rolled by the new policy would destroy American jobs, resulting in slower economic growth. That certainly is not what Trump claimed he would do with his slogans about America First and Make America Great Again.

The most interesting finding from the Penn Wharton budget model computer program was that simply doubling the number of immigrants from about 800,000 per year to 1.6 million would do the most to increase economic growth per person. The education level of the immigrants did not matter.

This larger influx would result in significantly more Gross Domestic

Product per capita, which would reach $83,700 in 2050. Leaving the number of immigrants at 800,000, but requiring that 55 percent arrive with high job skills, would mean no more than $76,100 per capita of economic output. Thus, more immigrants regardless of job skills is better for Americans overall by 10 percent.

The most troubling finding of this study was that the RAISE Act favored by Trump "could shave two percentage points off GDP growth and cause a loss of more than four million jobs" by the year 2040.

Kent Smetters, the Wharton business professor who worked on the computer model, noted that immigrants of all kinds are a "net positive" because they "tend to work pretty hard, they tend to have a very high attachment rate to the labor force, they are less likely to be on unemployment insurance" because they come to America in the hopes of improving their and their family's economics.

In addition, Smetters said, "as younger members of the workforce, immigrants also help pay for Social Security and Medicare for the elderly. That is a crucial benefit as the U.S.," like many other countries with modern economies, faces an aging population with a shrinking ratio of workers to retirees.

The Wharton model is available without charge, allowing people to experiment with policy options at www.budgetmodel.wharton.upenn.edu /immigration/.

Jim Acosta, a network television correspondent whose parents fled Castro's Cuba, asked at a White House press briefing about the RAISE Act, which favors English-speaking immigrants. His question drew a sharp, condescending response from the designated White House spokesman, Stephen Miller, a Steve Bannon associate who often sounds like a white nationalist.

Acosta brought up the poem in the Statue of Liberty's pedestal and its famous last lines:

> *Give me your tired, your poor,*
> *Your huddled masses yearning to breathe free,*
> *The wretched refuse of your teeming shore*
> *Send these, the homeless, tempest-tost to me,*
> *I lift my lamp beside the golden door!*

Acosta said the proposed immigration policy seemed to run counter to those ideals. Miller shot back that the poem was added to its pedestal later, while the statute is "a symbol of American liberty lighting the world."

What Miller didn't say, or didn't know, or perhaps knew but didn't want others to know, is that Lazarus's 1883 poem was critical to the efforts to raise money for the pedestal on which the statue stands. The statue was not completed until three years later, making her words integral.

This might seem an odd subject for the White House spokesman of the day to raise, but it stems from an active discussion among the people that Bannon calls the alt-right and critics call racists and white supremacists to develop a narrative that most immigrants are unworthy of America.

A leading racist, Richard Spencer, who says he was Miller's mentor, which Miller does not dispute, had denounced the Emma Lazarus poem three days before Trump became president.

"It's offensive that such a beautiful, inspiring statue was ever associated with ugliness, weakness, and deformity," Spencer tweeted. This theme was picked up a few days later by Rush Limbaugh, the right-wing radio talk show host. He told his audience that "the Statue of Liberty had absolutely nothing to do with immigration" and mused, "Why do people think that it does? Well, there was a socialist poet."

David Duke, the former KKK leader, attacked the poem and Lazarus in "The Jewish Led Alien Invasion," a chapter in one of his books filled with diatribes against Jews and others he hates.

In the fluid zone between white nationalists in the Trump White House and violent racists in Charlottesville, the Statute of Liberty has become a symbol of efforts to make America white again, although, of course, it never was all white.

An immigrant from Ireland, John Carney, took up the Acosta-Miller exchange. Carney is the economics editor at Breitbart, Bannon's gathering place for the like-minded.

Carney tweeted that what Breitbart and Trump call the "opposition" news media were engaged in "the Weaponization of the Statue of Liberty." He also pointed to political cartoons that used the statue and caricatures of Trump to argue visually that the president wants immigration restricted to white, English-speaking Christians.

Then Carney focused his attention on the September 2017 cover of

Vogue. The fashion magazine featured an Annie Leibovitz photograph of actress Jennifer Lawrence in a low-cut, tight-fitting red satin dress. Lawrence was leaning against a metal railing as if on the prow of a ship, the statue behind her, surrounded by water and clouds in luscious shades of blue.

Breitbart's Carney saw this as an attack on Trump's Make America Great Again theme, connecting it to the Acosta-Miller exchange. "We're going to have to create a full #MAGA shadow cultural industry because the Opposition Media can't even do fashion without attacking us."

But there was a problem with Carney insinuating that the *Vogue* cover was part of a journalistic cabal. Zara Rahim, the *Vogue* spokeswoman, informed Carney that the photo could not have anything to do with that August exchange in the White House press briefing room because "we shot this in June, buddy."

Trump regards Brietbart as a reliable source of information, just as he has made statements that trace back to the Russian propaganda website Sputnik, the neo-Nazi Daily Stormer, and InfoWars, where host Alex Jones carries on about the "interdimensional beings" secretly controlling American elites. Trump has been an InfoWars guest.

None of these information sources that Trump relies on considers refugees to be a crisis worthy of American help. None writes favorably or evenhandedly about people of color, especially regarding immigration. None pays heed to humanitarian crises caused by wars, famine, and other disruptions, even though 66 million people, nearly one percent of earth's population, were forced to live away from their homes in 2016.

That estimate by the United Nations High Commissioner for Refugees counted a third of these people as refugees. More than a third came from two predominantly Muslim countries, Afghanistan and Syria, where American military actions played a major role in forcing people to flee. But the sources of information Trump relies on share with him a bias against Muslims and Islam.

Nearly 85,000 people entered America in 2016 as refugees, about one tenth of legal immigrants. Other countries, many of them desperately poor, like Chad, allowed in far more refugees. Sweden, with 10 million people, has about half as many refugees as America with its more than 320 million people. To Miller, Limbaugh, Bannon, Carney, Jones, and the others, those 85,000 refugees are about 84,999 too many.

These "information" sources also keep up a steady alarmist tone about the border with Mexico even though illegal crossings into the United States fell sharply with the Great Recession and have been flat since, according to federal government data and reports by private organizations. Of the estimated 9 to 11 million people living in the United States without authorization, two thirds came more than a decade earlier, the Pew Research Center found.

Those crossing the border in 2017 were more likely to come from Central America and Asia than Mexico, whose economy has improved since NAFTA, the North American Free Trade Agreement, was signed in 1993. But to the sources of information Trump relies on, all immigrants look alike and all are to be feared and kept out unless they look and talk like people on the alt-right. And to Trump, foreign workers are bad, unless they serve his Mar-a-Lago customers, earning cheap wages with no tips.

PART VIII

CONCLUSION

The Con Unravels

As these pages show, based on his own words and deeds, Donald Trump is manifestly unfit to hold any public office. That Donald Trump legitimately holds office under our Constitution is beyond question. That he is a clear and present danger to the whole world should be obvious by now.

Trump lacks the emotional stability, knowledge, critical-thinking skills, and judgment to be commander in chief. Emotionally he remains the thirteen-year-old troublemaker his father sent off to a military academy, where by his own account brutality was common. Being stuck in the awkward year between childhood and maturity for nearly six decades is a terrible fate, one that has twisted Trump's personality and explains much of his narcissism, immature attitudes about women, disregard for others, and his imagined intellectual gifts shown by his frequent declaration that "I'm like a smart person."

Even by the standards of the incurious George W. Bush, Trump is appallingly ignorant. Not knowing a Shia Muslim from a Sunni Muslim or why this division within Islam matters deeply to American foreign policy decisions, Trump spews bigotry against all Muslims. George W. Bush constantly reminded the world that our response to 9/11 was not a war on Islam, that the faith was not the issue, but rather the abuse of it by zealots. Bush participated in Muslim religious events to emphasize that point.

Trump not only inflames hatred of all Muslims, he also allows himself to be used by the Saudis. They support the most violent faction of the Islamic religion and finance terrorists while Trump praises Riyadh for fighting against terrorism, unaware of how out of touch his words are.

More surprising than Trump's lack of knowledge of geopolitics is his ignorance of economics, the field in which he was given a bachelor's degree by the University of Pennsylvania. Anyone who did the work to earn such a degree would know that imposing a tariff on imports from Mexico to pay for his wall means that American consumers would bear the cost, not Mexicans.

Worse is Trump's faux patriotism.

That Trump's loyalties are divided, that he owes something to Moscow, is obvious from his many words of praise for Vladimir Putin, his years of lucrative financial transactions, and his hiring of Paul Manafort to run his campaign. Whether Trump is merely a fool or a knowing Kremlin agent is unresolved at this writing. What we know for sure is that the Trump campaign eagerly solicited the Kremlin's help to defeat Hillary Clinton, wanted to use Russian diplomatic links to secretly communicate with Moscow, and that Trump directly participated in lying and covering up that secret collaboration with a hostile foreign power.

That Trump has no regard for decency in politics is shown by his leading chants of "Lock her up" and asking people at rallies to pledge loyalty to him just as James Comey, the FBI director he fired, said he was asked to do in private. These are words and actions befitting a dictator, not an American president. But they also fit with Trump's philosophy. Those who turn the other cheek as Jesus Christ taught in the Sermon on the Mount are fools, idiots, and losers, Trump has said many times. His philosophy is revenge and violence against others, decidedly anti-Christian attitudes that have not dissuaded many prominent television preachers from their enthusiastic endorsements of him as a "fine Christian family man."

Trump maintains strong support among roughly a third of Americans. Many of them are old enough to have lived through all or part of the Cold War and yet some of them tell journalists, focus group leaders, and pollsters that, like Trump, they trust Putin's regime more than American intelligence agencies. During the Cold War, for sure, Republican politicians loudly denounced anyone who espoused such views as useful idiots, fellow travelers, and traitors.

This core of support, almost entirely among Republicans, means that sitting members of the House and Senate cannot go up against Trump unless they are confident they can win the next primary election. John Danforth, the former Republican senator from Missouri, said he was speaking out against Trump specifically because congressional Republicans cannot.

Their inaction may be profiles in cowardice, but it also shows how the system of checks and balances built into our Constitution is not working as intended.

Trump may be part of a larger global social force, a political tsunami of fear and rejection of the modern world and a nostalgic desire to go back to an imagined past of peace and simplicity. We see this force in the rise of fundamentalist Christians, Hindus, Jews, and Muslims as well as a new age of dictators from Putin to Turkey's Recep Tayyip Erdoğan and Egypt's Abdel Fattah el-Sisi to nationalists like India's Narendra Modi.

Great social waves, like tsunamis, cannot be stopped by holding up signs in protest. They must instead continue until their destructive energy dissipates. Our hope must be that the future will produce better leaders, not worse.

And then there are Trump's many delusions.

Trump claims to know more about the jihadis who created the Islamic State of Iraq and the Levant, or ISIL, than America's generals. He claims to know how to deal with North Korea, an impoverished cult state, and yet until the president of China gave him a long history lesson by telephone, Trump admits he had no knowledge of the history of conflict between the Chinese and Korean peoples. He claims to be the world's foremost expert on taxes. All that is nonsense, a con job that should have had people laughing at him, not voting for him.

For almost three decades I have been pointing out that Trump creates his own reality, a point on which his other leading biographers agree. What astonishes me is how many people blind themselves to his nonsense. Then again, denial is a powerful human emotion and this mass reaction is understandable among those beaten down by nearly four decades of government policies that stealthily take from the many to enrich the few.

Trump brilliantly tapped into the economic malaise that has afflicted much of the country after more than three decades of economic stagnation. It began to lift only in 2013. When the cries of people for help go unheeded, they will turn to anyone, even a demagogue, for relief.

Many of the economic changes in America and the world are beyond the control of a president or Congress. As we move from the industrial era into the still emerging digital era and, soon, the biological age, the world will be vastly richer, but many people may be worse off. For millions of Americans the harsh truth is that inefficiency created industrial jobs. As techniques to manufacture more and better products with less and less labor advance, those boring but good-paying factory jobs are only memories. Trump can claim he will change that, but he cannot. No president can.

The path to a better future is through investing in education, and especially science, as well as improving infrastructure. Trump's budget shows he is hostile to all of these, particularly science. Other politicians also have cut investments in the future. College, once free or cheap in many parts of the country, has become costly even for community college students. Not funding basic research today means America will be less prosperous than it could be in the future.

For more than two decades I have warned that the frustrations caused by Washington and state capitals adopting stealth government policies favoring the rich would one day explode in ways that would be harmful, not beneficial, to our democracy. In bestselling books, hundreds of articles, columns, and speeches I have documented how policies hardly anyone knew about take from the many in subtle ways and concentrate money in the pockets of the 32,000 or so Americans at the apex of the economic pyramid.

Trump is among those beneficiaries of modern America's silent plutocratic system of redistribution upward, a process that in Orwellian terms makes sure the pigs get the apples and milk because they claim they need them to help those animals who only get slop. That I explained these devices at great length in my books *Perfectly Legal, Free Lunch,* and *The Fine Print* shows that irony is not dead. Trump masterfully grasped the anxiety and fear among the economically oppressed who had been largely abandoned by the Democrats. His slogans showed his mastery of the art of persuasion.

To understand Trump's unfitness for office, step back for a moment and wipe from your mind the image Trump spent decades polishing through his faux reality television show, the books others wrote for him, and his manipulation of the conventions of journalism.

Imagine a man you never heard of sits down next to you at the start of a cross-country plane flight or a long bus ride. This older man, his yellowish hair long and combed over, wearing a nice suit with a long necktie, incessantly talks about himself.

You would get an earful of bluster about his wealth. Next would be his imagined smarts—"I have a very good brain"—a tale told in sixth-grade sentences, half-finished thoughts, and other verbal ingredients of what is politely called "word salad."

Imagine he started talking, as he did to black leaders in February, about Frederick Douglass in the present tense, more than a century after his death. This man tells you that Douglass is "an example of somebody who's done an amazing job and is getting recognized more and more, I notice."

Listen as he describes climate change as a "Chinese hoax" and says America should mine and burn more coal instead of developing renewable energy sources like the rest of the world. Imagine him urging steam power rather than "digital" catapults to launch jet fighters from aircraft carriers because "no one understands digital."

Imagine him telling you that he gets pleasure from destroying the lives of anyone who slights him. And imagine he tells you that the Mexican government is sending hordes of murderers and rapists across the border and that all blacks live in ghettos, uneducated and often unable to find work.

Now imagine you are a black businessman, the owner of profitable factories like my former next-door neighbor in Rochester. Or a federal judge born in America whose parents came from Mexico. Or one of the millions of Americans who owe their jobs to "the digital."

You would, I imagine, fear you were, to use a Trumpian term, stuck next to a nut job until your trip ended.

How can it be that millions of people do not see Trump for what he is—a narcissistic, ill-informed, thieving old blowhard? As the adage goes, poor people are crazy; rich people are eccentric.

Before the election, I predicted that, as president, Trump's behavior would become increasingly erratic, and it has. That is because of his own shortcomings, especially his desperate need for adoration, his self-centered thinking, and his ignorance of basic issues of diplomacy, economics, and geopolitics.

A month after the inauguration, thirty-five psychiatrists wrote a letter to the editor of *The New York Times* that made exactly this point:

> Mr. Trump's speech and actions demonstrate an inability to tolerate views different from his own, leading to rage reactions. His words and behavior suggest a profound inability to empathize. Individuals with these traits distort reality to suit their psychological state, attacking facts and those who convey them (journalists, scientists).
>
> In a powerful leader, these attacks are likely to increase, as his personal myth of greatness appears to be confirmed. We believe that the grave emotional instability indicated by Mr. Trump's speech and actions makes him incapable of serving safely as president.

A few months later, psychiatrist Prudence L. Gourguechon, a former president of the American Psychoanalytic Association, proposed judging Trump's fitness for office using the United States Army Field Manual on developing leaders. She distilled from its 188 pages five crucial qualities needed to lead:

- *Trust*
- *Discipline and self-control*
- *Judgment and critical thinking*
- *Self-awareness*
- *Empathy*

Not one of these is part of Trump's nature.

Trust. For years, he has said in talks and the books that bear his name that no one is to be trusted, especially those closest to you.

Discipline and Self-control. The Army manual says leaders maintain their composure under pressure and do not react "viscerally or angrily when receiving bad news or conflicting information," and do not allow "personal emotions to drive decisions or guide responses to emotionally charged situations." That's the opposite of Trump.

Judgment. That Trump asserts that the best advisers reside in his head and thus he does not need experts does not suggest sound judgment.

Critical Thinking. The Army manual notes that a leader adapts to new facts and "seeks to obtain the most thorough and accurate understanding possible" while also anticipating "first, second and third consequences of multiple courses of action." A trademark Trump characteristic runs counter to this. "We have no choice," he says about everything from banning Muslims from entering America to building his wall on the Mexican border to repealing Obamacare.

Self-awareness. Trump lies compulsively, telling so many made-up stories, imagined events, and absurd fabrications that he often stumbles over his own statements. That Trump contradicts himself without embarrassment, remorse, or even acknowledgment goes to the heart of his lack of self-awareness. Showing video clips of Trump denying he said something followed by earlier clips of him saying that which he denied have become staples of political comedy shows like *Saturday Night Live* and late night television.

On his first full day in office, the public got a full dose of how Trump just makes stuff up and insists it is reality. The first official statement read by Sean Spicer, the White House press secretary, insisted that Trump's was "the largest audience to witness an inauguration, period. Both in person and around the globe."

Never mind that photographs and transit ridership data show that Obama's second inaugural drew a bigger crowd than Trump's. Never mind that transit ridership at the 2009 inauguration was more than double that in 2017. Never mind that George W. Bush in 2001 and Bill Clinton in 1993 drew crowds that by such indicators as transit ridership and photographs were larger or at least equal. Never mind that as Spicer spoke, the largest mass demonstrations in American history, by far, were under way as about six million women and some men marched in Washington and more than 100 other cities to protest Trump's presidency.

Spicer's statement, obviously ordered by Trump as a test of his press secretary's loyalty—and which Spicer said after resigning that he regretted—used a litany of what could be called alternative facts to justify the crowd size claim. Labeling anything that does not comport with Trump's version of reality "fake news" is part of a strategy to muddy clear waters, sow confusion, and pose as the only honest person in a craven world of dissemblers.

Similarly, after denigrating American intelligence agencies, Trump insisted his dismissive remarks were made up by journalists, whom he calls "dishonest" and "among the most dishonest human beings on earth" and "totally dishonest." With those words he is really speaking of himself.

Empathy. As for empathy, Trump flew twice to Texas after Hurricane Harvey. The first time he boasted about the size of the crowd he drew in Corpus Christi, his wife's white athletic shoes not smudged by a speck of mud. On his second visit, he advised people at a feeding station to "have a good time." During the presidential campaign he denigrated John McCain's five years as a prisoner of war and later mocked Khizr and Ghazala Khan, whose Army officer son was killed in Afghanistan.

Later Trump denounced the people of Puerto Rico after hurricane Maria flattened the island, mocking how the island name is pronounced by locals, saying *pwear-toe-rico.* And on his brief visit he tossed rolls of paper towels to those in the small audience, a Trumpian twist on Marie Antoinette. He criticized the mayor of San Juan for pointing out that, contrary to Trump's claims of a great job of relief, people were dying for lack of water, food, medicine, and electricity and federal officials were slow to respond. Trump blamed the Puerto Ricans for refusing to help themselves. Lin-Manuel Miranda, creator of the musical *Hamilton,* noted the contrast between Trump's remarks on the American island hurricane and those that ravaged Florida and Texas. "I've never seen a sitting president attack the victims of a natural disaster before," Miranda said.

By every measure in the manual, had Trump become an Army officer instead of dodging the draft with his doctor's note about a bone spur in his foot, he would not have risen through the ranks.

Throughout his campaign, Trump predicted his presidency would be one win after another. "We're going to win so much you may even get tired of winning. And you'll say please, please, it's too much winning, we can't take it anymore."

That's not what happened. Still, many of his supporters refuse to accept that they got conned. It must be the fault of Democrats or news reporters, or anyone except Trump. Such is the power of adoration of the celebrity, not that much different from when the ancient Greeks invented tales of intimacy with the gods, producing demigods. Right after they invented demigods, hubris appeared. And we know how that turned out . . .

Trump arrived with no idea of how Washington works. The self-proclaimed great negotiator then started off on the wrong foot and kept on going.

The smart first move would have been to introduce an infrastructure bill to undo decades of malign neglect. Rebuilding failing highways and bridges, replacing unsafe dams, building modern airport terminals, and improving water and sewer systems would have created jobs for construction crews, engineers, and factory workers nationwide. It would have made life more pleasant and signaled a better future. And Democrats would have had to go along with such a bill.

Instead Trump put that on the back burner and demanded an immediate replacement of Obama's signature achievement, the Affordable Care Act.

A month after taking office, Trump met with governors to discuss the problems of repealing Obamacare. He came out of the closed-door session confessing his ignorance of what was common knowledge. "I have to tell you, it's an unbelievably complex subject. Nobody knew that health care could be so complicated."

That should have opened more eyes to Trump's con artistry since everyone else in America knew health care was extremely complicated.

His most extreme supporters, the neo-Nazis, call him "savior" in their online publications. Trump claims that mantle, tweeting as a candidate "I alone can solve" the problem of "radical Islamic terrorism." In accepting the Republican nomination for president, Trump declared "I alone can fix it." Instead of disgust at such an authoritarian claim, or mocking laughter, his words were greeted with enthusiastic applause by leaders of the party that says it stands for personal responsibility and maximum individual liberty (including openly carrying loaded military-grade weapons).

Trump's success in reaching the White House and his continued die-hard support among a third of the adult population reveals a much more serious problem than a crazy man being president.

Donald Trump is not the political disease afflicting America, he is a symptom.

That millions of people voted for a narcissistic, know-nothing con artist who has spent his entire life swindling others while repeatedly urging followers to commit criminal acts of violence against his critics reveals more about America than about Trump.

During the Constitutional Convention, Benjamin Franklin was supposedly asked, "What have we got, a republic or a monarchy?" to which he replied, "A republic—if you can keep it."

Franklin's point was that self-governance requires people to accept the burdens as well as the benefits of freedom. It means they are responsible for their fate and cannot just blame a crazy king or an uncaring despot or anyone else. They must, to be free, take personal responsibility and be actively engaged in shaping the policies that will affect not only their lives, but those of generations to come.

If the United States of America is to endure, it must be with a recognition that compromise, cooperation, and caring about the interests of those you dislike are the basic ingredients of success.

What we have seen since Watergate, unfortunately, is a widening chasm between the incentives of office seekers and the interests of the American people, a political divide that Trump recognized and brilliantly exploited. And now he uses his office to profiteer and to denigrate those who disagree with him, just as dictators and would-be dictators have always done.

Under our Constitution we determine our political fate. If we wish to turn in our citizenship responsibilities and outsource the work to power mongers, we can do so.

Democracies do not die dramatically. They slowly fade away.

In a democracy, we deal with many contending interests through cooperation and compromise. But ever since the anti-tax zealot Grover Norquist popularized the quip by Dick Armey, the former Texas congressman, that "bipartisanship is political date rape," we have seen a growing sense of my way or the highway.

We live in a time when many people denigrate those who have worked to make the most of the opportunities of living in this country, not in terms of monetary rewards but of developing their character, intellect, and judgment. We should oppose these crass tendencies. Our Constitution was born of the Enlightenment, of the idea that reason and intellect and vigorous public debate could produce better societies than those ruled by dogma and monarchs who claimed authority as their divine right.

"Our Constitution is not written to handle someone like Trump," the political scientist Jason Johnson told me. "That is the greatest danger and greatest harm he is to our country."

Johnson notes that the Federalist Papers, the structured debate over whether America should adopt the Constitution, shows that the Framers "envisioned presidents who might be dishonest, who might not have consistent ethical values, but they never envisioned a self-involved dictatorial capitalist, so we don't have a government designed to restrain someone who doesn't care about any of the norms. The British would just get rid of such a person" by calling elections.

In America, though, "everything is dependent on the moral will of existing political parties and Congress, and we are all suffering for that whether we recognize it or not." Johnson believes the failure of Congress to rein in Trump's profiteering, his dealings with the Kremlin, and his bellicosity will afflict America long after he leaves office. "For the next thirty-five years or so, the standard for what you can get away with as long as you are in power and stay in power has been lowered to a level I don't think any of us can fully appreciate today," he said.

America has yet to become the society that Martin Luther King dreamed of in 1963, in which we judge one another not by the color of our skin but the content of our character. Trump represents a diversion on the road to that much better society. He is emblematic of the tendency, magnified since the 1980s, to judge people by the content of their wallet, as if money had anything to do with character.

Our Constitution is meant to free the human spirit so we and our posterity may become something better than we were, better than we are today. Freedom is about choosing, but it is also about having to live with the consequences of the choices we make. If we choose to empower the dishonest, the ill prepared, the mean-spirited, and the emotionally im-mature, we will pay dearly.

Trump often speaks of a unified nation, revealing yet another aspect of his appalling ignorance about our nation. We were not founded to be united. We are not the Taliban, nor the Saudis, nor any other society built on the premise that every member will behave as those in power demand. No president should ever express his admiration for dictators and those who rule not because of popular support but with the iron fist and the gulag. Yet Trump has done exactly that with regard to power seekers in Russia, the Philippines, and Turkey, and even the fratricidal dictator in North Korea, whose power depends on maintaining his entire country as a prison.

Trump's presidency poses a challenge for America. What future will we choose? Do we want to slide toward autocracy in this and future admin-istrations? Or do we want a future that frees the human spirit even more?

ACKNOWLEDGMENTS

One person wrote this book, but the facts came from many people, far more than I will properly express my gratitude to below. To those I neglect to mention, be assured you have my appreciation and so do the readers.

This book is dedicated to Wayne Barrett, who in the late 1970s was the first journalist to start seriously covering Donald Trump instead of printing as fact whatever Trump said. Wayne worked at *The Village Voice* and yet had the deep trust of many law enforcement officials because of his doggedness and absolute integrity, as shown at his funeral, where politicians whose foibles and misconduct he laid bare in print, including New York governor Andrew Cuomo and Senator Chuck Schumer, came to honor his memory and express gratitude for reporting that persuaded them to become better public servants. Before he died, one day before Trump assumed office, Wayne entrusted me with his extensive Trump files. I have shared those files and my own with reporters from major news organizations, many of whom also helped with tying down key facts in this book.

Many academics took time to tutor me and point me to scholarly articles, often by those with whom they disagree, and to refine my understanding of complex issues. Especially helpful were Professors Douglas Brinkley of Rice University, a presidential historian; David Carlton of Vanderbilt, who studies Southern industrialization and deindustrialization; and Roger Conner of Vanderbilt Law, who for more than four decades has been a source for my reporting.

George Lakoff, the University of California cognitive scientist who wrote *Don't Think of an Elephant!* and other provocative books on how the ways politicians, journalists, and others frame issues affect popular perceptions and civic debate, patiently refreshed his past lessons for me on issue framing.

My Syracuse University College of Law colleagues Robert Ashford and Aviva Abramovsky, now dean at the University at Buffalo School of Law, promptly gave advice on legal issues. At the University of Minnesota Law School, I relied on the insights of professors Richard W. Painter, who served as chief ethics officer in the George W. Bush administration, and June Carbone and her husband, William K. (Bill) Black, who as a banking regulator was responsible for the more than three thousand criminal cases brought during the savings and loan scandals of the late 1980s and early 1990s.

The documentary filmmaker Libby Handros provided material related to her 1991 film, *Trump: What's the Deal?*, which Trump suppressed for a quarter century with litigation threats.

As years have turned into decades, my admiration for my literary agent, the lawyer Alice Martell, and her assistant, Stephanie Finman, at the Martell Literary Agency has steadily grown. Alice guided my nascent idea for an exposé of the casino industry and its regulators into my first book in 1992 and has nurtured seven more books with others planned. I am grateful that Bob Bender and Jonathan Karp of Simon & Schuster saw the value in this book documenting what Trump is doing and agreed to publish it.

It's Even Worse Than You Think is a sequel to my 2016 book, *The Making of Donald Trump,* published by Melville House Press, which in turn drew on *Temples of Chance,* my 1992 casino industry exposé, as well as the proposal for a movie about Trump that director Tim Burton commissioned me to write in 1999. In these works, I relied on public records to illuminate Trump's conduct, from his deep lifelong entanglements with heavyweight criminals, including a major drug trafficker for whom he risked his casino licenses for reasons that to this day have never been properly explained, to his appointments of manifestly unqualified cabinet secretaries.

This book was conceived in late 2016, after the elections, as my friends David Crook and Adam Leipzig joined me in founding DCReport.org, a nonprofit and nonadvertising news organization. DCReport covers what the current president and Capitol Hill politicians do, rather than what Trump tweets and they say. We are grateful to more than a thousand Americans who have made gifts of five dollars and up.

Many of the stories DCReport's writers broke later made their way into the mainstream news, though sadly some important issues did not. I am especially grateful to Jim Henry, DCReport's investigative economist. Jim, a lawyer, former McKinsey & Co. chief economist, and former General Electric executive, has devoted his life to exposing money laundering and illicit cash, work that helped me in writing parts of this book. At various places this book relies on the DCReport articles of Isabella Alves, Jillian S. Ambroz, Sarah Okeson, Vic Simon, and Laura Vecsey, who received tiny honoraria for yeoman work. Ambroz and Okeson also worked as reporters on this book.

We plan to continue DCReport long past this administration because of a need to cover our government, not just politics and controversy. For so long as our United States of America endures, the need to shine spotlights on the actions and inactions of our government will never diminish, nor will our duties as American citizens to be engaged with our government.

My hope, dear readers, is that you noticed the repeated use of the word "our" in the previous paragraph. As David Crook says, "It's our government. We own it. We ought to act like owners."

Like this book, DCReport.org grows from a belief that American journalism should refer to *our* Constitution and *our* government, instead of using *the,* which we consider alienating in that context. The use of *the* encourages the idea that our United States of America is a power unto itself rather than a creation of we the people for our benefit. The idea that our government is an alien force has long been promoted by some of the fringe ideologues I have tracked for nearly five decades, some of whom obtained high positions in the Trump administration.

We could not have launched DCReport.org without the help of Andy Alm and GoGo Lidz; the continuing social media skills of Tod Hardin at thisiscrowd.com; and the many volunteers who acted as copy editors, proofreaders, and tipsters. Thanks, too, to Ian Isaacs, introduced to us by the great and sadly late journalist Jack Rosenthal, for trying to develop the resources to expand our capacity to cover the actions, and inactions, of our government, not just what our politicians say about our government.

Writers Danelle Morton and Dana Kennedy offered encouragement when it was needed most. So did Julia Kagan, Joshua Greenman, and Harry Siegel. I am also grateful for the valuable assistance of Seth Heald, president of the Sierra Club in Virginia, Mieke Eoyang, Christine McEntee, the excellent Freedom of Information Act devotee Michael Ravnitsky, and many others who, because of my shortcomings, or their wish to remain uncredited, will not be named.

As always, I relied on help from some of my eight children, now long grown. Amy Boyle Johnston, a writer, photographer, and glass artist, researched the public record and had the daunting task of keeping my files organized. Amy, or Number Four as I call her sometimes, set aside completing her deeply researched biography of Rod Serling to find obscure documents, often making connections neither I nor anyone else had made between distinct events. Molly Leonard, a lawyer in the Toronto suburb of Brampton, took time from representing children in court proceedings to copyedit some chapters. So did her younger sister Kate, who makes eight, and who has worked as the script coordinator on *House of Cards*, *The Breaks*, and the forthcoming *The Looming Tower* while developing her own skills as a lyricist, comedy writer, and performer in Manhattan.

My loving wife of more than thirty-five ever better years, Jennifer Leonard, whose last name we gave our two daughters, was, as always, unsparing in her support both for this book and the Rochester Area Community Foundation, which she has led since 1993. Jennifer, like Molly and Kate a better writer than me, gave the honest appraisals we verbally preface with a warning that what comes next is "unvarnished criticism." She embodies my firm belief that your best friends tell you not just what you are glad to hear, but more importantly what you need to hear.

David Cay Johnston
Rochester, New York

NOTES

My policy is to promptly and forthrightly correct any errors. Readers who find any factual error are asked to point it out and send supporting documentation to davidcayjohnston@gmail.com.

THE TRUMP FACTOR

12 *"Moscow and Bejing are deeply envious"*: Kate Reilly, "Read Hillary Clinton's Speech on Donald Trump and National Security," *Time*, June 2, 2016 (with video), http://time.com/4355797/hillary-clinton-donald-trump-foreign-policy-speech-transcript/.

KLEPTOCRACY RISING

13 *known as The Beast*: Trump Inaugural Parade Motorcade, C-SPAN, Jan. 20, 2017, https://www.c-span.org/video/?422243-102/trump-inaugural-parade-motorcade.

13 *On the night before the Inauguration*: Matthew Nussbaum, "Spicer on Trump Going to Hotel: 'Shouldn't Be a Shocker,'" Politico, Jan. 19, 2017, http://www.politico.com/story/2017/01/2017-trump-inauguration-hotel-visit-233837.

15 *Average room rates*: "Donald Trump's Conflicts of Interest," Economist.com, Nov. 26, 2016, https://www.economist.com/news/business/21710828-weakness-trump-inc-may-pose-more-problem-its-sprawl-donald-trumps-conflicts.

15 *revenue per guest night was $653*: Jonathan O'Connell, "Trump D.C. Hotel Turns $2 Million Profit in Four Months," *Washington Post*, Aug. 10, 2017, https://www.washingtonpost.com/politics/trump-dc-hotel-turns-2-million-profit-in-four-months/2017/08/10/23bd97f0-7e02-11e7-9d08-b79f191668ed_story.html?utm_term=.8f752b647aa0.

16 *"during my term(s) in office":* Donald J. Trump, Twitter, Dec. 12, 2016, https://twitter.com/realdonaldtrump/status/808529888630239232?lang=en.

17 *13 cents:* Bruce Feirstein, "Trump's War on 'Losers': The Early Years," *Vanity Fair,* Aug. 12, 2015, https://www.vanityfair.com/news/2015/08/spy-vs-trump.

18 *separate lawsuit:* Daniel Wagner, "Here Is Donald Trump's Newly Released Videotaped Deposition," BuzzFeed, Sept. 30, 2016, https://www.buzzfeed.com/danielwagner/trump-video-depositions.

19 *revocable trust:* www.gsa.gov/portal/getMediaData?mediaId=157798.

20 *180-page report concluded:* John F. Berry and Ted Gup, "Inquiry Clears Carter Family's Peanut Business," *Washington Post,* Oct. 17, 1979, https://www.washingtonpost.com/archive/politics/1979/10/17/inquiry-clears-carter-familys-peanut-business/ca5371c9-f0a7-4809-9b7d-7a57e78b76b0/.

EMOLUMENTS

23 *early 1800s:* Norman L. Eisen, Richard Painter, and Laurence H. Tribe, "The Emoluments Clause: Its Text, Meaning, and Application to Donald J. Trump," Governance Studies at Brookings Institution, Dec. 16, 2016, https://www.brookings.edu/wp-content/uploads/2016/12/gs_121616_emoluments-clause1.pdf.

24 *NASA scientist accept:* United States Attorneys General, "Emoluments Clause Questions Raised by NASA Scientist's Proposed Consulting Arrangement with the University of New South Wales," Court Listener, Free Law Project, May 23, 1986, https://www.courtlistener.com/opinion/4343778/emoluments-clause-questions-raised-by-nasa-scientists-proposed-consulting/.

26 *profit, gain, benefit, and advantage:* Samuel Johnson, *A Dictionary of the English Language* (W. Strahan, 1755), https://books.google.com/books?id=cNrI9Y4bY_QC&q=%22emolument%22#v=onepage&q=%22Emolument%22&f=false; John Mikhail, "'Emolument' in Blackstone's Commentaries," balkin.blogspot, May 28, 2017, https://balkin.blogspot.com/2017/05/emolument-in-blackstones-commentaries.html.

26 *remains in print today:* A modern printed set sells new for about $450; there are many versions of the *Commentaries* in print, https://www.amazon.com/Blackstones-Commentaries-Constitution-Government-Commonwealth/dp/1886363153.

26 *extensive business holdings: Citizens for Responsibility and Ethics in Washington v. Donald J. Trump,* https://www.courthousenews.com/wp-content/uploads/2017/01/Emoluments.pdf.

27 *"their bottom line":* Author interview, June 17, 2017.

28 *pending in summer 2017:* Erika Kinetz, "Ivanka Trump Brand Applies for,
Wins More China Trademarks," *Chicago Tribune,* June 12, 2017, http://www.
chicagotribune.com/business/national/ct-ivanka-trump-china-trademarks
-20170612-story.html.

28 *the Trump family owned:* Sui-Lee Wee, "Trump Adds More Trademarks in
China," *New York Times,* June 13, 2017, https://www.nytimes.com/2017/06/13
/business/trump-china-trademarks.html.

28 *"decisions made that quickly":* Erika Kinetz, "China Approves 9 Trump Trademarks Previously Rejected," Associated Press, June 14, 2017, https://apnews
.com/a891967cfe12428cb2f7ad05f8fcf594/China-approves-9-Trump-trade
marks-previously-rejected.

29 *identify foreign government business:* Trump Organization Brochure, "Donation
of Profits from Foreign Government Patronage," https://democrats-oversight
.house.gov/sites/democrats.oversight.house.gov/files/documents/Trump%20
Org%20Pamphlet%20on%20Foreign%20Profits.pdf.

REFUSALS TO PAY

31 *lying, denying, or concealing:* Office of Government Ethics, Form 450, 5 CFR
Part 2634, Subpart I U.S., https://www.oge.gov/web/OGE.nsf/OGE%20Forms
/A3FD8C0DFF0A2DAF85257EC10065A07F/$FILE/oge450_accessible%20
(Jan2017).pdf?open.

32 *more than $50 million:* Executive Branch Personnel Public Financial Disclosure
Report (OGE Form 278e), Donald J. Trump, https://assets.documentcloud.org
/documents/3867112/Trump-Financial-Disclosure-2017.pdf.

33 *broke the story:* Jeff Ostrowski, "EXCLUSIVE: Donald Trump Sues Over
Taxable Value of Jupiter Golf Club," *Palm Beach Post,* July 13, 2017, http://
www.mypalmbeachpost.com/news/exclusive-donald-trump-sues-over
-taxable-value-jupiter-golf-club/LhGqsVNiBirUNR6JOAbUoI/.

34 *money for Russian oligarchs:* Brian Bandell, "Trump Boosts Loan on Doral
Golf Resort," *South Florida Business Journal,* Aug. 13, 2015, https://www
.bizjournals.com/southflorida/news/2015/08/13/trump-boosts-loan-on-doral
-golf-resort.html.

36 *ordered them out immediately:* Debra Cassens Weiss, "Trump's Gold Club
Must Pay $5.7M to Locked-Out Members, Judge Rules," *ABA Journal,* Feb. 2,
2017, http://www.abajournal.com/news/article/trumps_golf_club_must_pay
_5.7m_to_locked_out_members_judge_rules.

36 *Six months later Trump appealed:* Andy Reid, "Trump Golf Club Fighting
Millions in Reimbursements to Former Members," *Sun Sentinel,* Aug. 8, 2017,

http://www.sun-sentinel.com/local/palm-beach/fl-pn-trump-golf-lawsuit
-appeal-20170808-story.html.

36 *Gloria Fried:* Allan Dodds Frank, "Trump Organization Seeks Hefty Tax Break
for Westchester Golf Club," ABC News, June 21, 2017, http://abcnews.go.com
/Politics/trump-organization-seeks-hefty-tax-break-westchester-golf/story?id
=48179222.

APPOINTEES

39 *"subglacial speed":* Karen Yourish and Gregor Aisch, "The Top Jobs in Trump's
Administration Are Mostly Vacant: Who's to Blame?," *New York Times,* July
20, 2017, https://www.nytimes.com/interactive/2017/07/17/us/politics/trump
-appointments.html.

39 *124 nominees confirmed:* Kevin Uhrmacher and Kevin Schaul, "At August
Recess, Trump Remains Behind on Confirmations," *Washington Post,* Aug. 4,
2017, https://www.washingtonpost.com/graphics/2017/politics/slow-pace-of
-trump-confirmations/?utm_term=.66a5785ba9af.

39 *pipeline was empty, too:* Partnership for Public Service, "Political Appointee
Tracker," https://ourpublicservice.org/issues/presidential-transition/political
-appointee-tracker.php.

39 *took his oath:* Julie Hirschfeld Davis, "In Break with Precedent, Obama Envoys
Are Denied Extensions Past Inauguration," *New York Times,* Jan. 5, 2017,
https://www.nytimes.com/2017/01/05/us/politics/trump-ambassadors.html.

40 *36 of 188 ambassadors:* American Foreign Service Association, "Appointments—Donald J. Trump," http://www.afsa.org/appointments-donald-j-trump.

41 *"Want approvals":* Donald J. Trump, Twitter, June 5, 2017, https://twitter.com
/realdonaldtrump/status/871722020278587393?lang=en.

42 *"I want to thank him":* Gregory Korte and Jessica Estepa, "Trump Thanks
Vladimir Putin for Expelling U.S. Diplomats from Russia: 'We're Trying to Cut
Down Our Payroll,'" *USA Today,* Aug, 10, 2017, https://www.usatoday.com
/story/news/politics/onpolitics/2017/08/10/donald-trump-thanks-vladimir
-putin-expelling-u-s-diplomats/557356001/.

42 *Mieke Eoyang:* Author interview, July 31, 2017.

43 *Revolving Door Project:* Center for Economic and Policy Research, biography
of Jeff Hauser, http://cepr.net/about-us/staff/jeff-hauser-executive-director-of
-the-revolving-door-project.

43 *"wholly inadequate":* Remarks of Walter M. Shaub, Jr., Director, U.S. Office of
Government Ethics, as prepared for delivery at 4:00 p.m. on January 11, 2017,

at the Brookings Institution, https://www.brookings.edu/wp-content/uploads/2017/01/20170111_oge_shaub_remarks.pdf.

44 *"undermines confidence in government"*: David Smith, "Trump Risks US Being Seen as 'Kleptocracy,' Says Ex-Ethics Chief Walter Shaub," *The Guardian,* July 31, 2017, https://www.theguardian.com/us-news/2017/jul/31/trump-ethics-chief-walter-shaub-kleptocracy.

HIDING IN THE BUDGET

47 *first report on the Trade and Development Agency:* U.S. Trade and Development Agency Fiscal Year 2018 Congressional Budget Justification, n.d., https://www.ustda.gov/sites/default/files/Congressional%20Budget%20Justification%20-%20FY%202018.pdf.

50 *"doing business with North Korea":* Donald J. Trump, Twitter, Sept. 3, 2017, https://twitter.com/realDonaldTrump/status/904377075049656322.

50 *third largest buyer of American exports:* Office of the United States Trade Representative, "The People's Republic of China," n.d., https://ustr.gov/countries-regions/china-mongolia-taiwan/peoples-republic-china.

50 *"over 2,400 megawatts of new renewable energy":* U.S. Trade and Development Agency, "Our Mission," n.d., https://www.ustda.gov/about/mission.

51 *greater extraction and use of fossil fuels:* Mathew Daly and Josh Boak, Associated Press, "Trump Plan Would Expand Oil Drilling in Arctic and Atlantic," *PBS NewsHour,* June 29, 2017, http://www.pbs.org/newshour/rundown/trump-plan-expand-oil-drilling-arctic-atlantic/.

A MIGHTY JOB CREATOR

54 *signed five executive orders:* The White House, Office of the Press Secretary, "Presidential Memorandum Regarding Construction of the Keystone XL Pipeline," Jan. 24, 2017, https://www.whitehouse.gov/the-press-office/2017/01/24/presidential-memorandum-regarding-construction-keystone-xl-pipeline.

57 *"auto companies that are coming back":* Donald J. Trump, speech, Phoenix, Arizona, Aug. 22, 2017, https://www.c-span.org/video/?432748-1/president-trump-criticizes-dishonest-media-defends-charlottesville-remarks-rally-phoenix.

57 *technology, especially in Texas:* CNNMoney Staff, "Trump and Jobs: A Running Fact Check," CNNMoney, March 28, 2017, http://money.cnn.com/2017/02/17/news/companies/donald-trump-jobs-watch/index.html.

57 *soft demand from buyers:* Ibid.

58 *reporter Jason Stein of the* Milwaukee Journal Sentinel: Jason Stein, "Wisconsin's Offer to Foxconn Grew Substantially and Hit $3 Billion on Handwritten Note," *Milwaukee Journal Sentinel,* Aug. 31, 2017, http://www.jsonline.com /story/news/politics/2017/08/31/wisconsins-offer-started-handwrittento -foxconn-grew-substantially-over-negotiations-after-handwritte/622041001/.

58 *Trump never mentioned:* Fiona Tam, "Foxconn Factories Are Labour Camps: Report," *South China Morning Post,* Oct. 11, 2010, http://www.scmp.com /article/727143/foxconn-factories-are-labour-camps-report.

59 *much more skilled manufacturing workers:* Danielle Paquette, "The Real Reason Ford Abandoned Its Plant in Mexico Has Little to Do with Trump," *Washington Post,* Jan. 4, 2017, https://www.washingtonpost.com/news/wonk /wp/2017/01/04/the-real-reason-ford-abandoned-its-plant-in-mexico-has -little-to-do-with-trump/?utm_term=.cd076449759a.

59 *a lifelong Cadillac fan:* Mark Ehrenfreund and Jim Tankersley, "Donald Trump Has a Favorite Carmaker, and That Might Be a Problem," *Washington Post,* Dec. 22, 2016, https://www.washingtonpost.com/news/wonk/wp/2016/12/22 /donald-trump-has-a-favorite-carmaker-and-that-might-be-a-problem.

59 *associated with the Colombo crime family:* William Bastone, "Trump Limos Were Built with a Hood Ornament," The Smoking Gun, Sept. 22, 2015, http:// www.thesmokinggun.com/documents/celebrity/trump-and-staluppi-092157.

FORGETTING THE FORGOTTEN MAN

61 *killed the webpage:* Jordan Barab, "OSHA Covers Up Workplace Fatalities," Confined Space, Aug. 25, 2017, http://jordanbarab.com/confinedspace/2017 /08/25/osha-hides-workplace-fatalities/.

61 *prior to 2017:* United States Department of Labor, OSHA, website, "Fatality Inspection Data," https://www.osha.gov/dep/fatcat/dep_fatcat.html.

62 *"President Trump's War on Regulation":* White House website, "President Trump's War on Regulation Results in Near-Record High CEO Confidence," Feb. 8, 2017, https://www.whitehouse.gov/blog/2017/02/08/trumps-war-regulation -results-near-record-high-ceo-confidence.

62 *average thirteen per day:* United States Department of Labor, OSHA, website, "Commonly Used Statistics," https://www.osha.gov/oshstats/commonstats .html.

62 *killed on the job:* Jordan Barab, "Weekly Toll: OSHA Won't Tell You Who Died in the Workplace. We Will," Confined Space, Aug. 28, 2017, http://jordan barab.com/confinedspace/2017/08/28/weekly-toll-osha-wont-tell/.

63 *"no interest in worker issues, either":* Author interview, April 4, 2017.

63 *"contrary to the national interest"*: The White House, "President Trump Elimi-
nates Job-Killing Regulations," March 30, 2017, https://www.whitehouse.gov
/blog/2017/03/30/president-trump-eliminates-job-killing-regulations.

63 *"working people's health and safety"*: "Gorsuch Confirmation Hearing, Day 4,
Part I," C-SPAN, March 23, 2017, https://www.c-span.org/video/?425700-1
/final-day-gorsuch-confirmation-hearing-focuses-witness-testimomny&live.

63 *refuse dangerous tasks:* United States Department of Labor, OSHA, website,
"Workers' Right to Refuse Dangerous Work," https://www.osha.gov/right-to
-refuse.html.

63 *Truck driver Alphonse Maddin: TransAm Trucking, Inc. v. Administrative
Review Board, United States Department of Labor,* No. 15-9504, appeal from
the Department of Labor (except OSHA), ARB. No. 13-031, https://www.ca10
.uscourts.gov/opinions/15/15-9504.pdf.

65 *"dissent, Judge Gorsuch"*: Dick Durbin, press release, "Durbin: Gorsuch Has a
Troubling Record of Ruling Against Workers and Families," March 3, 2017,
https://www.durbin.senate.gov/newsroom/press-releases/durbin-gorsuch-has
-a-troubling-record-of-ruling-against-workers-and-families.

65 *A rule went into effect:* United States Department of Labor, OSHA, press release,
"US Labor Department Proposes Delay to Beryllium Rule Effective Date,"
March 1, 2017, https://www.osha.gov/news/newsreleases/national/03012017.

66 *where silica is used:* Centers for Disease Control and Prevention, "Silicosis
Mortality Trends and New Exposures to Respirable Crystalline Silica—United
States, 2001 2010," Feb. 13, 2015, https://www.cdc.gov/mmwr/preview
/mmwrhtml/mm6405a1.htm.

66 *"form the basis of lawsuits"*: Chamber letter by Neil Bradley, chief policy officer,
in Impact of Federal Regulations on Domestic Manufacturing (Docket No.
170302221-7221-01); DOC-2017-0001-0001.

67 *Driver fatigue:* Author interview, Sept. 11, 2017. Claybrook cited National
Highway Transportation Safety Administration data including "Traffic Safety
Facts 2015 Data," February 2017, https://crashstats.nhtsa.dot.gov/Api/Public
/Publication/812373.

67 *A notice in the Federal Register:* Federal Register, "Evaluation of Safety Sensitive
Personnel for Moderate-to-Severe Obstructive Sleep Apnea," Aug. 8, 2017, https://
www.federalregister.gov/documents/2017/08/08/2017-16451/evaluation
-of-safety-sensitive-personnel-for-moderate-to-severe-obstructive-sleep-apnea.

69 *World Economic Outlook:* International Monetary Fund, "World Economic
Outlook Update, July 2017," http://www.imf.org/en/Publications/WEO/Issues
/2017/07/07/world-economic-outlook-update-july-2017.

WASHINGTON APPRENTICE

73 *"take apart an engine blindfolded"*: White House Press Secretary Office, "Remarks by President Trump in Roundtable Discussion on Vocational Training with U.S. and German Business Leaders," March 17, 2017, https:// www.whitehouse.gov/the-press-office/2017/03/17/remarks-president-trump -roundtable-discussion-vocational-training-us-and.

75 *"the very near future as to GDP"*: White House Press Secretary Office, "Remarks by President Trump at Signing of an Executive Order on Apprenticeship and Workforce of Tomorrow Initiatives," June 15, 2017, https://www.whitehouse .gov/the-press-office/2017/06/15/remarks-president-trump-signing-executive -order-apprenticeship-and.

75 *The executive order declared*: White House Press Secretary Office, "Presidential Executive Order Expanding Apprenticeships in America," June 15, 2017, https://www.whitehouse.gov/the-press-office/2017/06/15/presidential -executive-order-expanding-apprenticeships-america.

THE TAX EXPERT

79 *to include Trump's name*: Rebecca Savransky, "NSC Officials Include Trump's Name as Often as Possible so He Reads Memos: Report," *The Hill*, May 17, 2017, http://thehill.com/homenews/administration/333788-nsc-official-include -trumps-name-as-often-as-possible-so-he-reads.

79 *sixth-grade grammar*: Justin Wm. Moyer, "Trump's Grammar in Speeches 'Just Below 6th Grade Level,' Study Finds," *Washington Post*, March 18, 2016, https://www.washingtonpost.com/news/morning-mix/wp/2016/03/18 /trumps-grammar-in-speeches-just-below-6th-grade-level-study-finds/.

79 *two administrative trials*: David Cay Johnston, "New Evidence Donald Trump Didn't Pay Taxes," Daily Beast, June 15, 2016, http://www.thedailybeast.com /new-evidence-donald-trump-didnt-pay-taxes.

81 *"It's never below zero"*: Louis Jacobson, "Donald Trump Gets Claim About U.S. GDP Doubly Wrong," PolitiFact, June 16, 2015, http://www.politifact.com/ truth-o-meter/statements/2015/jun/16/donald-trump/donald-trump-says-us -gdp-never-negative-ter//.

82 *actors paid fifty bucks*: Aaron Couch and Emmet McDermott, "Donald Trump Campaign Offered Actors $50 to Cheer for Him at Presidential Announcement," *Hollywood Reporter*, June 17, 2015, http://www.holly woodreporter.com/news/donald-trump-campaign-offered-actors-803161.

82 *"we have an amazing code"*: Tom McCarthy and Ben Jacobs, "Donald Trump Unveils Tax Plan with Cuts for Poorest and Richest Americans," *The Guardian*, Sept. 28, 2015, https://www.theguardian.com/us-news/2015/sep/28/donald -trump-unveils-tax-plan.

83 *from 1967 through 2012*: Chad Stone, Danilo Trisi, Arloc Sherman, and Emily Horton, "A Guide to Statistics on Historical Trends in Income Inequality," Center on Budget and Policy Priorities, Nov. 7, 2016, https://www.cbpp.org /research/poverty-and-inequality/a-guide-to-statistics-on-historical-trends -in-income-inequality.

88 *"a whole different ballgame"*: Mathew J. Belvedere, "A 'Revved Up Economy' Will Help Pay for My Agenda, Trump Says," CNBC, Feb. 28, 2017, https:// www.cnbc.com/2017/02/28/a-revved-up-economy-will-help-pay-for-my -agenda-trump-says.html.

89 *Steve Mnuchin and Gary Cohn*: "The 1-Page White House Handout on Trump's Tax Proposal," CNN, April 26, 2017, http://www.cnn.com/2017/04/26/politics /white-house-donald-trump-tax-proposal/index.html.

TRUMP'S TAX RETURN

93 *the tax return story at DCReport.org*: David Cay Johnston, "Trump Earned $153 Million in 2005; He Paid $36.6 Million in Taxes," DCReport.org, March 14, 2017, https://www.dcreport.org/2017/03/14/taxes/.

94 *sent anonymously to* The New York Times: David Barstow, Susanne Craig, Russ Buettner, and Megan Twohey, "Donald Trump Tax Records Show He Could Have Avoided Taxes for Nearly Two Decades, The Times Found," *New York Times*, Oct. 1, 2016, https://www.nytimes.com/2016/10/02/us/politics /donald-trump-taxes.html.

94 *the New York* Daily News: Nicole Hensley and Rich Schapiro, "Trump Tax Returns Surface: The Donald's $916M Loss in 1995 Means He Could Have Avoided Paying for 18 Years," New York *Daily News*, Oct. 2, 2106, http://www .nydailynews.com/news/politics/trump-tax-records-show-avoided-paying-20 -years-article-1.2814176.

97 *"That makes me smart"*: Daniella Diaz, "Trump: 'I'm Smart' for Not Paying Taxes," CNN, Sept. 27, 2016, http://www.cnn.com/2016/09/26/politics/donald -trump-federal-income-taxes-smart-debate/index.html.

99 *Joseph Weichselbaum, a mob associate*: William Bastone, "Trump Vouched for Cocaine Trafficker," The Smoking Gun, Feb. 16, 2016, ttp://www

.thesmokinggun.com/documents/celebrity/the-donald-and-the-dealer
-173892. "Trump: Cocaine Dealer? What Cocaine Dealer?" The Smoking
Gun, March 1, 2016, http://www.thesmokinggun.com/documents/celebrity
/trump-dge-report-weichselbaum-563821. David Cay Johnston, "Just What
Were Donald Trump's Ties to the Mob?" Politico Magazine, May 22, 2016,
http://www.politico.com/magazine/story/2016/05/donald-trump-2016-mob
-organized-crime-213910.

100 *risked his casino license:* David Cay Johnston, "The Drug Trafficker Donald
Trump Risked His Casino Empire to Protect," The Daily Beast, Oct. 19, 2016,
https://www.thedailybeast.com/the-drug-trafficker-donald-trump-risked
-his-casino-empire-to-protect; see also *Trump: The Deals and the Downfall,*
Wayne Barrett (New York: HarperCollins 1992), where the story broke, and
Libby Handros documentary.

TRUMP'S WALL

104 *20 percent tariff on Mexican imports:* Gregory Korte and David Jackson,
"Trump Mulls 20% Border Tax on Mexico; Aides Later Call It Just an Option,"
USA Today, Jan. 26, 2017, https://www.usatoday.com/story/news/politics
/2017/01/26/trump-propose-20-mexican-border-tax-pay-wall/97099374/.

107 *$4 billion per year:* United States Energy Information, "U.S. Net Imports from
Mexico of Crude Oil and Petroleum Products, Monthly, https://www.eia.gov
/opendata/qb.php?sdid=PET.MTTNTUSMX2.M.

110 *"They'll be very happy to pay":* Jake Miller, "Mexico Will 'Be Very Happy to Pay'
for Border Wall, Trump Says," CBS News, May 1, 2017, https://www.cbsnews
.com/news/mexico-will-be-very-happy-to-pay-for-border-wall-trump-says
/. Accessed Sept. 2, 2017.

110 *Attorney General Jeff Sessions: This Week with George Stephanopoulos,*
"Transcript 4-23-17: Attorney General Jeff Sessions and Xavier Becerra," ABC
News, April 23, 2017, http://abcnews.go.com/Politics/week-transcript-23-17
-attorney-general-jeff-sessions/story?id=46955082. Accessed Sept. 2, 2017.

110 *children sixteen and younger:* Treasury Inspector General for Tax Administration, "Individuals Who Are Not Authorized to Work in the United States
Were Paid $4.2 Billion in Refundable Credits," July 7, 2011, https://www
.treasury.gov/tigta/auditreports/2011reports/201141061fr.pdf. Accessed Sept.
2, 2017.

110 *$7.6 billion:* Joint Committee on Taxation Staff, "Description of the Budget
Reconciliation Legislative Recommendations Relating to Social Security
Number Requirements for the Refundable Portion of the Child Tax Credit,"

April 18, 2012, https://www.jct.gov/publications.html?func=startdown&id
=4421.

111 *Census Bureau data showed:* United States Census Bureau, "Trade in Goods with
Mexico," https://www.census.gov/foreign-trade/balance/c2010.html.

POLLUTERS' PARADISE

115 *sued the EPA fourteen times:* "Pruitt v. EPA: 14 Challenges of EPA Rules by
the Oklahoma Attorney General," *New York Times,* Jan. 14, 2017, https://www
.nytimes.com/interactive/2017/01/14/us/politics/document-Pruitt-v-EPA-a
-Compilation-of-Oklahoma-14.html.

115 *"the EPA's activist agenda":* Justin Worland, "What You Need to Know About
Scott Pruitt, Trump's Pick for EPA," *Time,* Dec. 7, 2016, http://time.com/4594238
/donald-trump-scott-pruitt-epa/.

116 *told to not take any notes:* Coral Davenport and Eric Lipton, "Scott Pruitt Is
Carrying Out His E.P.A. Agenda in Secret, Critics Say," *New York Times,* Aug.
11, 2017, https://www.nytimes.com/2017/08/11/us/politics/scott-pruitt-epa
.html.

116 *"Chinese hoax":* Louis Jacobson, "Yes, Donald Trump Did Call Climate Change
a Chinese Hoax," PolitiFact, June 3, 2016, http://www.politifact.com/truth-o
-meter/statements/2016/jun/03/hillary-clinton/yes-donald-trump-did-call
-climate-change-chinese-h/.

116 *"as you do your work":* Scott Pruitt, speech to EPA staff, Feb. 21, 2017, https://
www.c-span.org/video/?424362-1/administrator-scott-pruitt-addresses-epa
-employees.

120 *"degraded environment":* Jacqueline Thomsen, "Top EPA Official Resigns over
Direction of Agency Under Trump," *The Hill,* Aug. 1, 2017, http://thehill.com
/news-by-subject/energy-environment/344825-top-epa-official-resigns-over
-direction-of-agency-under.

GO FOIA YOURSELF

124 *less than a third of Obama's five-year average:* Eric Katz, "EPA Has Slashed Its
Criminal Investigation Division in Half," *Government Executive,* Aug. 24, 2017,
http://www.govexec.com/management/2017/08/epa-has-slashed-its-criminal
-investigation-division-half/140509/.

INTERIOR PURGING

133 *673-page document:* U.S. Global Change Research Program Climate Science Speacial Report (CSSR), Fifth-Order Draft, June 28, 2017, https://assets .documentcloud.org/documents/3920195/Final-Draft-of-the-Climate -Science-Special-Report.pdf.

134 *seventy-four questions:* "Questions Posed by President-Elect Trump's Transition Team to Energy Department Officials," *Washington Post,* https://www .washingtonpost.com/apps/g/page/politics/questions-posed-by-president -elect-trumps-transition-team-to-energy-department-officials/2143/.

134 *Senator Edward Markey:* Edward J. Markey, letter to Donald J. Trump, Dec. 9, 2016, https://www.markey.senate.gov//imo/media/doc/2016-12-09-Markey -PresidentTrump-DOE.pdf.

STRIPPING SCIENCE

138 *"the world's greatest person":* Greg Miller, Julia Vitkovskaya, and Reuben Fischer-Baum, " 'This Deal Will Make Me Look Terrible': Full Transcripts of Trump's Calls with Mexico and Australia," *Washington Post,* Aug. 3, 2017, https://www .washingtonpost.com/graphics/2017/politics/australia-mexico-transcripts/.

138 *Science and Technology Policy:* The White House, National Science and Technology Council webpage, https://www.whitehouse.gov/ostp/nstc#Documents_Reports.

138 *policy office webpage:* The White House, National Science and Technology Council webpage, "OSTP News and Public Releases," https://www.whitehouse .gov/ostp/news.

138 *urgent scientific and technological issues:* The White House, Office of Science and Technology Policy, "NSTC Documents and Reports," https://obamawhite-house.archives.gov/administration/eop/ostp/nstc/docsreports.

138 *atmospheric, oceanic, and food safety science:* "Tracking How Many Key Positions Trump Has Filled So Far," *Washington Post,* https://www.washingtonpost .com/graphics/politics/trump-administration-appointee-tracker/database /?add-filter=science-positions&tid=a_inl. Last accessed Sept. 14, 2017.

139 *profitable products and services:* Mick Mulvaney, "Memorandum for the Heads of Executive Departments and Agencies," Aug. 17, 2017, https://www.whitehouse .gov/sites/whitehouse.gov/files/omb/memoranda/2017/m-17-30.pdf. Accessed Sept. 10, 2017.

139 *infesting cattle herds:* Goldengooseaward.org, "2016: The Sex Life of the Screwworm Fly," https://www.goldengooseaward.org/awardees/screwworms.

141 *according to the Commerce Department:* Justin Antonipillai and Michelle K.

Lee, "Intellectual Property and the U.S. Economy: 2016 Update," Economics and Statistics Administration and United States Patent and Trademark Office, Sept. 2016, https://www.uspto.gov/sites/default/files/documents /IPandtheUSEconomySept2016.pdf.

STOCKING THE SWAMP

145 *a Boeing 777 generates only 110,000 horsepower:* Alexis C. Madrigal, "A Single Boeing 777 Engine Delivers Twice the Horsepower of All the Titanic's," *The Atlantic,* Dec. 30, 2011, https://www.theatlantic.com/technology/archive/2011 /12/a-single-boeing-777-engine-delivers-twice-the-horsepower-of-all-the -titanics/250698/.

146 *$50 billion worth:* Catherine Traywick, "Energy Projects Worth $50 Billion Are Stalled Until Trump Fills Empty Posts," Bloomberg News, May 5, 2017, https://www.bloomberg.com/news/articles/2017-05-05/trump-s-delay-stalls -50-billion-of-energy-projects-in-pipeline.

146 *"The jihad has begun":* Marie Cusick, "Utility Regulator Slams Pipeline Opponents," StateImpact/NPR, March 21, 2017, https://stateimpact.npr.org /pennsylvania/2017/03/21/utility-regulator-slams-pipeline-opponents/.

150 *had moved out of more than a decade before:* Sean Sullivan and Glen Boshart, "FERC's Bay: Transition Team Knew I Would Leave; Chair Swap Got Lost in the Mail," SNL, Feb. 1, 2017, http://www.snl.com/web/client?auth=inherit#news /article?id=39289785&cdid=A-39289785-10531.

DIPLOMACY

155 *"express their feelings":* Mathew J. Belvedere, "Commerce's Wilbur Ross Sees a 'Big Sea Change' in Saudi Arabia Regarding Women in Business," CNBC, May 22, 2017, https://www.cnbc.com/2017/05/22/commerces-wilbur-ross-sees-a -big-sea-change-in-saudi-arabia-regarding-women-in-business.html; Patrick Wintour, "UN Accuses Saudi Arabia of Using Terror Laws to Suppress Free Speech," *The Guardian,* May 4, 2017, https://www.theguardian.com/world /2017/may/04/un-accuses-saudi-arabia-of-using-terror-laws-to-suppress -free-speech; United Nations, "The Universal Declaration of Human Rights," http://www.un.org/en/universal-declaration-human-rights/.

155 *"organizing a demonstration":* United States Department of State, "Country Reports on Human Rights Practices for 2016," https://www.state.gov/j/drl/rls /hrrpt/humanrightsreport/index.htm#wrapper.

156 *aside from soccer matches:* Janine Di Giovanni, "When It Comes to Beheadings,

ISIS Has Nothing over Saudi Arabia," *Newsweek,* Oct. 14, 2014, http://www
.newsweek.com/2014/10/24/when-it-comes-beheadings-isis-has-nothing
-over-saudi-arabia-277385.html.

156 *convicted murderer:* Cornell Center on the Death Penalty Worldwide, "Death
Penalty Database: Qatar," Jan. 1, 2010, https://www.deathpenaltyworldwide
.org/country-search-post.cfm?country=Qatar.

157 *Trump's Riyadh speech:* President Trump's Speech to the Arab Islamic American
Summit, May 21, 2017, https://www.whitehouse.gov/the-press-office/2017/05
/21/president-trumps-speech-arab-islamic-american-summit.

157 *Abandonining that history:* Ibid.

158 *Saudis fund the Taliban:* Carlotta Gall, "Saudis Bankroll Taliban, Even as King
Officially Supports Afghan Government," *New York Times,* Dec. 6, 2016,
https://www.nytimes.com/2016/12/06/world/asia/saudi-arabia-afghanistan
.html.

158 *Trump had interests:* Stephen Rex Brown, "EXCLUSIVE: Donald Trump Made
Millions from Saudi Arabia, but Trashes Hillary Clinton for Saudi Donations
to Clinton Foundation," Sept. 4, 2016, http://www.nydailynews.com/news
/politics/exclusive-donald-trump-made-millions-saudi-government-article
-1.2777211.

159 *Trump said he would have a conflict:* Ashley Dejean, "Donald Trump Has a
Conflict of Interest in Turkey. Just Ask Donald Trump," *Mother Jones,* April 18,
2017, http://www.motherjones.com/politics/2017/04/trump-turkey-erdogan
-conflict-interest/.

159 *"we need to use":* Wikileaks.org, https://wikileaks.org/podesta-emails/emailid
/3774.

160 *started providing $110 million annually:* Phil Stewart, "Exclusive: U.S. to
Spend Up to $550 Million on African Rapid Response Forces," Reuters,
Aug. 6, 2014, http://www.reuters.com/article/us-africa-summit-military
/exclusive-u-s-to-spend-up-to-550-million-on-african-rapid-response-forces
-idUSKBN0G623J20140807.

160 *"life-saving potential":* The White House, "FACT SHEET: U.S. Support for
Peacekeeping in Africa," Aug. 6, 2014, https://obamawhitehouse.archives.gov/
the-press-office/2014/08/06/fact-sheet-us-support-peacekeeping-africa.

160 *without direct American involvement:* United States Department of State, "U.S.
Peacekeeping Capacity Building Assistance," Jan. 25, 2017, https://www.state.
gov/t/pm/rls/fs/2017/266854.htm.

TRADE

164 *"will to survive"*: The White House, "Remarks by President Trump to the People of Poland," July 6, 2017, https://www.whitehouse.gov/the-press-office /2017/07/06/remarks-president-trump-people-poland-july-6-2017.

165 *A new trade deal:* "A New Trade Deal Between the EU and Japan," *The Economist,* July 8, 2017, https://www.economist.com/news/finance-and -economics/21724830-besides-slashing-tariffs-cheese-and-cars-it-sends -message-donald-trump.

165 *"the world's largest free"*: James Kanter, "The E.U.-Japan Trade Deal: What's in It and Why It Matters," *New York Times,* July 6, 2017, https://www.nytimes. com/2017/07/06/business/economy/japan-eu-trade-agreement.html.

165 *Jean-Claude Juncker:* Remarks by European Commission President Juncker at the joint press briefing with Donald Tusk, President of the European Council, and Shinzō Abe, Prime Minister of Japan, on the occasion of the EU-Japan Summit, European Commission Press Release, July 6, 2017, http://europa.eu /rapid/press-release_SPEECH-17-1926_en.htm.

165 *Donald Tusk:* Remarks by President Donald Tusk at the press conference of the EU-Japan summit in Brussels, July 6, 2017, http://www.consilium.europa.eu /en/press/press-releases/2017/07/06-tusk-remarks-press-conference-eu-japan -summit.

166 *counted in the hundreds:* David Cay Johnston, "The Troubled Trade Deal with South Korea," Reuters, July 31, 2012, http://blogs.reuters.com/david-cay -johnston/2012/07/31/the-troubled-trade-deal-with-south-korea/.

168 *tertiary or college education:* Tables A1.1 and A1.2 Educations at a Glance 2017: OECD Indicators, http://www.keepeek.com/Digital-Asset-Management/oecd /education/education-at-a-glance-2017_eag-2017-en#page53.

170 *"China almost certainly is"*: Author interview, July 3, 2017.

171 *Kurt Eichenwald wrote in* Newsweek: Kurt Eichenwald, "How Donald Trump Ditched U.S. Steel Workers in Favor of China," *Newsweek,* Oct. 3, 2016, http:// www.newsweek.com/how-donald-trump-ditched-us-steel-workers-china -505717.

171 *"The normal mechanism"*: Dean Baker, "Trump Takes Credit for Redistrib-uting From Workers and Communities to Corporations," Beat the Press blog, http://cepr.net/blogs/beat-the-press/trump-takes-credit-for-redistributing -from-workers-and-communities-to-corporations.

DIGITAL DELUSIONS

173 *most expensive ship ever built:* "US Navy Receives Its Most Expensive Ship Ever," NavalToday.com, June 1, 2017, http://navaltoday.com/2017/06/01/us -navy-receives-its-most-expensive-ship-ever/.

173 *"They just gave me this beautiful jacket":* Kalhan Rosenblatt, "President Trump Goes 'Top Gun' in Navy Jacket and Hat," NBC News, March 2, 2017, https:// www.nbcnews.com/news/us-news/president-trump-goes-top-gun-navy -jacket-cap-n728361.

174 *Trump vowed to grow the Navy:* Hope Hodge Seck, "Aboard *Ford,* Trump Promises 12 Carriers, Record Navy Growth," Military.com., March 2, 2017, http://www.military.com/daily-news/2017/03/02/aboard-ford-trump -promises-12-carriers-record-navy-growth.html.

175 *the Stockholm International Peace Research Institute calculated:* Stockholm International Peace Research Institute, "SIPRI Military Expenditure Database," https://www.sipri.org/databases/milex.

175 *the Trump White House cited a figure of $585 billion:* The White House, "Budget of the U.S. Government: A New Foundation for American Greatness," https://www .whitehouse.gov/sites/whitehouse.gov/files/omb/budget/fy2018/budget.pdf.

177 *"the challenges that we face":* Associated Press, "Fact-checking What Trump Has Taken Credit For," CBS, March 6, 2017, https://www.cbsnews.com/news /fact-checking-what-trump-has-taken-credit-for/.

177 *seven hundred fewer sailors:* "Gerald R. Ford Class Aircraft Carrier," Military. com., http://www.military.com/equipment/gerald-r-ford-class-aircraft-carrier.

177 *"how you don't build a ship":* David Martin, "New Warship 'Poster Child for How You Don't Build a Ship,' Says Ex-Navy Secretary," CBS, March 2, 2017, https://www.cbsnews.com/news/uss-gerald-r-ford-poster-child-for-how-you -dont-build-a-ship-says-former-navy-secretary/.

178 *in an interview with* Time *magazine:* Zeke J. Miller, "Read Donald Trump's Interview with Time on Being President," *Time,* May 11, 2017, http://time.com /4775040/donald-trump-time-interview-being-president/.

180 *They wore miniskirts:* Robin Eberhardt, "Trump Shown Photo of Afghan Women in Miniskirts: Report," *The Hill,* Aug. 22, 2017, http://thehill.com/ policy/defense/347446-mcmaster-showed-trump-1970s-photos-of-afghan -women-wearing-miniskirts-in.

PROMISES AND PERFORMANCES

185 *"What the hell do you have to lose?"*: Tom LoBianco and Ashley Kilough, "Trump Pitches Black Voters: 'What the Hell Do You Have to Lose,'" CNN, Aug. 19, 2016, http://www.cnn.com/2016/08/19/politics/donald-trump-african -american-voters/index.html.

185 *"Were you paid $1,500 to be a thug?"*: Donald Trump, campaign speech in Kinston, North Carolina, Oct. 26, 2016, https://www.c-span.org/video /?417502-1/donald-trump-campaigns-kinston-north-carolina.

185 *C. J. Cary:* Amy B. Wang, "Trump Booted a Black Man from His Rally and Called Him a 'Thug.' Turns Out He Is a Supporter," *Washington Post,* Oct. 29, 2016.

186 *"a lot of people don't know"*: Donald Trump, campaign speech in Charlotte, North Carolina, Oct. 26, 2016, https://www.c-span.org/video/?417505-1 /donald-trump-proposes-new-deal-urban-america.

186 *In an uncharacteristically subdued voice:* Tim Funk and Jim Morrill, "Donald Trump Promises 'A New Deal for Black America' at Spirit Square," *Charlotte Observer,* Oct. 26, 2016, http://www.charlotteobserver.com/news/politics -government/election/article110546817.html.

187 *got to speak at all:* Walter M. Kimbrough, "My Statement: White House HBCU Event," medium.com., https://medium.com/@HipHopPrez/my -statement-white-house-hbcu-event-bf51a619194a. Feb. 27, 2017.

187 *"their white peers"*: Ibid.

187 *"bow down"*: Jason M. Breslow, "The FRONTLINE Interview: Omarosa Manigault," *Frontline,* Sept. 27, 2016, http://www.pbs.org/wgbh/frontline /article/the-frontline-interview-omarosa-manigault/.

188 *"all of our people"*: Donald Trump, Feb. 27, 2017, https://www.whitehouse. gov/the press office/2017/02/28/remarks-president-trump-signing-hbcu -executive-order.

188 *Called "skinny"*: Office of Management and Budget, "America First: A Budget Blueprint to Make America Great Again," https://www.whitehouse.gov/sites /whitehouse.gov/files/omb/budget/fy2018/2018_blueprint.pdf.

188 *"would undermine opportunity"*: Jamaal Abdul-Alim, "Hartle: Trump Education Budget an 'Assault on College Affordability,'" *Diverse,* http://diverse education.com/article/96740/.

190 *"not reflective of that sentiment"*: JL Carter Sr., "Trump Budget Proposal Gives HBCU Community the 'Burning Sands' Treatment," *HBCU Digest,* March 16, 2017, https://www.hbcudigest.com/trump-budget-proposal-gives-hbcu -community-the-burning-sands-treatment/.

190 *Johnny one-note education policy:* Betsy DeVos, "Statement from Secretary of Education Betsy DeVos Following Listening Session with Historically Black College and University Leaders," Feb. 28, 2017, https://www.ed.gov/news/press-releases/statement-secretary-education-betsy-devos-following-listening-session-historically-black-college-and-university-leaders.

193 *"willfully impervious":* Stephen Henderson, "Betsy DeVos and the Twilight of Public Education," *Detroit Free Press,* Dec. 3, 2016, updated Dec. 6, 2016, http://www.freep.com/story/opinion/columnists/stephen-henderson/2016/12/03/betsy-devos-education-donald-trump/94728574/.

BANKERS BEFORE BRAINS

197 *annual disclosure report to shareholders:* U.S. Securities and Exchange, Form 10-K, 2016, for Bridgepoint Education, Inc., http://d18rn0p25nwr6d.cloudfront.net/CIK-0001305323/c9270e18-c8d7-4d2a-902e-622ce040a8dc.pdf.

198 *"company was under investigation":* Patricia Cohen, "Betsy DeVos's Hiring of For-Profit College Official Raises Impartiality Issues," *New York Times,* March 17, 2017, https://www.nytimes.com/2017/03/17/business/education-for-profit-robert-eitel.html.

199 *a host of Education Department regulations:* U.S. Department of Education, Regulatory Reform Task Force Progress Report, May 2017, https://www2.ed.gov/documents/press-releases/regulatory-reform-task-force-progress-report.pdf.

199 *Hansen sought to roll back:* Annie Waldman, "For-Profit Colleges Gain Beachhead in Trump Administration," ProPublica, March 14, 2017, https://www.propublica.org/article/for-profit-colleges-gain-beachhead-in-trump-administration.

201 *charged a lot and delivered little: Massachusetts et al. v. United States Department of Education and Betsy DeVos,* United States District Court, District of Columbia, https://assets.documentcloud.org/documents/3889617/Filed-Complaint-Massachusetts-Et-Al-v-DeVos.pdf.

ABOVE THE LAW

207 *Donald Trump flew to Phoenix:* Donald J. Trump, Speech at Phoenix, Arizona, Aug. 22, 2017, https://www.c-span.org/video/?432748-1/president-trump-criticizes-dishonest-media-defends-charlottesville-remarks-rally-phoenix.

213 *stabbing, followed by arrests:* Justin Jouvenal, "Teen Charged in Va. Gang Slaying Told Victim She'd 'See Her in Hell,' According to Testimony," *Washington Post,* May 11, 2017, https://www.washingtonpost.com/local/public-safety/suspects -in-ms-13-related-killing-of-15-year-old-girl-to-appear-in-court/2017/05/10 /715512e5-1941-434c-ba36-5b2805650b7b_story.html.

216 *"not tolerate roughing up of prisoners":* Suffolk County Police Department, Twitter, July 28, 2017, https://twitter.com/SCPDHq/status/891038888315244544.
police chiefs denounced: Brian M. Rosenthal, "Police Criticize Trump for Urging Officers Not to Be 'Too Nice' with Suspects," *New York Times,* July 29, 2017, https://twitter.com/SCPDHq/status/891038888315244544.

218 *told* The Washington Post: Phillip Rucker and Ellen Nakashima, "Trump Asked Sessions About Closing Case Against Arpaio, an Ally Since 'Birtherism,'" *Washington Post,* Aug. 26, 2017, https://www.washingtonpost.com/politics /trump-asked-sessions-about-closing-case-against-arpaio-an-ally-since -birtherism/2017/08/26/15e5d7b2-8a7f-11e7-a94f-3139abce39f5_story.html.

219 *"time and resources into these cases":* Ramsey Cox, "Sessions: Obama Abuses 'Pardon Power,'" *The Hill,* April 24, 2014, http://thehill.com/blogs/floor-action /senate/204261-sessions-obama-is-abusing-pardon-power.

WOUNDING THE VETERANS

221 *"Making Our Military Strong Again":* https://www.whitehouse.gov/making-our -military-strong-again.

222 *more than 2.3 million veterans:* Veterans Benefits Administration Annual Benefits Report Fiscal Year 2000, Feb. 2001, https://www.benefits.va.gov /REPORTS/abr/fy2000_abr_v3.pdf.

222 *By 2015 almost 4.2 million veterans received disability benefits:* Veterans Benefits Administration 2015 Report on Compensation, https://www .benefits.va.gov/REPORTS/abr/ABR-Compensation-FY15-05092016.pdf.

223 *Fred Trump believed his son needed discipline:* Paul Schwartzman and Michael E. Miller, "Confident. Incorrigible. Bully: Little Donny Was a Lot Like Candidate Donald Trump," *Washington Post,* June 22, 2016, https://www .washingtonpost.com/lifestyle/style/young-donald-trump-military-school /2016/06/22/f0b3b164-317c-11e6-8758-d58e76e11b12_story.html?utm_term =.d2519be8e498.

223 *he could not recall which foot:* Craig Whitlock, "Questions Linger About Trump's Draft Deferments During Vietnam War," *Washington Post,* July 21, 2015, https://www.washingtonpost.com/world/national-security/questions-linger

-about-trumps-draft-deferments-during-vietnam-war/2015/07/21/257677bc
-2fdd-11e5-8353-1215475949f4_story.html?utm_term=.51db4e249c49.

223 *"I feel like a great and very brave soldier"*: Ale Russian, "Trump Boasted of
Avoiding STDs While Dating: Vaginas Are 'Landmines . . . It Is My Personal
Vietnam,'" *People,* Oct. 28, 2016, http://people.com/politics/trump-boasted
-of-avoiding-stds-while-dating-vaginas-are-landmines-it-was-my-personal
-vietnam/.

223 *"They're stockbrokers that were in Vietnam"*: Lois Romano, "Donald Trump,
Holding All the Cards The Tower! The Team! The Money! The Future!,"
Washington Post, Nov. 15, 1984, https://www.washingtonpost.com/archive
/lifestyle/1984/11/15/donald-trump-holding-all-the-cards-the-tower-the
-team-the-money-the-future/8be79254-7793-4812-a153-f2b88e81fa54/?utm
_term=.3379ae9ce06a.

224 *"but a lot of people can't handle it"*: Daniel White, "Read Donald Trump's
Remarks to a Veterans Group," *Time,* Oct. 3, 2016, http://time.com/4517279
/trump-veterans-ptsd-transcript/.

224 *"the number one thing we have to do"*: Ibid.

224 *"This will take the place of Twitter"*: Donald J. Trump, speech, July 26, 2016,
https://www.c-span.org/video/?c4613502/realdonaldtrump-will-take-place
-twitter.

224 *"and get it taken care of"*: Donald J. Trump, speech, July 11, 2016, https://www.c
-span.org/video/?412560-1/donald-trump-delivers-remarks-veterans-issues.

225 *Trump signed into law:* White House website, "President Trump Signs Veterans
Accountability and Whistleblower Protection Act," June 23, 2017, https://www
.whitehouse.gov/blog/2017/06/23/president-trump-signs-veterans-account
ability-and-whistleblower-protection-act.

225 *These veterans would see their income plunge:* Richard Sisk, "Elderly Vets Could
Face Benefits Cut Under Trump Budget," military.com, May 24, 2017, http://
www.military.com/daily-news/2017/05/24/elderly-vets-face-benefits-cut
-trump-budget.html.

226 *seven thousand of these veterans were age eighty or older:* Rep. Mark Takano website:
"Rep. Mark Takano Questions VA Secretary Shulkin About Trump Budget," May
24, 2017, http://takano.house.gov/view/rep_mark-takano-questions-va-secretary
-shulkin-about-trump-budget.

226 *"a long, stressful summer"*: Leo Shane III, "VA Secretary Backs Off Plan to Cut
Elderly Vets' Benefits," *Military Times,* June 14, 2017, https://www.militarytimes
.com/news/pentagon-congress/2017/06/14/va-secretary-backs-off-plan-to
-cut-elderly-vets-benefits/.

226 *And the budget called for eliminating the $3.5 million:* Jennifer McDermott,

"Advocates of Homeless Vets Fear Trump Budget Could Hurt Them," Associated Press, March 28, 2017, https://apnews.com/2c4ff33242a34530a2723ffd92fe0d98 /veteran-homelessness-trumps-budget-could-hurt-efforts.

227 *More than 70,000 of them are veterans:* Harry Stein, "Trump's Hiring Freeze Breaks Faith with America's Veterans," *The Hill,* Jan. 27, 2017, http://thehill .com/blogs/pundits-blog/the-administration/316467-trumps-hiring-freeze -breaks-faith-with-americas.

227 *federal workforce was not bloated:* Christopher Ingraham, "The Trump Administration Just Told a Whopper About the Size of the Federal Workforce," *Washington Post,* Jan. 23, 2017, https://www.washingtonpost.com/news/wonk /wp/2017/01/23/the-trump-administration-just-told-a-whopper-about-the -size-of-the-federal-workforce/?tid=ptv_rellink&utm_term=.b945ec21da32.

227 *the Obama administration had hired more claims examiners:* Stein, "Trump's Hiring Freeze Breaks Faith with America's Veterans."

227 *The annual savings would total about $20 million in 2018:* Nikki Wentling, "Budget Calls for Cuts to VA Programs as Tradeoff for Extending Choice," *Stars and Stripes,* May 23, 2017, http://www.military.com/daily-news/2017/05 /23/budget-calls-cuts-va-programs-tradeoff-extending-choice.html.

THE ROAD TO CHARLOTTESVILLE

229 *"I am the least racist person":* Marc Fisher, "Donald Trump: 'I Am the Least Racist Person,'" *Washington Post,* June 10, 2016, https://www.washing-tonpost.com/politics/donald-trump-i-am-the-least-racist-person/2016 /06/10/eac7874c-2f3a-11e6-9de3-6e6e7a14000c_story.html?utm_term =.ad194d14092f.

229 *The Southern Poverty Law Center:* "Hate Map," https://www.splcenter.org/hate -map.

230 *ready for war:* Todd Gitlin, "The Well-Armed, Uniformed Militiamen Whose Pictures You May Have Missed," *Moyers & Company,* Aug. 28, 2017, http:// billmoyers.com/story/militiamen-charlottesville-violence//.

231 *first-aid kits:* Joanna Walters, "Mistaken for the Military: The Gear Carried by the Charlottesville Militia," *The Guardian,* Aug. 15, 2017, https://www .theguardian.com/us-news/2017/aug/15/charlottesville-militia-security-gear -uniforms.

231 *"had better equipment than our State Police had":* Harrison Jacobs, "VA Governor Defends Charlottesville Response: Militia Members Had 'Better' Guns than Police," *Business Insider,* Aug. 13, 2017, http://www.businessinsider.com/virginia

-gov-mcauliffe-defends-charlottesville-police-better-semiautomatic-guns
-white-nationalists-2017-8.

231 *"I don't know"*: Alan Zimmerman, "In Charlottesville, the Local Jewish
Community Presses On," ReformJudiasm.org., Aug. 14, 2017, https://reform
judaism.org/blog/2017/08/14/charlottesville-local-jewish-community-presses.

231 *may not use a BB gun or a slingshot*: Kitsap County, http://www.codepublishing
.com/WA/KitsapCounty/html/Kitsap10/Kitsap1012.html#10.12.080. Amended
in 2009 to delete the phrase "or carry any firearm."

232 *"carried out on a stretcher, folks"*: Donald J. Trump, speech, Feb. 22, 2016,
https://www.c-span.org/video/?405003-1/donald-trump-campaign-rally-las
-vegas.

232 *"I would never kill them"*: Theodore Schleifer, "Donald Trump on reporters: 'I
would never kill them,'" CNN.com, Dec. 21, 2015, http://www.cnn.com/2015
/12/21/politics/trump-putin-killing-reporters/index.html.

233 *"The polls say"*: Reuters, "Donald Trump: I Could Shoot Somebody and Not
Lose Votes—Video," *The Guardian,* Jan. 24, 2016, https://www.theguardian
.com/us-news/video/2016/jan/24/donald-trump-i-could-shoot-somebody
-and-not-lose-votes-video.

233 *"the same attitude"*: https://archive.org/details/CSPAN_20160125_083500
_Donald_Trump_Campaign_Rally_in_Muscatine_Iowa.

233 *"right smack between the eyes"*: Jeremy Diamond, "Trump Calls Orlando
shooter a 'son of a b——,'" CNN, June 17, 2016, http://www.cnn.com/2016/06
/17/politics/donald-trump-orlando-shooter/index.html.

233 *"she wouldn't be prosecuted, OK?"*: Jeremy Diamond, "Trump: Clinton Could
Shoot Somebody and Not Be Arrested," CNN, Sept. 9, 2016, http://www.cnn
.com/2016/09/09/politics/donald-trump-hillary-clinton-shoot-somebody
/index.html.

237 *In Germany, Chancellor Angela Merkel:* Agence France-Press, "Merkel
Condemns 'Disgusting' Far-Right Violence in US," Aug. 14, 2017, https://
www.thelocal.de/20170814/merkel-condemns-disgusting-virginia-far-right
-violence.

238 *The Nazi leader said:* Bruce Loebs, "Hitler's Rhetorical Theory," *Relevant
Rhetoric* 1, 2010, http://relevantrhetoric.com/Hitler%27s%20Rhetorical%20
Theory.pdf.

239 *"associating with David Duke"*: Nancy Dillon and Adam Edelman, "Trump
Plays Dumb When Asked About Endorsement from Former KKK Leader
David Duke," Feb. 28, 2016, http://www.nydailynews.com/news/politics/trump
-plays-dumb-endorsement-kkk-leader-article-1.2546509.

239 *The Nazi news site then called Frazier:* Andrew Anglin, "Trump Attacks His-

trionic Black Bastard Who Resigned From Council Over Alleged Misstatement,"
Daily Stormer, Aug. 14, 2017, https://dailystormer.ai/trump-attacks-histrionic
-black-bastard-who-resigned-from-council-over-alleged-misstatement/.

IMMIGRATION

242 *"came in totally legally"*: Rebecca Savransky, "Trump Promises Press Conference
on Melania's Immigration Story," *The Hill,* Aug. 9, 2016, http://thehill.com
/blogs/ballot-box/presidential-races/290935-trump-on-wifes-immigration
-story-she-came-in-totally.

243 *"No exceptions"*: Donald J. Trump, Statement on Position on Visas, March 3,
2016, http://www.presidency.ucsb.edu/ws/index.php?pid=113898.

243 *$88,000 or less:* Characteristics of H-1B Specialty Occupation Workers, Table 12,
https://www.uscis.gov/sites/default/files/USCIS/Resources/Reports%20and%20
Studies/H-1B/h-1B-FY16.pdf.

244 *"theft of American prosperity"*: Glenn Thrush, Nick Wingfield, and Vindu
Goel, "Trump Signs Order That Could Lead to Curbs on Foreign Workers,"
New York Times, April 18, 2017, https://www.nytimes.com/2017/04/18/us
/politics/executive-order-hire-buy-american-h1b-visa-trump.html.

244 *"suggest reforms"*: The White House, "Presidential Executive Order on Buy
American and Hire American," April 18, 2017, https://www.whitehouse.gov
/the-press-office/2017/04/18/presidential-executive-order-buy-american-and
-hire-american.

244 *"That's not accurate"*: "Transcript of the Republican Presidential Debate in
Detroit," *New York Times,* March 4, 2016, https://www.nytimes.com/2016/03/04
/us/politics/transcript-of-the-republican-presidential-debate-in-detroit.html.

244 *temporary low-skill, low-paid jobs:* United States Department of Homeland
Security, July 17, 2017, press release, "DHS Provides Relief to American
Businesses in Danger of Suffering Irreparable Harm," https://www.dhs.gov
/news/2017/07/17/dhs-provides-relief-american-businesses-danger-suffering
-irreparable-harm.

245 *Locally four people wanted work:* Jeff Ostrowski, "Trump Not the Only
Employer Hiring Foreign Workers for Low-Wage Jobs," *Palm Beach Post,*
March 7, 2016, http://www.mypalmbeachpost.com/business/employment
/trump-not-the-only-employer-hiring-foreign-workers-for-low-wage-jobs/.

245 *Made in America Week:* The White House, "Made in America Week Recap,"
July 24, 2017, https://www.whitehouse.gov/blog/2017/07/24/made-america
-week-recap.

245 *fifteen chambermaids:* Jeremy Singer-Vine, Jessica Garrison, and Ken Bensinger,

"More Foreign Workers Requested by Trump's Mar-a-Lago," BuzzFeed, https://www.buzzfeed.com/jsvine/trumps-florida-clubs-want-to-hire-more-foreign-workers. The actual Labor Department records are available: For cooks: https://lcr-pjr.doleta.gov/index.cfm?event=ehLCJRExternal.dspJobOrderView&frm=lcjr&task=view_job_order&view=external&lcjr_id=116826; for waiters: https://lcr-pjr.doleta.gov/index.cfm?event=ehLCJRExternal.dspJobOrderView&frm=lcjr&task=view_job_order&view=external&lcjr_id=116833; for chambermaids: https://lcr-pjr.doleta.gov/index.cfm?event=ehLCJRExternal.dspJobOrderView&frm=PJR&task=view_job_order&view=external&lcjr_id=116824.

246 *supported the RAISE Act:* Staff, "Full Speech: Donald Trump Affirms Hard-Line Immigration Plan," *The Hill,* Aug. 31, 2016, http://thehill.com/blogs/pundits-blog/presidential-campaign/294055-full-speech-donald-trump-affirms-hardline.

247 *by the year 2040:* University of Pennsylvania, Wharton, report, "The RAISE Act: Effect on Economic Growth and Jobs," Aug. 10, 2017, http://www.budgetmodel.wharton.upenn.edu/issues/2017/8/8/the-raise-act-effect-on-economic-growth-and-jobs; University of Pennsylvania, Wharton, report, "The Real Costs of the RAISE Act," Aug. 11, 2017, http://knowledge.wharton.upenn.edu/article/the-real-costs-of-the-raise-act/.

247 *Kent Smetters, the Wharton business professor:* Kent Smetters, "The Real Costs of the RAISE Act," Knowledge@Wharton, Aug. 11, 2017, http://knowledge.wharton.upenn.edu/article/the-real-costs-of-the-raise-act/.

247 *Acosta brought up:* Josiah Ryan, CNN, "CNN's Acosta, White House Aide Clash over Immigration at Briefing," Aug. 2, 2017, http://money.cnn.com/2017/08/02/media/jim-acosta-stephen-miller-immigration/index.html.

249 *That estimate:* UNHCR, United Nations Refugee Agency, "Figures at a Glance; Statistical Yearbooks," http://www.unhcr.org/en-us/figures-at-a-glance.html.

250 *9 to 11 million people:* Jens Manuel Krogstad, Jeffrey S. Passel, and D'Vera Cohn, "5 Facts About Illegal Immigration in the U.S.," Pew Research Center, April 27, 2017, http://www.pewresearch.org/fact-tank/2017/04/27/5-facts-about-illegal-immigration-in-the-u-s/.

THE CON UNRAVELS

253 *brutality was common:* Michael D'Antonio, "The Men Who Gave Trump His Brutal Worldview," *Politico,* March 29, 2016, http://www.politico.com/magazine/story/2016/03/2016-donald-trump-brutal-worldview-father-coach-213750.

253 *"I'm like a smart person"*: Chris Cillizza, "Donald Trump Is a 'Smart Person' in Case You Forgot," *Washington Post*, Dec. 12, 2016, https://www.washingtonpost .com/news/the-fix/wp/2016/12/12/donald-trump-doesnt-need-a-daily -intelligence-briefing-according-to-donald-trump/?tid=pm_pop&utm_term =.825ab1db95f4.

255 *ISIL:* Mark Thompson, "Donald Trump's Coming Clash with the Military Generals," *Time,* Sept. 11, 2016, http://time.com/4486862/donald-trumps -coming-clash-with-the-military-generals/.

257 *Frederick Douglass:* Lucy Clarke-Billings, "Does President Trump Know That Slave Activist Frederick Douglass Is Dead?," *Newsweek,* Feb. 2, 2017, http:// www.newsweek.com/does-president-donald-trump-know-black-activist -frederick-douglass-dead-551584.

258 *thirty-five psychiatrists:* Richard A. Friedman, "Is It Time to Call Trump Mentally Ill?," *New York Times,* Feb. 17, 2017, https://www.nytimes.com/2017 /02/17/opinion/is-it-time-to-call-trump-mentally-ill.html.

258 *A few months later, psychiatrist Prudence L. Gourguechon:* Prudence L. Gourguechon, "Is Trump Mentally Fit to Be President? Let's Consult the U.S. Army's Field Manual on Leadership," *Los Angeles Times,* June 16, 2017, http://beta.latimes.com/opinion/op-ed/la-oe-gourguechon-25th-amendment -leadership-mental-capacities-checklist-20170616-story.html.

259 *"around the globe":* Elle Hunt, "Trump's Inauguration Crowd: Sean Spicer's Claim Versus the Evidence," *The Guardian,* Jan. 22, 2017, https://www.the guardian.com/us-news/2017/jan/22/trump-inauguration-crowd-sean-spicers -claims-versus-the-evidence.

260 *Later Trump denounced:* Chris Cillizza, "Trump Sent 18 Tweets on Puerto Rico on Saturday, and Made Things a Whole Lot Worse," CNN.com, Oct. 1, 2017, http://www.cnn.com/2017/10/01/politics/trump-tweets-puerto-rico/index. html.

INDEX